HR Question and Answer BOOK

Burton J. Fishman, Esq.
Judith E. Kramer, Esq.
Barbara S. Magill, Esq.
Kathleen J. Raynsford, Esq.

Thompson Publishing Group, Inc.
1725 K St. NW, 7th Floor
Washington, DC 20006
(202) 872-4000 (Editorial Offices)
1-800-677-3789 (Customer Service)

THOMPSON

THOMPSON

Thompson Publishing Group, Inc.

Thompson Publishing Group is a trusted name in providing professionals with authoritative analysis of laws and regulations that help businesses develop regulatory compliance strategies. Since 1972, thousands of professionals in business, government, law and academia have relied on Thompson Publishing Group for the most authoritative, timely and practical guidance available.

Thompson offers looseleaf services, books, specialty newsletters, audio conferences and online products in a number of subject and regulatory compliance areas. These Thompson products provide insightful analysis, practical guidance and real-world solutions to the challenges facing Human Resource professionals today and beyond. More information about Thompson's product offerings is available at http://www.thompson.com.

To order any Thompson products or additional copies of this book, please contact us:

Call: 1-800-677-3789
Online: www.thompson.com
Fax: 1-800-999-5661
Email: service@thompson.com
Mail: Thompson Publishing Group
Subscription Service Center
PO Box 26185, Tampa, FL 33623-6185

Authors: Burton J. Fishman, Esq.
Judith E. Kramer, Esq.,
Barbara S. Magill, Esq.
Kathleen J. Raynsford, Esq.

Production: Laurie S. Clark
Cover Design: Ellen Hamilton
Indexer: Kate Mertes

Acknowledgment

We would like to thank Daniel B. Abrahams of the law firm Epstein Becker & Green, PC, Washington, DC, for his contributions to Chapter 2: Compensation. The checklists and decision charts (pp. 44-55) provided for use in determining the applicability of various white-collar exemptions were developed by Mr. Abrahams and first appeared in the *Employer's Guide to the Fair Labor Standards Act* published by Thompson Publishing Group.

HR Question and Answer Book is published by
Thompson Publishing Group, Inc., 1725 K St. NW, 7th Floor, Washington, DC 20006.

ISBN-10: 1-930872-99-2
ISBN-13: 978-1-930872-99-8

Printed in the United States

About this Book

Like all human resource professionals, you face risks every day. Most often, these risks are in the form of questions for which you do not have answers. The *HR Question and Answer Book* is designed for you. Based on questions and topics you have asked about, this book focuses on the information you need to do your job on a day-to-day basis.

The 201 questions cover the HR life cycle from **Recruiting and Hiring** to **Termination** – and everything in between – to address the concerns you have and the tasks you need to perform regarding **Compensation, Workplace Culture, Employee Conduct** and **Leave and Benefits**. The questions are those that have been asked of us by clients or submitted to Thompson Publishing Group, Inc., by subscribers. They come from real workplace situations, so they are certain to reflect actual problems with which you must deal.

Our answers are written by legal experts and consultants, some of whom have HR backgrounds like yours. They are based on best practices in the field and will help you avoid pitfalls and litigation, and improve the overall management of your workforce.

The answers provide complete but to-the-point responses. Many begin with a "yes" or "no" and then elaborate, so you will understand the reasoning behind the answer. When appropriate, charts, tables, checklists, policies and forms are included so you can move quickly from the answer right into action.

To assist you further, this book is organized so you can find what you need quickly and easily. At the top of each page is the subject area that is discussed and the question numbers. The questions are numbered consecutively. All of them are listed at the beginning of the book, and each chapter has a list on the second page of the questions in that chapter.

The table of contents lists every question in the book. In addition, a detailed index at the back of the book provides all the key words you need to find the answer you want. For example, if you have a question about how to know if an employee qualifies for the administrative exemption for overtime purposes under the Fair Labor Standards Act (FLSA), you can find the answer by looking up "FLSA," "exemption," "administrative exemptions," or even "overtime" in the index.

The policies and forms follow the question to which they apply. Each one has a number, keyed to the question. When a policy or form applies to a subsequent answer, it is cross-referenced in that answer so you can go back and find it easily.

If you want to delve deeper into a particular subject, you will find reference sources at the end of most questions. And at the back of the book are "plain-English" summaries of most of the employment laws referred to in the answers.

We think you will find this to be the easiest to use and most informative book of its kind.

About the Authors

Burton J. Fishman, Esq.

Burton J. Fishman is of counsel with Fortney & Scott, LLC, a Washington, D.C., firm specializing in labor and employment law. A former U.S. Labor Department deputy solicitor, he is co-chairman of the American Bar Association's Federal Legislative Development Committee. He devotes his practice to developing the "law of the workplace," an interdisciplinary approach that offers employers counsel and representation on a broad range of matters growing out of government regulation of business. He has written more than 70 books and articles on employment law.

Judith E. Kramer, Esq.

Judith E. Kramer is of counsel with Fortney & Scott and is primarily engaged in counseling management on employment-related compliance and enforcement issues involving the U.S. Department of Labor and other federal agencies. Prior to joining Fortney & Scott, she served as deputy solicitor of Labor, the highest-ranking career position in the DOL Solicitor's Office. She also served as a trial and appellate attorney at the Civil Rights Division of the U.S. Department of Justice. She is a cum laude graduate of the Northwestern University School of Law.

Barbara S. Magill, Esq.

Barbara S. Magill is a senior managing editor at Thompson Publishing Group. She has written and edited numerous books on employment law and has particular expertise on the Americans With Disabilities Act, the Family and Medical Leave Act and the Uniformed Services Employment and Reemployment Rights Act. She served as an HR generalist prior to joining Thompson, with responsibility for benefits, equal employment opportunity and the company's affirmative action plan, and before that was in private law practice in Illinois.

Kathleen J. Raynsford, Esq.

Kathleen J. Raynsford is of counsel with Fortney & Scott. Her employment law expertise includes wage and hour, state and federal employment discrimination and workplace harassment. She helps management develop and administer affirmative action plans, workforce reductions and equal employment opportunity training programs. She also handles Office of Federal Contract Compliance Programs audits. Before joining Fortney & Scott, she was the associate general counsel, Labor-Personnel at the National Railroad Passenger Corporation (Amtrak).

Table of Contents

Table of Contents

Discrimination/Harassment

Disability

Gender

National Origin

Age

Recruiting and Hiring

1

Introduction

We begin at the beginning: recruiting and hiring. Many HR specialists think that this is the single most difficult task they are asked to perform. And, of course, hiring the right person makes a real contribution to any company. Having the right person in the job makes your life a lot easier.

But, as human resource professionals know, hiring an employee is not as simple as running an ad on the Internet or in the newspaper, asking a few questions of some candidates and offering a job to one of them. There are many practical and legal issues to consider first. And there are so many ways to go wrong: a poorly designed application, an inaccurate job description, an incomplete background check, even an off-handed comment during a job interview.

By answering some of the questions our clients most often ask us about hiring, we hope to avoid these and other pitfalls. The subjects in this chapter include affirmative action and nepotism; background checks and job references; illegal immigrants and I-9 forms; interviewing and job descriptions; testing; and staying clear of the ADA in general.

Sample policies, forms and checklists are included with the answers to help you find practical solutions to your problems. For further information, sources are listed when appropriate at the end of each answer.

Although the answers were written by employment law attorneys, they are meant to be practical, not legal advice. Because every situation is fact specific and state laws vary considerably, you should consult your own lawyer for legal advice.

Questions in This Chapter

Affirmative Action and EEO

1. Q: What am I supposed to do when no minorities apply for a job opening? I'm worried about breaking the employment discrimination rules – all the qualified applicants for a CPA job are white men.

A: Assuming you are confident that the essential qualifications for the CPA position are current, accurate and job-related, the first step is to assess the diversity of your applicant pool compared to the availability of such positions in the surrounding geographic area.

For example, federal contractors may compare the applicant pool against availability statistics from their affirmative action plans and/or the software utilized to create those plans. As a practical matter, for employers who are not federal contractors but are located in urban areas where it appears unusual that no qualified women or minority candidates applied for the vacancy, the next step is to examine the ways the vacancy was advertised. All employment advertisements should emphasize that the company is an "Equal Opportunity" employer. It also may be advantageous to include the statement that "qualified women and minority candidates are encouraged to apply."

Expand recruitment efforts beyond the immediate geographic area, to include minority and gender-specific professional organizations, employee associations and affinity groups, as well as minority and female educational institutions. To the extent that outside recruiters or "headhunters" are utilized, they should be encouraged to tap sources of minority and female candidates to increase diversity within the applicant pool. It may also be useful to ask any current female or minority incumbents whether they are aware of qualified candidates, or other recruitment resources. All of these efforts should be documented.

That said, it is important to review what the employer should *not* do. It is never permissible or appropriate to hire an otherwise unqualified candidate from any protected group over other qualified male, non-minority applicants simply to increase diversity. Reverse discrimination claims are on the rise, and the Equal Employment Opportunity Commission has expressed interest in pursuing such charges more aggressively than it has in the past.

At all times, the focus should remain on increasing diversity within the applicant pool. After the applicant pool has been narrowed to only those meeting the basic qualifications for the position, all candidates must receive equal consideration, without regard to gender or ethnicity.

2. Q: Can I reject a candidate because of gaps in her job application? I know employment gaps are an issue for a lot of mothers returning to the workplace.

A: No. A policy or practice of rejecting applicants based on gaps in employment history may adversely impact female candidates who leave the workforce temporarily due to pregnancy or to care for their children. This may result in liability for sex discrimination under Title VII of the 1964 Civil Rights Act and state anti-discrimination laws.

You would have to defend such a policy on the grounds of business necessity, a difficult task. For example, you would have to be able to show that rejecting all candidates with gaps in their employment history, both male and female, has resulted in a better quality of new hire. You would then have to produce evidence of that. For example, you would need to show that the policy increased productivity, reduced turnover, and/or there were fewer terminations for performance-related issues.

Any apparent gaps in employment history should be fully explored with the candidate before a decision is made. To facilitate this effort, the application form should specifically state that any gaps in employment history must be fully explained, in writing. See the sample employment application forms beginning with Fig. 2-A.

FIG. 2-A
SAMPLE 1:
APPLICATION FOR EMPLOYMENT

Position Desired:________________________ [ ] Part time [ ] Full time Date: ________

Name: ____
(Print) Last First Middle

Present
Address: ____
Street and Number City State

Have you ever worked for this company before? [ ] Yes [ ] No
If Yes, please give dates and position(s) held: ________________________

Have you ever pled guilty or "no contest" to, or been convicted of a serious misdemeanor or felony (convictions for marijuana-related offenses that are more than two years old need not be listed). [ ] Yes [ ] No
If Yes, please give the date(s) and details:

____

Have you been arrested for any matters for which you currently are out on bail or on your own recognizance pending trial? [ ] Yes [ ]No
If Yes, please give the date(s) and details:

____

Note: Answering "Yes" to these questions does not constitute an automatic bar to employment. Factors such as age and time of the offense, seriousness and nature of the violation, and rehabilitation will be taken into account. In answering these questions, do not include the following: (1) minor traffic infractions, (2) convictions for which the record has been sealed or expunged, (3) referrals to or participation in any diversion programs, or (4) marijuana-related offenses that occurred over two years ago.

Record of Previous Employment

Please list the names of your present and previous employers in chronological order with the present, or most recent, employer first. Be sure to account for all periods of time including military service and any periods of unemployment. If self-employed, give the name of the firm or business and supply business references. Use additional pages if needed.

Present or Most Recent Employer	Employed	Position or Title	Reason for Leaving
____________ Name of company or firm ____________ Address ____________ City, State, Zip Code ____________ Area Code and Telephone	From (mo/yr) ______ To (mo/yr)	__________ Name and Title of last supervisor	

HFHRT013

1

continued on next page

FIG. 2-A (CONT.)

Previous Employer	Employed	Position or Title	Reason for Leaving
______ Name of company or firm ______ Address ______ City, State, Zip Code ______ Area Code and Telephone	Employed From (mo/yr) ______ To (mo/yr)	Position or Title ______ Name and Title of last supervisor	Reason for Leaving
Previous Employer ______ Name of company or firm ______ Address ______ City, State, Zip Code ______ Area Code and Telephone	Employed From (mo/yr) ______ To (mo/yr)	Position or Title ______ Name and Title of last supervisor	Reason for Leaving
Previous Employer ______ Name of company or firm ______ Address ______ City, State, Zip Code ______ Area Code and Telephone	Employed From (mo/yr) ______ To (mo/yr)	Position or Title ______ Name and Title of last supervisor	Reason for Leaving
Previous Employer ______ Name of company or firm ______ Address ______ City, State, Zip Code ______ Area Code and Telephone	Employed From (mo/yr) ______ To (mo/yr)	Position or Title ______ Name and Title of last supervisor	Reason for Leaving

Have you ever been terminated or asked to resign from any job? [ ] Yes [ ] No
If Yes, please explain circumstances: ______________________________

____

Please explain fully any gaps in your employment history: ______________________________

____

May we contact your current employer? [ ] Yes [ ] No. If No, please explain: ______________

____

Please indicate any actual experience, special training or qualification that you have that you feel is relevant to the position for which you are applying: ______________________________

____

____

2

continued on next page

FIG. 2-A (CONT.)

Have you ever used another name? [ ]Yes [ ] No
If so, what other names?

Is any additional information relative to any change of name, use of an assumed name, or nickname necessary to enable a check on your work and educational records? [ ] Yes [ ] No
If Yes, please explain: ____________________

If hired, can you provide proof that you are authorized to work in the United States on an unrestricted basis? [ ] Yes [ ] No.

If hired, can you provide proof that you are over 18 years of age? [ ] Yes [ ] No.

Are you capable of satisfactorily performing the essential job duties of the position, with or without reasonable accommodation, for which you are applying? (Please review the attached job description.)
[ ] Yes [ ] No.

Do you have adequate transportation to and from work? [ ] Yes [ ] No.

Education

School Name	**Years Completed** (circle one)	**Diploma /Degree**	**Describe Course of Study or Major**	**Describe Specialized Training, Experience, Skills and Extra-Curricular Activities**
Elementary:	**4 5 6 7 8**			
High School:	**9 10 11 12**			
College/University:	**1 2 3 4**			
Graduate/Professional:	**1 2 3 4**			
Trade/Correspondence:				
Other:				

Personal References
Please list at least three persons who know you well – *not* previous employers or relatives.

Name	**Occupation**	**Address (Street, City and State)**	**Telephone Number**	**Number of Years Known**

I certify that all of the information that I have provided on this application is true and accurate.

Date ____________ **Signature of Applicant** ____________

3

continued on next page

Fig. 2-A (cont.)

Applicant's Statement & Agreement

Work Rules. In the event of my employment with [COMPANY], I agree to comply with all rules and regulations of [COMPANY].

Drug/Alcohol Test. I understand that [COMPANY] reserves the right to require me to submit to a test for the presence of drugs in my system prior to employment and at any time during my employment to the extent permitted by law.

Medical Examination. I understand that any offer of employment may be contingent upon the passing of a physical examination. I consent to the disclosure of the results of any physical examination or related tests to [COMPANY]. I understand that should I decline to sign this consent or decline to take any of the above-described tests, my application for employment may be rejected or my employment may be terminated.

Background Investigation. I understand that [COMPANY]'s consideration of my application includes an investigation of the information I have provided on this application and other relevant information such as my driving record and criminal record, if any. I understand that should I decline to consent to such an investigation, my application for employment may be rejected or my employment may be terminated.[1]

Bond. I understand that bonding may be a condition of employment. If it is, I will be so advised either before or after hire and a bond application will have to be completed.

Arbitration Agreement. I understand that as a condition of employment, I will be asked to sign an arbitration agreement. I understand that should I decline to sign an arbitration agreement, my application for employment may be rejected or my employment may be terminated.[2]

At-Will Employment. If hired, I further agree as follows: My employment and compensation are terminable at will, are for no definite period, and my employment and compensation may be terminated by [COMPANY] (employer) at any time and for any reason whatsoever, with or without good cause at the option of either [COMPANY] or myself. No implied, oral or written agreements contrary to the express language of this agreement are valid unless they are in writing and signed by the President of the Company [or majority owner or owners if [COMPANY] is not a corporation]. This agreement takes the place of all prior and contemporaneous agreements, representations, and understandings between me and [COMPANY].

[Insert if collective bargaining agreements: Notwithstanding the foregoing, the terms of any collective bargaining agreement will apply to any applicant hired to work in a position subject to a collective bargaining agreement.]

I hereby certify that all the information that I have provided on this application or any other document filled out in connection with my employment, and in any information that I have provided during any interview, is true and correct. I have withheld nothing that would, if disclosed, affect this application unfavorably. I understand that if I am employed and any such information is later found to be false or incomplete in any respect, I may be dismissed.

If you have any questions regarding this agreement, please ask a Company representative before signing.

---

[1] *This clause does not satisfy an employer's obligation under the FCRA to obtain an applicant's consent to a background investigation. Please consult with counsel regarding the appropriate consent procedures.*

[2] *This clause should not be included unless the Company has an arbitration policy in place. Any arbitration policy should be implemented only after consulting with counsel.*

4

continued on next page

Fig. 2-A (cont.)

I hereby acknowledge that I have read the above statements and agreements and understand the same.

MY SIGNATURE BELOW ATTESTS TO THE FACT THAT I HAVE READ, UNDERSTAND, AND AGREE TO BE LEGALLY BOUND BY ALL OF THE ABOVE TERMS.

____________________ DATE

____________________ Signature of Applicant

5

Fig. 2-B
Sample 2:
Application for Employment

Date ________

We appreciate your interest in working at **[Company Name]**. As an equal opportunity employer, our employment practices are in accordance with the laws that prohibit discrimination due to race, sex, sexual orientation, age, disability, or national origin. This application form was designed for use by persons applying for various types of positions — professional, technical, clerical, and administrative. Please answer only the questions that apply. All information will be treated confidentially.
PLEASE TYPE OR PRINT

Name ____
Last First Middle Social Security No.

Address ____
Street Apartment No.

____
City State Zip

E-Mail Address ____

Telephone No. (   ) ______________ Business Telephone No. (   ) ______________

Are you an U.S. citizen? _ Yes _ No If naturalized, date of citizenship and country of birth________________

If no, type of Visa and expiration date ____________ Alien Registration #________________

List any other names used

____

Position and salary desired ____

Date available ____

How were you referred to us? _ Newspaper Ad _ School _ On my own _ the Company Employee _ Agency _ Other

Name of Referral Source ____

Have you ever been employed here before? _ Yes _ No If yes, give date ________________

Education and Training

	Name of School	**City and State**	**Major Subject**	**Degree/Diploma and Number of Years Attended**
High School				
College/ University				
College/ University				
Other				

List awards, scholarships, honors received (include publications, inventions, technical awards, etc.) ________________

____

List professional certifications or designations, and date received ________________

continued on next page

Fig. 2-B (cont.)

Employment History

This portion of the application must be completed even if a resume is submitted. Starting with the most recent employer, list full- and part-time jobs, summer or volunteer work during the last 10 years. Include periods of military service, self-employment, and unemployment. Please leave no unexplained gaps. Attach separate sheet if necessary.

1	Last or Present Employer	Telephone ( )
	Address	Employed (Month and Year) From To
	Supervisor's Name and Title	Reason for Leaving
	State Job Title and Describe your work	
2	Last or Present Employer	Telephone ( )
	Address	Employed (Month and Year) From To
	Supervisor's Name and Title	Reason for Leaving
	State Job Title and Describe your work	
3	Last or Present Employer	Telephone ( )
	Address	Employed (Month and Year) From To
	Supervisor's Name and Title	Reason for Leaving
	State Job Title and Describe your work	

We may contact the employers listed above unless you indicate those you do not want us to contact.	Do Not Contact Employer Number(s) ________ Reason ________________

continued on next page

FIG. 2-B (CONT.)

References: Professional Colleagues

Name First M.I. Last	Employer/Position	Business Address	Business Phone No.
1			
2			
3			

This application will be kept in the Company's active files only until the position for which it was submitted is filled. If the applicant is not hired, the applicant must complete a new application to be considered for employment.

I hereby authorize the Company, either on its own or by and through an agent, to thoroughly investigate my references, work record, education and other matters related to my suitability for employment, such as criminal convictions, and, further, authorize my present employer or any former employer or any other party, including any Government or law enforcement agency and the references I have listed, to disclose to the Company any and all letters, reports and other information related to my work records, without giving me prior notice of such disclosure, except those which would indicate age, race, creed, color, sex, sexual orientation, or national origin. In addition, I hereby release the Company, my former employers, and all other persons, corporations, partnerships and associations from any and all claims, demands or liabilities arising out of or in any way related to such investigation or disclosure. I agree to abide by all rules and regulations of the company, and I understand that false statements or consequential omissions of any kind are sufficient grounds for denying employment or for dismissal.

I have read and understand the above statement. This application is complete and accurate to the best of my knowledge.

Signature ______________________________ Date ____________________

3. Q: What can you tell me about the new EEO-1 Report?

A: The EEO-1 Report – formally known as the "Employer Information Report" – is a government form requiring many employers to provide a count of their employees by job category and then by ethnicity, race and gender. It must be filed by: (1) employers with federal government contracts of $50,000 or more and 50 or more employees; and (2) employers who do not have a federal government contract but have 100 or more employees. The EEO-1 report is submitted to both the EEOC and the Department of Labor, Office of Federal Contract Compliance Programs (OFCCP).

The EEO-1 report must be filed annually with the EEOC by September 30. It must use employment numbers from any pay period in July through September of that year. Starting with surveys due by Sept. 30, 2007, pertaining to any single pay period between July 2007 and September 2007, a new EEO-1 Report must be used. On the new form, a few of the categories have been changed:

- a new category titled "Two or more races" has been added;
- "Asian or Pacific Islander" are divided into two separate categories: "Asian" and "Native Hawaiian or other Pacific Islander;"
- "Black" is renamed as "Black or African American;"
- "Hispanic" is renamed as "Hispanic or Latino;" and
- self-identification of race and ethnic categories is strongly endorsed, as opposed to visual identification by employers.

Note that race and ethnicity have been separated so that an employee can be identified both as "Hispanic" and as "Black" or "White." Employers should first ask if an employee is Hispanic or Latino (ethnicity) and second ask what race or races the employee considers him- or herself to be. This is called the "two-question format." Employers may ask employees to specify particular races, but they are not required to do so. If employees list several specific races even though the employer asked if they consider themselves to be "two or more races," these employees should be counted in the "Two or more races" category. The employer should preserve the detailed race information because it is an employment record.

Changes are also being made to the job categories on the EEO-1 report. First, the current category of "Officials and Managers" will be divided into two levels based on responsibility and influence within the organization:

- Executive/Senior Level Officials and Managers (plan, direct and formulate policy, set strategy and provide overall direction; in larger organizations, within two reporting levels of CEO)
- First/Mid-Level Officials and Managers (direct implementation or operations within specific parameters set by Executive/Senior Level Officials and Managers; oversee day-to-day operations)

The revised EEO-1 also will move business and financial occupations from the Officials and Managers category to the Professionals category to improve data for analyzing trends in mobility of minorities and women within Officials and Managers.

More information about the revised EEO-1 is available on the EEOC's website at http://www.eeoc.gov/eeo1/index.html.

Background Checks

4. Q: Can I ask job applicants about any past arrests or convictions?

A: The answer is "no" for arrest records and "yes" for convictions.

Any questions about an applicant's arrest record are improper and may lead to liability for employment discrimination. The Equal Employment Opportunity Commission (EEOC) and many states prohibit the use of arrest records for employment decisions because they are inherently biased against applicants in protected classes, particularly minority group members.

An applicant may be asked about prior felony convictions, if job related. However, rejecting an applicant based on a prior conviction gets a little more complicated. According to the EEOC, an employer must establish a business necessity for relying on an applicant's conviction record based on three factors:

1. the nature and gravity of the offense;
2. how "old" the conviction record is (recent, versus 20 years ago); and
3. how the offense relates to the job for which the candidate has applied.

For example, a conviction for theft certainly is related to an applicant's eligibility for any position handling money or inventory. Alternatively, a "youthful" conviction for reckless driving may not preclude an otherwise qualified candidate from employment in an entry-level office job. Any misrepresentations on the employment application concerning criminal history may provide an alternative basis for rejection or immediate termination of the candidate, even if the offense itself is not sufficient.

If prior criminal history will be considered in hiring decisions, the employment application form should include at least the following:

1. an appropriate question concerning prior criminal convictions, excluding minor traffic offenses (e.g., "Have you ever been convicted of a crime, other than a minor traffic offense? If so, please explain");
2. an explicit warning that any misstatements or misrepresentations on the application form will constitute grounds for the candidate's immediate rejection or termination from employment if he or she has been hired; and
3. a statement signed by each applicant acknowledging that they will be subject to a background investigation, including a criminal background check.

See Fig. 4-A for the types of questions that may not and may be asked.

Sources: EEOC's Revised Policy Statement on the Use of Conviction Records by Employers in Making Employment Decisions.

Fig. **4**-A
Job Application and Pre-Employment Questions

According to the EEOC, the following are examples of questions that may not be asked on a job application or during an interview.

- Have you ever had or been treated for any of the following conditions or diseases?
- Have you been treated in the past three years for any conditions or diseases and, if so, what were they?
- Have you ever been hospitalized? If so, for what condition?
- Have you ever been treated by a psychiatrist or psychologist? If so, for what condition?
- Have you ever been treated for any mental condition?
- Is there any health-related reason you may not be able to perform the job for which you are applying?
- Have you had a major illness in the last five years?
- How many days were you absent from work because of illness last year?
- Do you have any physical defects that preclude you from performing certain kinds of work? If yes, describe such defects and specific work limitations.
- Do you have any disabilities or impairments that may affect your performance in the position for which you are applying?
- Are you taking prescribed drugs?
- Have you ever been treated for drug addiction or alcoholism?
- Have you ever filed for workers' compensation insurance?

Pre-employment questions that may be asked –

- Can you meet the requirements of the attendance policy?
- Can you perform the tasks of this position with or without an accommodation?
- Describe or demonstrate how you would perform this function, with or without an accommodation. (Such a question may be asked of applicants who have a known disability that might prevent them from performing a job function. If the disability would not interfere with a job function, however, the person could be asked only to demonstrate job performance if all other candidates must do so.)
- Do you use illegal drugs?
- Have you ever been arrested for driving under the influence?
- Do you have the required licenses and degrees to perform this job?

5. Q: How can I find out about an applicant's workers' comp history? I don't want to hire someone who's likely to go out on workers' comp.

A: The simple answer is, you can't, at least not right away, if you have 15 or more employees, because you are covered by the Americans With Disabilities Act (ADA).

To help prevent discrimination against individuals with disabilities in hiring, the ADA prohibits employers from asking *job applicants* any questions about disabilities, including attempting to elicit information about physical or mental conditions that could be disabilities. That means employers cannot ask about accidents that caused injuries (including workers' compensation claims), medications a potential employee is taking, health insurance claims the person made or any medical treatments the individual had or is undergoing.

Employers covered by the ADA cannot ask about health on application forms or in interviews *before* a hiring decision is made. *After* an individual is offered a job, an employer may make medical history inquiries and even require a medical examination and condition an employment offer on the results of a medical examination, *if* all entering employees in the same job category are required to take the same exam or provide the same information.

If the medical information the employer obtains screens out individuals with disabilities, the exclusionary criteria must be job-related and consistent with business necessity. That means, you have to justify it on the basis that individuals in that job have to have the physical ability to do certain things. There also must be a serious effort to determine if a reasonable accommodation would enable the person to perform the job's essential functions despite the disability. But remember, the ADA applies only to individuals with disabilities. If you discover that an applicant is a serial user of workers' comp and no disability is involved, you can factor that applicant's history into your hiring decision.

After an individual is hired and working, an employer may require a medical examination or make medical inquiries, as long and they are job-related and consistent with business necessity. And, of course, voluntary medical examinations and medical histories that are part of an employee health program are permitted.

Any medical information, regardless of when it is obtained, must be kept confidential and available only on a need-to-know basis, such as to supervisors who need to know about work restrictions, first aid and safety personnel, or government officials. The information should be kept in files separate from all other personnel records.

Example: If an employee is injured while on the job, gathering workers' compensation information would be both job-related and a business necessity. Therefore, an employer may ask questions about workplace injuries that happen after an employee is hired.

Sources: 29 C.F.R. §§1630.13 and 14; EEOC Enforcement Guidance: Workers' Compensation and the ADA; EEOC Enforcement Guidance: Pre-employment Disability-Related Questions and Medical Examinations.

6. Q: Is there a way to learn more about applicants' prior job performance? Whenever I check job references, all I get are useless "neutral references."

A: Yes, but it may not be easy or productive. Fear of litigation has led many employers to adopt a "name, rank and serial number" policy when it comes to giving out information about former employees. This is the "neutral reference," verifying only dates of employment, position held and salary. But there are some ways to elicit additional information.

It is essential to lay the groundwork for a constructive reference check. Employers should ensure that the employment application form includes a clear, easily readable statement notifying candidates that a pre-hire background check is required, and that providing false information on the application form constitutes grounds for rejection of the applicant or immediate termination if the falsehood is discovered after hire. The application should also require that gaps in employment be identified and explained.

All candidates should be asked to sign a reference check release form, documenting their consent to have references contacted, performance reviews obtained, credit and criminal background checks performed, and waiving any claims against present, former or prospective employers based on the references given.

The form should also advise candidates that a failure to consent to such checks by signing the release disqualifies them from further consideration. A completed form can be faxed to reluctant references to encourage a more candid report. See Fig. 6-A for a Release and Authorization for Public Records Form.

Do not rely solely on the references the candidate suggests, because these generally are "pre-approved" contacts with glowing reviews. Moreover, it may be difficult to locate former co-workers or supervisors who have moved on to other employers. One option is to ask the primary references for more names, or press the candidate further. While he or she may be reluctant to approve a call to a current boss, the candidate may be willing to identify a current co-worker, who can speak confidentially. Also, consider asking the candidate to identify anyone who should not be contacted, and why.

Although most reference checks are done by phone, it may be helpful to fax a short questionnaire asking for numerical ratings, including space for written comments. Reluctant references may be more responsive to a request to rate the candidate's job performance on a scale of 1 to 5, for example.

Follow-up questions are essential as well, such as "Could you be more specific?" or "Could you give me an example?" Subtle cues, such as long pauses after probing questions and tone of voice may indicate a reluctance to say something negative, and should not be ignored. It may even be productive to ask reluctant references whether their failure to provide information signifies a problem with the candidate.

Finally, always ask whether the candidate is eligible or ineligible for rehire, and whether it is company policy not to rehire former employees. The type of response given may be revealing.

Fig. 6-A

To Be Used When Procuring Information From Public Records Without The Services Of A Consumer Reporting Agency

RELEASE AND AUTHORIZATION FOR PUBLIC RECORDS

DISCLOSURE: A PUBLIC RECORD MAY BE PROCURED FOR EMPLOYMENT PURPOSES.

I voluntarily and knowingly authorize, for employment purposes only, [COMPANY] to obtain public records, which may include records documenting an arrest, indictment, conviction, civil judicial action, tax lien or outstanding judgment.

I voluntarily and knowingly release from all liability all persons, companies and corporations requesting and/or supplying information for such public records, except that such release shall not be implied to waive any rights I may have to correct errors or misstatements contained in the public records obtained pursuant to this agreement.

SIGNATURE DATE	CA APPLICANTS <u>ONLY</u>: You have the right to receive a copy of any public record that is ordered pursuant to your authorization. ☐ I wish to waive my right to be furnished with a copy of a public record should any be ordered.
FULL NAME (*type or print legibly*)	DRIVER'S LICENSE NUMBER STATE OF ISSUE
STREET ADDRESS	DATE OF BIRTH
CITY, STATE, ZIP	
SOCIAL SECURITY NUMBER	

HFHRT031

This application will be kept in the Company's active files only until the position for which it was submitted is filled. If the applicant is not hired, the applicant must complete a new application to be considered for employment.

I hereby authorize the Company, either on its own or by and through an agent, to thoroughly investigate my references, work record, education and other matters related to my suitability for employment, such as criminal convictions, and, further, authorize my present employer or any former employer or any other party, including any Government or law enforcement agency and the references I have listed, to disclose to the Company any and all letters, reports and other information related to my work records, without giving me prior notice of such disclosure, except those which would indicate age, race, creed, color, sex, sexual orientation, or national origin. In addition, I hereby release the Company, my former employers, and all other persons, corporations, partnerships and associations from any and all claims, demands or liabilities arising out of or in any way related to such investigation or disclosure. I agree to abide by all rules and regulations of the company, and I understand that false statements or consequential omissions of any kind are sufficient grounds for denying employment or for dismissal.

I have read and understand the above statement. This application is complete and accurate to the best of my knowledge.

Signature ______________________________ Date ____________________

7. Q: What should I know about genetic discrimination laws?

A: Genetic discrimination is focused on prohibiting the use of genetic information about potential health problems when making employment decisions. For example, if a woman has the gene that tends to predict breast cancer, genetic discrimination laws would prevent an employer or health insurer from rejecting that person based on that information. Over 30 states have passed laws prohibiting genetic discrimination. In most cases, these laws also provide that genetic information may not be sought or disclosed.

At the federal level, HIPAA already prohibits the use of genentic information in group health insurance contexts. A federal genetic discrimination law is pending. Both Houses of Congress have passed laws, but single bill has not yet been approved and signed into law.

I-9 Forms

8. Q: Do I have to check ID documents for everybody I hire? I usually hire people I've known for years, so I know they're okay.

A: You need to make sure that everyone you *hire* is authorized to work in the United States. You do not need to see identification papers for everyone you interview, but you *do* need to fill out an Employment Eligibility Verification form – commonly referred to as the "I-9" (see Fig. 8-A for a copy of the form) – for everyone you hire.

You must have an I-9 on file for every employee hired after Nov. 6, 1986, even if you have known the employee for years and are sure he or she is legally residing in the United States and is authorized to work.

At the time you hire an employee, you must make sure that the employee completes Section 1 of the I-9. Then, within three business days of the date of hire, you must complete Section 2 of the form by examining evidence of the employee's identity and employment eligibility, and recording the document title (for example, "U.S. Passport," "Permanent Resident Card" or "Driver's License"), the issuing authority, the document number, the expiration date of the document (if any) and the date employment began.

You should not continue to employ a person who cannot present acceptable documents. The third page of the I-9 form provides a list of acceptable documents.

Remember, you cannot insist on any particular form of documentation. List A on page 3 of the I-9 form contains documents that establish both identity and employment eligibility. List B contains documents that establish identity only, and List C includes documents that establish employment eligibility only.

The so-called "green cards" (permanent resident cards) are on List A. They establish *both* the employee's identity and employment eligibility. But it is entirely appropriate for an employee to show you a different document from List A, such as a U.S. passport, an unexpired temporary resident card, an unexpired foreign passport with a stamp or form indicating unexpired employment authorization, or one of the other documents on List A.

It is also appropriate for the employee to show you a document from List B to establish identity, such as a voter registration card, a driver's license issued by a state, a school I.D. card with a photograph or a hospital record *and* a document from List C to establish employment eligibility, such as a U.S.

> What Do I Do With Completed I-**9**s?
>
> Completed I-9s should be kept for three years after the date of hire, or one year after the date employment ends, whichever is *later*. The departments of Justice, Labor and the Office of Homeland Security have the authority to inspect your company's I-9 forms to make sure they are filled out properly and that your employees are authorized to work in the United States.
>
> There are no special rules about where the forms should be filed. It makes sense to keep them all together, rather than in individual employees' personnel files, so they are easier to produce for inspection. But as a practical matter, it makes good sense to keep a copy in each employee's personnel folder as well.

Social Security card, a certification of birth abroad issued by the U.S. State Department, or an original or certified copy of a U.S. birth certificate.

If you insist on seeing a specific document, say a green card, with the intent of discriminating against an applicant because of his or her national origin or citizenship status, you may be considered to have committed document abuse. The employee can file a complaint against your company with the Office of Special Counsel for Immigration-Related Unfair Employment Practices in the Civil Rights Division of the Department of Justice.

By the way, hiring "guys from the neighborhood" sounds pretty innocuous, but make sure that it's not just a way of avoiding hiring people who are "different," such as women and minorities.

Sources: 8 U.S.C. §§1324a and b; 8 C.F.R. §1274a.2.

Fig. 8-A

Department of Homeland Security
U.S. Citizenship and Immigration Services

OMB No. 1615-0047; Expires 03/31/07

Employment Eligibility Verification

INSTRUCTIONS

PLEASE READ ALL INSTRUCTIONS CAREFULLY BEFORE COMPLETING THIS FORM.

Anti-Discrimination Notice. It is illegal to discriminate against any individual (other than an alien not authorized to work in the U.S.) in hiring, discharging, or recruiting or referring for a fee because of that individual's national origin or citizenship status. It is illegal to discriminate against work eligible individuals. Employers **CANNOT** specify which document(s) they will accept from an employee. The refusal to hire an individual because of a future expiration date may also constitute illegal discrimination.

Section 1- Employee. All employees, citizens and noncitizens, hired after November 6, 1986, must complete Section 1 of this form at the time of hire, which is the actual beginning of employment. **The employer is responsible for ensuring that Section 1 is timely and properly completed.**

Preparer/Translator Certification. The Preparer/Translator Certification must be completed if Section 1 is prepared by a person other than the employee. A preparer/translator may be used only when the employee is unable to complete Section 1 on his/her own. However, the employee must still sign Section 1 personally.

Section 2 - Employer. For the purpose of completing this form, the term "employer" includes those recruiters and referrers for a fee who are agricultural associations, agricultural employers or farm labor contractors.

Employers must complete Section 2 by examining evidence of identity and employment eligibility within three (3) business days of the date employment begins. If employees are authorized to work, but are unable to present the required document(s) within three business days, they must present a receipt for the application of the document(s) within three business days and the actual document(s) within ninety (90) days. However, if employers hire individuals for a duration of less than three business days, Section 2 must be completed at the time employment begins. **Employers must record: 1)** document title; **2)** issuing authority; **3)** document number, **4)** expiration date, if any; and **5)** the date employment begins. Employers must sign and date the certification. Employees must present original documents. Employers may, but are not required to, photocopy the document(s) presented. These photocopies may only be used for the verification process and must be retained with the I-9. **However, employers are still responsible for completing the I-9.**

Section 3 - Updating and Reverification. Employers must complete Section 3 when updating and/or reverifying the I-9. Employers must reverify employment eligibility of their employees on or before the expiration date recorded in Section 1. Employers **CANNOT** specify which document(s) they will accept from an employee.

- If an employee's name has changed at the time this form is being updated/reverified, complete Block A.
- If an employee is rehired within three (3) years of the date this form was originally completed and the employee is still eligible to be employed on the same basis as previously indicated on this form (updating), complete Block B and the signature block.
- If an employee is rehired within three (3) years of the date this form was originally completed and the employee's work authorization has expired **or** if a current employee's work authorization is about to expire (reverification), complete Block B and:
  - examine any document that reflects that the employee is authorized to work in the U.S. (see List A **or** C),
  - record the document title, document number and expiration date (if any) in Block C, and
  - complete the signature block.

Photocopying and Retaining Form I-9. A blank I-9 may be reproduced, provided both sides are copied. The Instructions must be available to all employees completing this form. Employers must retain completed I-9s for three (3) years after the date of hire or one (1) year after the date employment ends, whichever is later.

For more detailed information, you may refer to the Department of Homeland Security (DHS) Handbook for Employers, (Form M-274). You may obtain the handbook at your local U.S. Citizenship and Immigration Services (USCIS) office.

Privacy Act Notice. The authority for collecting this information is the Immigration Reform and Control Act of 1986, Pub. L. 99-603 (8 USC 1324a).

This information is for employers to verify the eligibility of individuals for employment to preclude the unlawful hiring, or recruiting or referring for a fee, of aliens who are not authorized to work in the United States.

This information will be used by employers as a record of their basis for determining eligibility of an employee to work in the United States. The form will be kept by the employer and made available for inspection by officials of the U.S. Immigration and Customs Enforcement, Department of Labor and Office of Special Counsel for Immigration Related Unfair Employment Practices.

Submission of the information required in this form is voluntary. However, an individual may not begin employment unless this form is completed, since employers are subject to civil or criminal penalties if they do not comply with the Immigration Reform and Control Act of 1986.

Reporting Burden. We try to create forms and instructions that are accurate, can be easily understood and which impose the least possible burden on you to provide us with information. Often this is difficult because some immigration laws are very complex. Accordingly, the reporting burden for this collection of information is computed as follows: **1)** learning about this form, 5 minutes; **2)** completing the form, 5 minutes; and **3)** assembling and filing (recordkeeping) the form, 5 minutes, for an average of 15 minutes per response. If you have comments regarding the accuracy of this burden estimate, or suggestions for making this form simpler, you can write to U.S. Citizenship and Immigration Services, Regulatory Management Division, 111 Massachuetts Avenue, N.W., Washington, DC 20529. OMB No. 1615-0047.

NOTE: This is the 1991 edition of the Form I-9 that has been rebranded with a current printing date to reflect the recent transition from the INS to DHS and its components.

EMPLOYERS MUST RETAIN COMPLETED FORM I-9
PLEASE DO NOT MAIL COMPLETED FORM I-9 TO ICE OR USCIS

Form I-9 (Rev. 05/31/05)Y

continued on next page

FIG. 8-A (CONT.)

Department of Homeland Security
U.S. Citizenship and Immigration Services

OMB No. 1615-0047; Expires 03/31/07

Employment Eligibility Verification

Please read instructions carefully before completing this form. The instructions must be available during completion of this form. ANTI-DISCRIMINATION NOTICE: It is illegal to discriminate against work eligible individuals. Employers CANNOT specify which document(s) they will accept from an employee. The refusal to hire an individual because of a future expiration date may also constitute illegal discrimination.

Section 1. Employee Information and Verification. To be completed and signed by employee at the time employment begins.

Print Name: Last | First | Middle Initial | Maiden Name

Address *(Street Name and Number)* | Apt. # | Date of Birth *(month/day/year)*

City | State | Zip Code | Social Security #

I am aware that federal law provides for imprisonment and/or fines for false statements or use of false documents in connection with the completion of this form.

I attest, under penalty of perjury, that I am (check one of the following):
☐ A citizen or national of the United States
☐ A Lawful Permanent Resident (Alien #) A ______
☐ An alien authorized to work until ______
(Alien # or Admission #) ______

Employee's Signature | Date *(month/day/year)*

Preparer and/or Translator Certification. *(To be completed and signed if Section 1 is prepared by a person other than the employee.) I attest, under penalty of perjury, that I have assisted in the completion of this form and that to the best of my knowledge the information is true and correct.*

Preparer's/Translator's Signature | Print Name

Address *(Street Name and Number, City, State, Zip Code)* | Date *(month/day/year)*

Section 2. Employer Review and Verification. To be completed and signed by employer. Examine one document from List A OR examine one document from List B and one from List C, as listed on the reverse of this form, and record the title, number and expiration date, if any, of the document(s).

	List A	OR	List B	AND	List C
Document title:	______		______		______
Issuing authority:	______		______		______
Document #:	______		______		______
Expiration Date *(if any)*:	______		______		______
Document #:	______				
Expiration Date *(if any)*:	______				

CERTIFICATION - I attest, under penalty of perjury, that I have examined the document(s) presented by the above-named employee, that the above-listed document(s) appear to be genuine and to relate to the employee named, that the employee began employment on *(month/day/year)* ______ **and that to the best of my knowledge the employee is eligible to work in the United States. (State employment agencies may omit the date the employee began employment.)**

Signature of Employer or Authorized Representative | Print Name | Title

Business or Organization Name | Address *(Street Name and Number, City, State, Zip Code)* | Date *(month/day/year)*

Section 3. Updating and Reverification. To be completed and signed by employer.

A. New Name *(if applicable)* | B. Date of rehire *(month/day/year) (if applicable)*

C. If employee's previous grant of work authorization has expired, provide the information below for the document that establishes current employment eligibility.

Document Title: ______ Document #: ______ Expiration Date (if any): ______

I attest, under penalty of perjury, that to the best of my knowledge, this employee is eligible to work in the United States, and if the employee presented document(s), the document(s) I have examined appear to be genuine and to relate to the individual.

Signature of Employer or Authorized Representative | Date *(month/day/year)*

NOTE: This is the 1991 edition of the Form I-9 that has been rebranded with a current printing date to reflect the recent transition from the INS to DHS and its components.

Form I-9 (Rev. 05/31/05)Y Page 2

continued on next page

FIG. 8-A (CONT.)

LISTS OF ACCEPTABLE DOCUMENTS

LIST A

Documents that Establish Both Identity and Employment Eligibility

1. U.S. Passport (unexpired or expired)
2. Certificate of U.S. Citizenship *(Form N-560 or N-561)*
3. Certificate of Naturalization *(Form N-550 or N-570)*
4. Unexpired foreign passport, with *I-551 stamp or* attached *Form I-94* indicating unexpired employment authorization
5. Permanent Resident Card or Alien Registration Receipt Card with photograph *(Form I-151 or I-551)*
6. Unexpired Temporary Resident Card *(Form I-688)*
7. Unexpired Employment Authorization Card *(Form I-688A)*
8. Unexpired Reentry Permit *(Form I-327)*
9. Unexpired Refugee Travel Document *(Form I-571)*
10. Unexpired Employment Authorization Document issued by DHS that contains a photograph *(Form I-688B)*

OR

LIST B

Documents that Establish Identity

1. Driver's license or ID card issued by a state or outlying possession of the United States provided it contains a photograph or information such as name, date of birth, gender, height, eye color and address
2. ID card issued by federal, state or local government agencies or entities, provided it contains a photograph or information such as name, date of birth, gender, height, eye color and address
3. School ID card with a photograph
4. Voter's registration card
5. U.S. Military card or draft record
6. Military dependent's ID card
7. U.S. Coast Guard Merchant Mariner Card
8. Native American tribal document
9. Driver's license issued by a Canadian government authority

For persons under age 18 who are unable to present a document listed above:

10. School record or report card
11. Clinic, doctor or hospital record
12. Day-care or nursery school record

AND

LIST C

Documents that Establish Employment Eligibility

1. U.S. social security card issued by the Social Security Administration *(other than a card stating it is not valid for employment)*
2. Certification of Birth Abroad issued by the Department of State *(Form FS-545 or Form DS-1350)*
3. Original or certified copy of a birth certificate issued by a state, county, municipal authority or outlying possession of the United States bearing an official seal
4. Native American tribal document
5. U.S. Citizen ID Card *(Form I-197)*
6. ID Card for use of Resident Citizen in the United States *(Form I-179)*
7. Unexpired employment authorization document issued by DHS *(other than those listed under List A)*

Illustrations of many of these documents appear in Part 8 of the Handbook for Employers (M-274)

Form I-9 (Rev. 05/31/05)Y Page 3

9. Q: Do I have to fire an employee if I discover later that he showed me a phony ID when I hired him?

A: No. First, talk to the employee and give him another opportunity to provide proper I-9 documentation. If he provides the proper documents, you should correct the information on the original I-9 to reflect those documents. If he cannot show you acceptable documents, you should terminate his employment.

While this is an unfortunate situation, your company can face criminal or civil penalties for employing someone who is not authorized to work in this country.

Remember, you are not required to be a document expert or to try to figure out if a document is genuine. Normally, an employer will be considered to have complied with the law if a document reasonably looked genuine and if it reasonably appeared to belong to the person presenting it.

But if you think an employee's documents do not look right – either because the document appears not to be genuine or because you have reason to suspect that it belongs to someone else – you should refuse to accept the document and ask for other documentation. Many employers have learned that once they ask for additional or more accurate papers, the employee disappears before the employers can act.

You can also seek assistance from a government office to determine whether the document is authentic and pertains to your employee. You can call a local office of the U.S. Citizenship and Immigration Services (part of the Department of Homeland Security) or the Office of Business Liaison of the Citizenship and Immigration Services.

Sources: 8 U.S.C. §1324a (e) and (f); 8 U.S.C. §1324a (b)(6); 8 C.F.R. §1274a.2(b)(1)(ii).

Interviewing

10. Q: How can I find out if an applicant can do a physically demanding job without getting in trouble? I'm thinking about requiring a medical certification from certain applicants.

A: The Americans With Disabilities Act (ADA) recognizes that physical qualification standards may be necessary for certain jobs. As long as you can show that your physical standards are job-related and consistent with business necessity, you may ask a job applicant how they would perform a specific task. Remember, the ADA protects against discrimination based on disability; it does not address whether you have demanding standards for demanding jobs as long as they do not implicate disabilities.

You also may require that applicants take a physical agility test. Again, the test must be job related, necessary for your business and must be given to all similarly situated applicants. If you are hiring firefighters, for example, you can require that applicants demonstrate their ability to climb ladders while carrying appropriate equipment.

What you cannot do before making a job offer is require a medical examination of an applicant. Nor are you permitted to ask about medical conditions, past or present, or disabilities. For example, questions such as, "Have you ever been treated for any of the following conditions," followed by a list, are not permitted, nor are questions about prescription medications or hospitalizations.

Sources: 20 C.F.R. §1630.14(b); EEOC's Enforcement Guidance: Pre-employment Disability-Related Inquiries and Medical Examinations; EEOC's ADA Technical Assistance Manual on Title I, §4.4.

11. Q: What am I not allowed to ask a job applicant? I'm confused about what I can and can't say.

A: I'm not surprised. This is one of the most confusing areas of the law and it is very easy to go astray.

The first rule of job interviewing must always be that any questions asked should be job-related. It is never discriminatory to ask about prior job experience, education or skills that are necessary prerequisites for performing the job to be filled. You should not ask anything that does not involve a bona fide occupational qualification. You also should not ask anything that might tend to affect a protected group (women, minorities or people with disabilities) differently than other applicants.

Many questions employers ask are not inherently discriminatory, but basing employment decisions on the answers is. For example, is it really necessary to know whether an applicant is married at the interview stage? Once the question is asked, it may be hard to prove the answer did not affect your hiring decision, so it is best if you just don't ask.

The same is true for asking an applicant age-related questions. It is not discriminatory, *per se*. But basing a hiring decision on age may violate the Age Discrimination in

Employment Act. Unless age is a bona fide occupational qualification, you should not ask an applicant about his or her birth date.

Similarly, gender-related questions such as pregnancy plans and the number and ages of children can be discriminatory if the answers are used to reject a female applicant. Unless the questions are directly related to performance of the job at issue, you should not ask them.

Some questions are less obvious. Questions about arrest records (as opposed to convictions) may be discriminatory because minorities have a disproportionately higher number of arrests than non-minorities. Some states prohibit refusing to hire applicants on the basis of arrest records and using arrest records as an employment criteria also may violate Title VII of the 1964 Civil Rights Act. For those reasons, it is best to not ask questions about arrests.

Other questions to avoid include anything about child care arrangements or prior salaries, because they tend to have a negative impact on women. Some states even prohibit asking information about prior salaries for that reason. The theory is you should pay a new employee what he or she is worth, so information about past salaries is not job-related.

Questions about modes of transportation, length of residence at a current address, home ownership and the like tend to impact unfavorably on minorities and should be avoided unless they involve a bona fide occupational qualification.

With many questions, the problem is not that you as an employer ask them – you may have a legitimate reason for wanting to know the answers – but the issue is timing. You can ask the question, but not before making a legitimate offer to hire.

Questions about citizenship and proof of eligibility to work in the United States fall into this category. Unless citizenship is a bona fide occupational qualification, you should not ask about it until after you have hired the employee and request information for purposes of filling out the federal I-9 form required by the Immigration Reform and Control Act.

Timing is also an issue with questions about physical and mental impairments. If you are covered by the Americans With Disabilities Act, questions about health history, including questions regarding health information you need for insurance purposes, may be obtained only after you have offered the applicant a job.

If the applicant has an obvious disability or volunteers information about a disability during the interview, you may ask whether he or she would need a reasonable accommodation and what that might be. In that case you also can ask how the applicant would perform specific job functions.

To avoid potential discrimination claims, you must be careful not to ask follow-up questions about the disability itself. Stick to questions about the applicant's ability to perform the essential function of the job, which are always legitimate, and to reasonable accommodation issues.

Required Affirmative Action

Some employers are required to meet diversity standards in their workforce. As part of that, job applicants must be identified in terms of protected categories – race, gender, disability. Race and gender usually will be obvious, but disability may not be.

The Equal Employment Opportunity Commission has said that to meet affirmative action requirements, job applicants may be asked to voluntarily supply information about disabilities. Employers must clearly state that the information is intended for use solely in connection with affirmative action and is strictly voluntary. The information should be kept confidential and separate from the rest of the application process so that the person or panel doing the hiring is not influenced by it.

Interview Procedures

You should standardize your interview procedures. Managers who will be interviewing job applicants should receive training that includes being told why some questions are unwise.

Standardized job-related questions should be prepared and used by everyone who does interviewing for your company. Having a script that everyone uses not only prevents improper questions, but creates a better basis for comparison of applicants. See 15 Rules for Interviews, Fig. 11-A.

Sources: 42 U.S.C. §§12112(c) and (d); 29 C.F.R. §1607; 29 C.F.R. §1630.13(a); EEOC's Enforcement Guidance: Pre-employment Disability-Related Inquiries and Medical Examinations; EEOC's Job Advertising and Pre-Employment Inquiries Under ADEA.

Fig. 11-A
Fifteen Rules for Pre-employment Interviews Under the ADA

1. Questions that elicit information about the existence, nature, or scope of a disability are prohibited. Questions about an applicant's ability to perform major life activities are considered to be disability-related and should be avoided.
2. An employer may ask about an applicant's ability to perform a job only within the framework of stated essential functions. Thus, after offering a job description or stating the requirements, an employer may ask if the applicant can meet those requirements, with or without an accommodation.
3. An employer may ask about non-medical qualifications (such as licenses, degrees, and certifications) and, if they are required of all similarly situated employees, the employer need make no allowance or accommodation for a disabled applicant.
4. An employer may ask if an applicant with an ***obvious*** disability needs an accommodation to participate in the hiring process, *but* whatever knowledge of the applicant's disability is acquired can and will be held against the employer in a subsequent discrimination suit. An employer may require the applicant to provide documentation regarding the disability in question and its functional limitations if the disability appears to be unrelated to the job.
5. If an applicant with a ***hidden*** disability asks for an accommodation for the hiring process or for an accommodation to demonstrate how a job would be performed, employers may require documentation to satisfy themselves that the applicant has a covered disability.
6. Even if all applicants are not asked, an employer may ask a disabled applicant to describe or demonstrate how the job would be performed ***only if*** (1) the applicant's obvious disability creates a reasonable belief in the employer that the disability may affect the applicant's ability to perform the job ***or*** (2) the applicant discloses that he or she has a hidden disability that creates this same reasonable belief.
7. Employers ***may ask*** if an applicant requires an accommodation to perform the job ***if*** the request:
    - is based on a reasonable belief that an obvious disability will require an accommodation;
    - comes after the applicant has disclosed a hidden disability that creates the same belief; or
    - comes after the applicant tells the employer that an accommodation will be required.
8. Despite the reasonableness of an employer's belief that even a manifest disability will require an accommodation, if the applicant denies that an accommodation is needed, the employer *may not* pursue the subject. However, an employer who reasonably believes that an accommodation will be needed *may*, in this circumstance, ask that the applicant describe or demonstrate how the job will be performed, even if all applicants are not asked to do so.
9. Even if an employer asks about the nature and scope of an accommodation properly and pursuant to the EEOC's rules, the employer will be presumed to have actual knowledge of the disability in any subsequent discrimination suit arising from the employer's failure to hire the applicant.
10. An employer may ask about all non-disabilty-related conditions of employment, including ability to meet attendance requirements.

continued on next page

FIG. 11-A (CONT.)

11. Employers ***may not*** ask about lawful drug use; the response will likely reveal the existence of many disabilities. However, if an applicant tests positive for illegal drug use, an employer may ask about lawful drug use. ***Please note,*** this could prompt the revisions of most drug-testing programs which usually ask about lawful drug use prior to the test, so that the lab can screen for specific false positives.
12. Employers may ask about illegal drug use, but ***be careful.*** Even though Congress has expressly identified drug use as not being a disability, the EEOC recognizes ***prior*** drug addiction (as opposed to current drug use) as a disability. Thus, an employer ***may*** ask "Have you ever used illegal drugs? When was the last time you did so?", but an employer ***may not*** ask "Have you ever been addicted to drugs?"
13. Government contractors ***may*** ask applicants to "self-identify" as individuals with disabilities, for purposes of complying with affirmative action requirements. Other employers may do so only if they are participating in affirmative action program, even voluntarily. In all circumstances, the disclosure must be voluntary and can be used only to benefit the self-identifying applicants.
14. However an employer learns of an employee's disability or other medical information, the information must be kept confidential and should be kept separate from the personnel function. e.g., unrelated to decisions about hiring, promotion, pay, or termination.
15. All tests, including medical tests, that seek information about impairments are prohibited. Agility tests and demonstrations of an ability to do the job or to meet fixed standards (e.g., typing tests) are permitted. The job-relatedness of the test is crucial. After a conditional offer of employment, a medical exam is permitted if all similarly-situated applicants are examined.

Job Descriptions

12. Q: How specific should our job descriptions be? Are just "essential functions" enough?

A: The more specific the job description is, the better it will serve to define the position and the skills an applicant needs to perform necessary tasks. But you do not have to include everything an employee does. The key is to identify essential tasks, those things that the job was created to do and without which there would be no need for the position. It will also make it a lot easier to conduct a job interview.

Job descriptions serve a number of purposes. They identify bona fide job requirements, which are the basis for minimum hiring qualifications and compensation. They can also provide promotion tracks and criteria on which to base performance appraisals and are useful in determining whether an employee is exempt from overtime requirements. Identifying essential job functions helps to determine the physical requirements for that job, which in turn clarifies who would be qualified to do it.

That is important because under the Americans With Disabilities Act, only qualified individuals need to be considered. A "qualified individual" is one who, with or without a reasonable accommodation, can perform a job's essential functions. The Family and Medical Leave Act (FMLA) also uses essential functions. A covered employee can take FMLA leave for "serious health conditions," which are defined as those that leave the worker unable to perform the essential functions of his or her job.

Employers are not required by any federal law to have job descriptions. However, written job descriptions that are prepared prior to advertising or interviewing applicants for a position are considered evidence, along with other relevant factors, that a particular task is essential. That can be important if someone charges you with discrimination for failure to hire them. If your defense is that the applicant could not do the job, your job description can back you up.

If you do decide to prepare job descriptions, make sure they describe all of the essential tasks the employee needs to do, especially those that are physical. Do a job analysis. Your current employees can help you with that.

Job descriptions should be detailed enough to be thorough, and specific enough to be clear. Describe tasks in some detail. For example, don't just say, "job requires heavy lifting." Instead, say, "job requires employee to lift without assistance widgets weighing up to 50 pounds." The percentage of time spent on each task should be included, if possible. (See Sample General Position Job Description, Fig. 12-A.) And job descriptions should be reviewed and updated periodically to keep them accurate.

Sources: 29 U.S.C. §2612(a)(1)(D); 29 C.F.R. §1630.2; EEOC Technical Assistance Manual §2.3(a).

Fig. 12-A
Sample General Position Job Description

The ADA prohibits discrimination against qualified individuals with disabilities. To determine whether an individual is qualified, the essential functions of each job should be identified. Essential job functions are those that are intrinsic to the position, and the individual who holds the job must be able to perform with or without reasonable accommodation.

Title:

Department:

Reports To:

Date:

POSITION PURPOSE AND OBJECTIVES
This is a short, general summary of the overall purpose and objectives of the position. This section should include statements describing the job's primary responsibility, the end results the job is expected to accomplish, and the degree of freedom to act (e.g., "under direct supervision," "under indirect supervision," "independently").

ESSENTIAL JOB FUNCTIONS
Each job has a number of tasks, duties and responsibilities that comprise the means of accomplishing the job's purpose and objectives. This section provides a list of those essential job functions. This is a crucial part of the Job Description because an employer is not obligated to accommodate an essential function.

Where possible, as with certain "white collar" jobs, the statement can include a description of what the function is and why it is required. For example, "Reviews and approves all personnel requisitions and payroll authorizations for accuracy and compliance with performance, salary review and administration guidelines."

In compiling this list, arrange the functions by area of responsibility and priority. List the functions within each area in order of importance. Also, when appropriate, note the timeliness and/or frequency of functions as appropriate (e.g., daily, weekly, monthly). But remember, this is not a work assignment sheet; it is a generalized description.

All position guides should include the following "Essential Functions":

1. Must be able to come to work promptly and regularly.
2. Must be able to take direction and work well with others.
3. Must be able to work under the stress of deadlines.
4. Must be able to concentrate and perform accurately

HFCMP002

continued on next page

Fig. 12-A (cont.)

5. Must be able to react to change productively and to handle other tasks as assigned.

KNOWLEDGE, SKILLS AND ABILITIES REQUIRED

This section details the specific knowledge, skills and abilities required to perform the various functions of the job. Each statement should include what is required and why it is required. For example, "Employee must know how to use Lotus 1-2-3 to maintain various budget and expense reports."

These statements should be stated as minimum requirements to accomplish the essential job functions and should be supported by the essential job functions listed above. Any physical abilities required by the job also should be detailed in this section (e.g., "Ability to repeatedly lift and carry 25 lbs. for periods of one to two hours in order to load bundles onto trucks") or in the "Essential Functions," if appropriate. This section may also be expanded to include "Minimum Qualifications," below.

SUPERVISORY RESPONSIBILITY

This section details the scope of the position's supervisory responsibility; a list of jobs that report to the incumbent should be included.

WORKING CONDITIONS

If there are unique or unusual conditions different from a normal office environment, they should be listed here. Working conditions should be inherent to the job; in other words, the job cannot be performed without exposure to the conditions described in this section, *e.g.*, "most of the work is outdoors, regardless of the weather."

MINIMUM QUALIFICATIONS

This section lists the minimum education, experience, or combination of education and experience required to obtain the job. It is important that these qualifications be stated as minimums; if they are inflated, they may screen out people who are qualified to do the work.

SUCCESS FACTORS

There are certain personal characteristics that contribute to an individual's ability to excel in a particular job. This section of the position guide should list those characteristics that the supervisor expects will result in successful performance of the job.

Testing Issues

13. Q: Can I ask an applicant to take a physical exam? After I offered one applicant the job, she told me about her history of sick leave absences, and now I'm having second thoughts about hiring her.

A: Maybe. Questioning how many sick days a candidate missed in a previous job prior to extending a conditional job offer violates the Americans With Disabilities Act (ADA).

Of course, if the candidate volunteers information concerning her sick leave history, there is no violation as long as the disclosure is truly voluntary, which may have been the case here. Also, you can ask *after* a job offer has been made. The thing to remember is that you cannot request, persuade, coerce or otherwise pressure a job applicant to get him or her to disclose medical information prior to a job offer.

Now, to physical exams. You may require candidates to undergo post-offer physical examinations, as long as *all* entering employees in the same job category have to have those examinations and any medical information obtained is kept confidential. Such examinations do not have to be limited to the individual's ability to perform job functions, nor do they have to be job related or consistent with business necessity. Moreover, the job offer can be conditioned on the exam results.

After you have offered an applicant a job, you may ask about the individual's workers' compensation history, prior sick leave usage, illnesses/diseases/impairments and general physical and mental health, as long as the same inquiries are made of all individuals in the same job category. Disability-related questions and medical examinations at the post-offer stage do not have to be related to the job. After basic medical information from all candidates has been received, specific individuals may be asked for more medical information if the follow-up examinations or questions are medically related to the previously obtained medical information.

If responses to medical inquiries or the results of a medical exam result in withdrawal of the conditional offer of employment, you must be able to show the action is job related and a business necessity, and that there is no reasonable accommodation that would enable the individual to perform the job's essential functions. The Equal Employment Opportunity Commission has recognized that the fact that an individual has taken sick leave or had a doctor's appointment is not confidential medical information.

Accordingly, you may require the candidate who disclosed sick leave information to undergo a post-offer physical examination, as long as other candidates for the position are examined as well. You also may ask questions concerning her prior use of sick leave in this context.

If you choose to reject the candidate based on information she provided on her own about prior sick leave, without relying on the examination results, you have articulated a basic business reason for your decision that is legally sufficient if reliable attendance is related to the job in question – as is virtually always the case.

However, if you rely on the exam results in deciding to reject the candidate, you must be prepared to establish business necessity, usually a more onerous prospect, and you must show that there was no reasonable accommodation that would have enabled the applicant to perform the job's essential functions.

See the checklist, "Job Application and Pre-Employment Questions," Fig. 4-A.

> **Sources:** 42 U.S.C. §12112(d); 29 C.F.R. §1630.13(a); EEOC Enforcement Guidance: Pre-employment Disability-Related Inquiries and Medical Examinations.

14. Q: Are honesty or integrity tests legal? I have a lot of cash-handling jobs and higher "losses" than I want.

A: Maybe. It depends in part on where your company is located, and in part on the type of test.

Described by some as a "paper-and-pencil polygraph," honesty or integrity tests first became popular after polygraph testing of applicants and employees was outlawed nearly 20 years ago. Many employers have turned to honesty testing to compensate for the lack of meaningful references from previous employers beyond verifying position, salary and dates of employment, and because it is inexpensive (as little as $25 per test).

Honesty tests should not just be pulled off the Internet and administered to employees. There are a number of complicated issues involving possible employment discrimination to be considered. At a minimum, if you wish to give honesty tests to your employees, you should:

- Consider which employees need to take an honesty or integrity test. Concerns about honesty may be greater for some positions than others. Blanket administration of the test companywide or for all entry-level positions may undercut claims that the test is job-related or justified by business necessity.
- Gather a wide number of tests from various testing companies before selecting any one test.
- Identify the type of validation the testing company used to prove the worth of its test. Insist on being given the actual validation test results and have that data independently analyzed. An expert will be able to determine if the validation is sufficient, or whether additional validation is required to justify using the test for the purposes you intend.
- Ask the testing company whether this or any other test they have developed has been the subject of any litigation or claim of discrimination. If the answer is "yes," find out when, where, by whom and what the outcome was. An Internet search might be wise as well. Find out if the results of the test are or will be "gender-normed."
- Review and have a lawyer review every question on the test to make sure the questions posed do not violate an applicant's privacy rights, or seek medical or disability-related information that would violate the Americans With Disabilities Act (ADA) or state disability discrimination laws.

- Obtain written consent from each applicant or employee before he or she takes the test.
- Keep test results confidential – even from the employee's manager and particularly from co-workers.

Employers that use these tests should heed the following warnings:

- Do not consider the test results a substitute for a criminal background check.
- If using the test in Rhode Island or California, do not rely solely on results of the test in determining whether the applicant is or is not qualified.
- Do not use a test that has not been validated for the particular jobs at issue at your particular company.

As you can see, using an honesty test raises issues. Here are a few.

Use prohibited: Although there is currently no federal regulation of integrity testing, a few states restrict the use of such tests under anti-polygraph statutes. Only one state – Massachusetts – bans employers outright from using paper-and-pencil honesty exams.

Both California and Rhode Island preclude honesty and integrity tests from serving as the "primary basis" for an employment decision. In Wisconsin, employees may challenge an honesty test as "unfair." Some state laws that ban polygraph testing are worded so broadly that it is difficult to determine precisely which tests are illegal, and the ban may be interpreted to include written honesty exams.

Discrimination: Gender bias is a potential problem with honesty testing because women's and men's tests are scored differently, a potential violation of Title VII of the 1964 Civil Rights Act and state anti-discrimination laws. To date, research has shown that integrity testing does not appear to adversely impact minority candidates. However, every test is different, and no employer should assume that a particular test will produce the same results as other tests.

Honesty testing also raises issues under the ADA and similar state disability discrimination laws, which prohibit employers from asking questions whose answers might "provide evidence that would lead to identifying a mental disorder or impairment." Employers should examine honesty tests question-by-question to determine whether any particular question goes beyond permissible limits under the ADA or state anti-discrimination laws.

These tests have also been criticized for their possible invasion of privacy and self-incrimination, when employers go too far in attempting to "psych out" their employees' character. Every question in such an exam should be reviewed for potential invasion of applicant privacy. This includes questions concerning medical conditions, disability or private, personal matters. Liability may also result from the careless use and/or disclosure of test data, particularly when an employee is hired despite his or her test results. Access to confidential information obtained during honesty testing and the overall test result should be strictly limited to those with a need to know.

Reliability: Another concern is some candidates' ability to "fake" honesty or "beat the test" by choosing what they think the employer wants to hear. This problem affects all demographics and creates "false negatives," because the scores indicate that these candidates are honest when they are not. False positives are also an issue – that is, testing may result in a high number of truthful people being erroneously labeled as liars. That can create potential liability for the employer to a rejected candidate for employment or promotion.

Sources: EEOC's Uniform Guidelines on Employee Selection Procedures, 29 C.F.R. Part 1607 (2004); EEOC Compliance Manual, §6903.

Compensation

2

Introduction

Often before an employee is even hired, you have a number of compensation issues to resolve. Is this going to be an exempt or nonexempt employee? What are the federal rules concerning what category your various jobs fit into? You also have to decide what schedule your various employees are going to have. Your business might require shift work. If your employees are office workers, you might want to have a flexible schedule, but with core hours for everyone. What are the rules concerning pay and flextime?

Minimum wage is simple, but what if your state has a different wage floor than the federal law? Overtime, deductions, mistakes, pre- and post-work time – these are all questions you might have at various times. The Fair Labor Standards Act controls these situations and more on the federal level, and this chapter tells you what the law says. It also points out when you need to check your own state's laws.

Independent contractors, part-time and temporary employees can serve a real need at different times. But there are compensation as well as practical issues with each. This chapter addresses some of those. Included are policies, forms and checklists where appropriate.

Questions in This Chapter

FLSA Issues

Definitions

15. Q: What are "exempt" employees?

A: "Exempt" employees are employees who are exempted from the minimum wage and/or the overtime requirements of the FLSA.

Generally, the exemptions are based on a recognition that certain jobs have duties and responsibilities that are not related to hourly output. Thus, all exemptions from the overtime pay requirement should be narrowly related to the duties of the employees involved. Further, these employees are not deemed to need the protection of the FLSA, either because they are highly paid or because they are protected by other laws. Some of the exemptions may have had their origins in political considerations. Certain professions, such as lawyers, doctors and teachers, are excluded from coverage by the statute.

There are many FLSA exemptions. The best known and most commonly used are the so-called "white-collar exemptions" – the executive, administrative, professional, computer employee and outside sales exemptions. Each type of exemption has different criteria for qualifications that must be carefully reviewed by employers (see specific exemptions for more information on requirements for white-collar exemptions).

Sources: 29 C.F.R. §541.602; 29 U.S.C. §213.

16. Q: How do I determine who is exempt – like an executive, for example?

A: First, make sure you really do know what an exempt employee is. The exemption from overtime pay requirements is based on a recognition that certain jobs have duties and responsibilities that are not related to hourly output. Thus, all exemptions from the overtime pay requirement should be narrowly related to the duties of the employees involved. The different exemptions that are available all reflect duties that meet the general criterion that the employee's labors are assessed on a qualitative, rather than a quantitative, basis. Sometimes these are difficult decisions because the criteria are often complicated and unclear.

With respect to the executive exemption, the charts beginning on the next page should assist you. The first is a checklist, which includes many of the most important criteria (see Checklist for Executive Exemption, Fig. 16-A). The second chart will help you through the questions you should ask when making the decision (see Executive Exemption Decision Chart, Fig. 16-B).

Fig. 16-A
Checklist for Executive Exemption "Standard" Test

- ☐ 1. Is the employee paid not less than $455 per week (or $380 per week, if employed in American Samoa by employers other than the federal government), exclusive of board, lodging or other facilities?

- ☐ 2. Is the employee paid on a salary basis? With certain limited exceptions, he or she must:
  - experience no reduction in salary for variations in the quality and quantity of work;
  - experience no deductions for partial-day absences; and
  - receive each pay period a pre-determined amount constituting all or part of his or her compensation.

- ☐ 3. Does the employee's "primary duty" consist of managing the enterprise or a customarily recognized department or subdivision thereof?
  - The primary duty means the principal, main, major or most important duty that the employee performs.
  - The primary duty must be managing a customarily recognized department or subdivision, not a mere collection of employees assigned from time to time to a specific job or series of jobs.

- ☐ 4. Does the employee regularly and customarily supervise two or more employees?
  - The employee must supervise two full-time employees or the equivalent (for example, one full-time and two half-time employees).
  - Employees supervised must be employed in the department that the "executive" is managing.
  - A shared responsibility for the supervision of the same two (or more) employees in the same department does not fulfill the requirement; however, a single department can have more than one manager if there is a ratio in the department of at least two full-time equivalents to each manager.

- ☐ 5. Does the employee have the authority to hire or fire other employees or are the employee's suggestions and recommendations as to the hiring, firing, advancement, promotion or any other change of status of other employees given particular weight?
  - To determine whether an employee's suggestions and recommendations are given "particular weight," factors to be considered include, but are not limited to, whether it is part of the employee's job duties to make such suggestions and recommendations; the frequency with which such suggestions and recommendations are made or requested; and the frequency with which the employee's suggestions and recommendations are relied upon.

Source: Daniel B. Abrahams, *Employer's Guide to the Fair Labor Standards Act* (Thompson Publishing Group).

Fig. 16-B
Executive Exemption Decision Chart

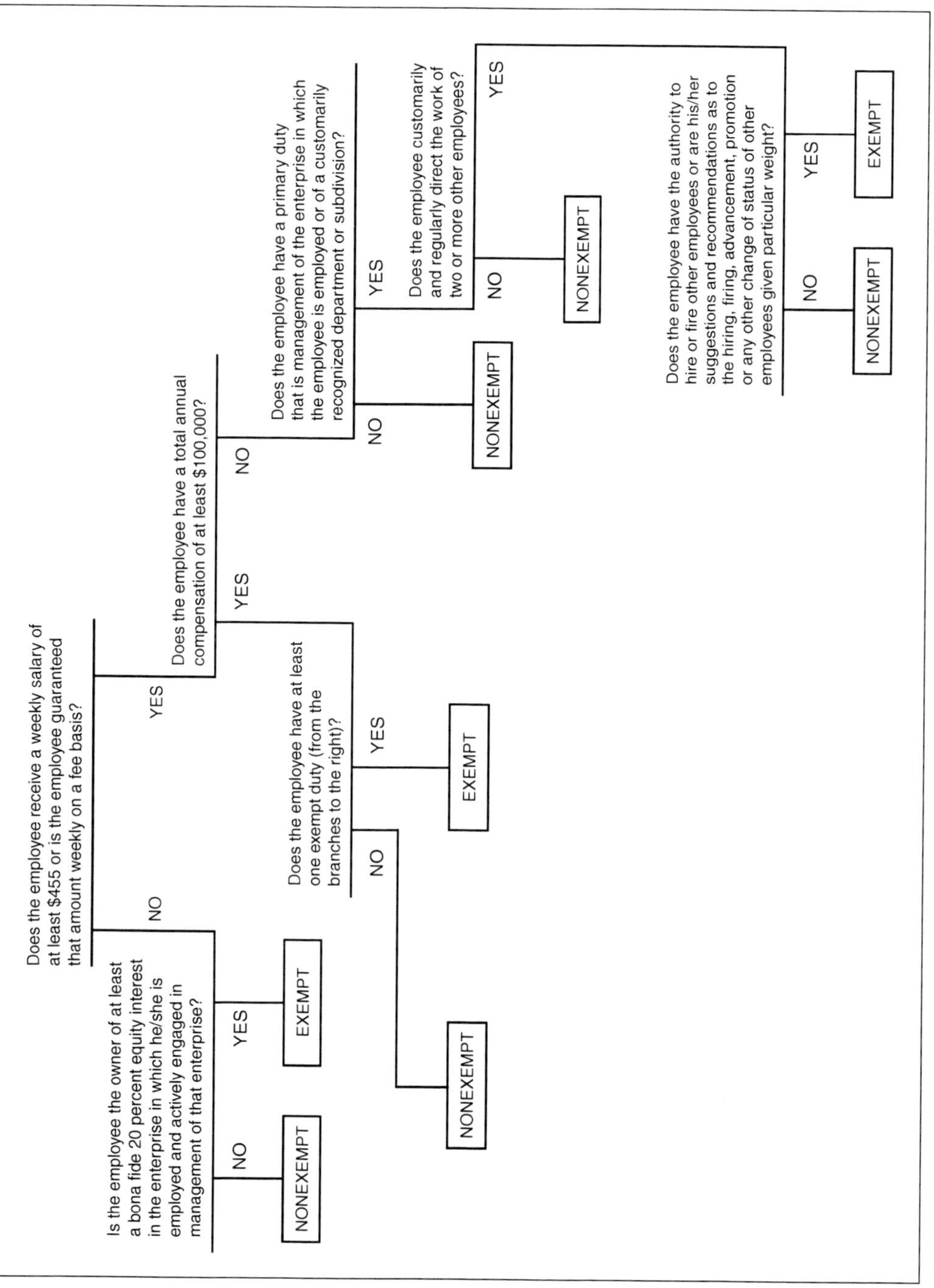

Source: Daniel B. Abrahams, *Employer's Guide to the Fair Labor Standards Act* (Thompson Publishing Group)

17. Q: How can I determine whether an executive is highly compensated?

A: The chart below, Fig. 17-A, should assist you. The Checklist for Executive Exemption "Highly Compensated Employee" Test includes many of the most important criteria for determining just who your highly compensated executives are. The Executive Exemption Decision Chart, Fig. 16-B, will help you through the questions you should ask when making the decision.

Fig. 17-A
Checklist for Executive Exemption "Highly Compensated Employee" Test

- ☐ 1. Is the employee's total annual compensation at least $100,000?
- ☐ 2. Is the employee paid not less than $455 per week (or $380 per week, if employed in American Samoa by employers other than the federal government), exclusive of board, lodging or other facilities?
- ☐ 3. Is the employee paid on a salary basis? With certain limited exceptions, he or she must:
    - experience no reduction in salary for variations in the quality and quantity of work;
    - experience no deductions for partial-day absences; and
    - receive each pay period a pre-determined amount constituting all or part of his or her compensation.
- ☐ 4. Does the employee regularly and customarily perform one or more exempt duties?

Source: Daniel B. Abrahams, *Employer's Guide to the Fair Labor Standards Act* (Thompson Publishing Group).

18. Q: How can I determine whether an administrative employee is exempt?

A: The different exemptions all reflect duties that meet the general criterion that the employee's labors are assessed on a qualitative rather than a quantitative basis. Sometimes these are difficult decisions because the criteria are often complicated and unclear. This is particularly true for administrative employees.

The Checklist for Administrative Exemption "Standard" Test, Fig. 18-A, includes the most important criteria for determining whether someone is an exempt administrative employee. The Checklist for Administrative Exemption "Highly Compensated Employee" Test, Fig. 18-B, will help you with highly compensated administrative employees, and the Administrative Exemption Decision Chart, Fig. 18-C, will help you through the questions you should ask when making the decision about whether an employee meets the requirements of an exempt administrative employee.

Fig. 18-A
Checklist for Administrative Exemption "Standard" Test

- ☐ 1. Is the employee paid not less than $455 per week (or $380 per week, if employed in American Samoa by employers other than the federal government), exclusive of board, lodging or other facilities?

- ☐ 2. Is the employee paid on a salary basis? With certain limited exceptions, he or she must:

  - experience no reduction in salary for variations in the quality and quantity of work;
  - experience no deductions for partial-day absences; and
  - receive each pay period a pre-determined amount constituting all or part of his or her compensation.

  Alternatively, is the employee paid on a fee basis?

- ☐ 3. Does the employee's "primary duty" consist of the performance of office or non-manual work directly related to the management or general business operations of the employer or the employer's customers?

  - The primary duty means the principal, main, major or most important duty that the employee performs.
  - The employee should not be a "blue-collar" worker or a "production worker" (except that if the organization's business is producing management services or other business operations for clients, then a production worker may be exempt).

- ☐ 4. Does the employee have a primary duty that includes the exercise of discretion and independent judgment with respect to matters of significance?

  - Exercising "discretion and independent judgment" involves comparing and evaluating possible courses of conduct, and acting or making a decision after the various possibilities have been considered.
  - Use of manuals and standard operating procedures does not preclude exemption if the manuals contain or relate to highly technical, scientific, legal, financial or other similarly complex matters that can be understood or interpreted only by those with advanced or specialized knowledge or skills.

Source: Daniel B. Abrahams, *Employer's Guide to the Fair Labor Standards Act* (Thompson Publishing Group).

Fig. 18-B
Checklist for Administrative Exemption "Highly Compensated Employee" Test

- ☐ 1. Is the employee's total annual compensation at least $100,000?
- ☐ 2. Is the employee paid not less than $455 per week (or $380 per week, if employed in American Samoa by employers other than the federal government), exclusive of board, lodging or other facilities?
- ☐ 3. Is the employee paid on a salary basis? With certain limited exceptions (see ¶322), he or she must:
    - Experience no reduction in salary for variations in the quality and quantity of work;
    - Experience no deductions for partial-day absences; and
    - Receive each pay period a pre-determined amount constituting all or part of his or her compensation.
- ☐ 4. Does the employee regularly and customarily perform one or more exempt administrative duties involving office or non-manual work *either* –
    - Directly related to management or general business operations of the employer or the employer's customers; *or*
    - Including the exercise of discretion and independent judgment.

Source: Daniel B. Abrahams, *Employer's Guide to the Fair Labor Standards Act* (Thompson Publishing Group).

Fig. 18-C
Administrative Exemption Decision Chart

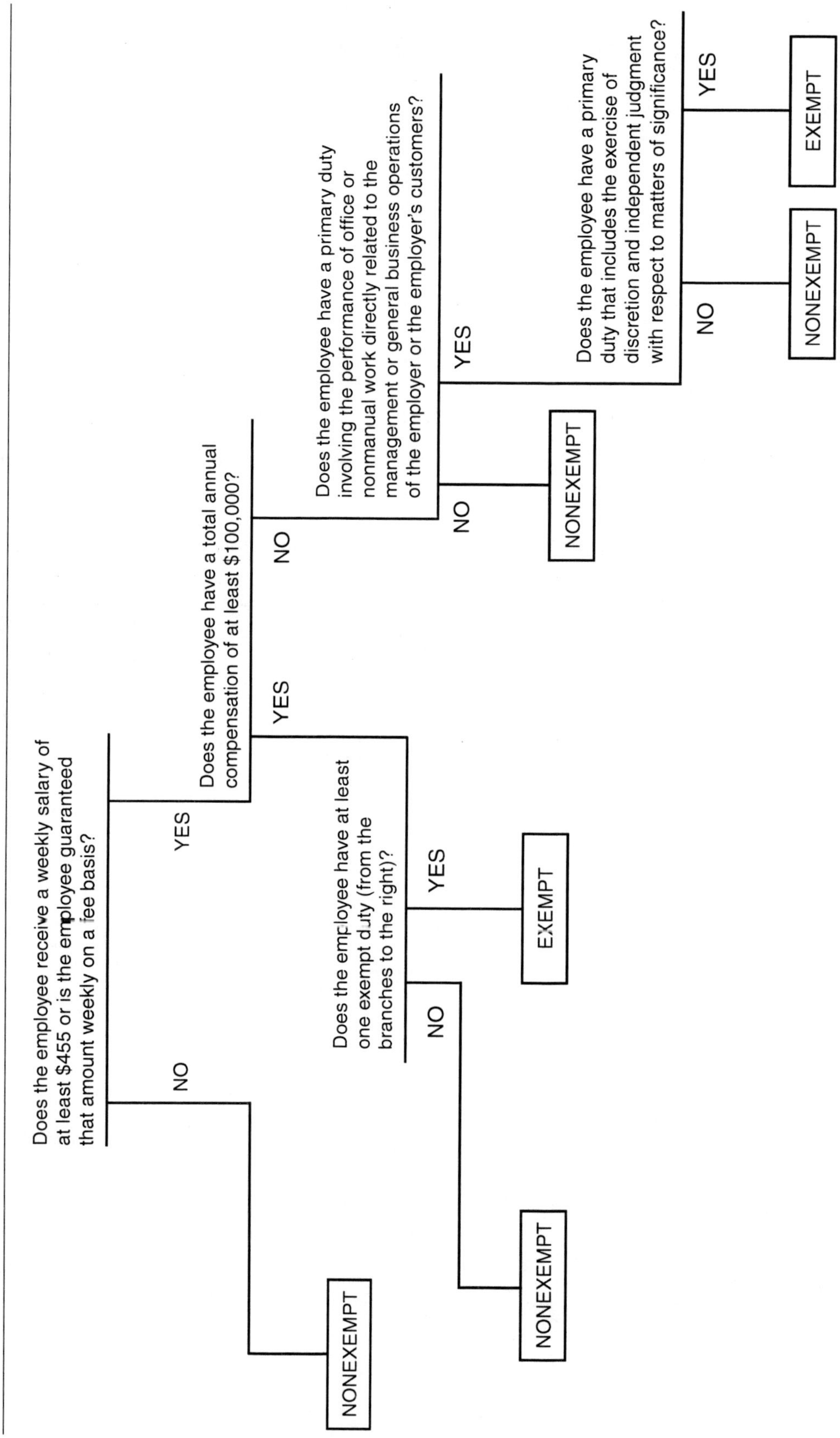

Source: Daniel B. Abrahams, *Employer's Guide to the Fair Labor Standards Act* (Thompson Publishing Group).

19. Q: How can I determine whether a professional employee is exempt?

A: There are *two* professional employee exemptions – one for *learned* professionals and another for *creative* professionals – and they have different criteria. With respect to the learned professional exemption, the charts that follow should assist you. The first, Fig. 19-A, is a checklist that includes many of the most important criteria for determining who is a learned professional. The second checklist, Fig. 19-B, is for highly compensated learned professional employees. The third chart, Fig. 19-C, will help you through the questions you should ask when making the decision about who qualifies for the learned professional exemption.

With respect to the creative professional exemption, the checklist, Fig. 19-D, includes many of the most important criteria for determining who qualifies. The second checklist, Fig. 19-E, is for highly compensated creative professional employees. The chart, Fig. 19-F, will help you through the questions you should ask when making the decision about whether someone is a creative professional employee.

Fig. 19-A
Checklist for "Learned" Professional Exemption "Standard" Test

❑ 1. Is the employee paid on a salary or fee basis not less than $455 per week (or $380 per week, if employed in American Samoa by employers other than the federal government), exclusive of board, lodging or other facilities?

a. Is the employee paid on a salary basis? With certain limited exceptions, he or she must:

- experience no reduction in salary for variations in the quality and quantity of work;
- experience no deductions for partial-day absences; and
- receive each pay period a pre-determined amount constituting all or part of his or her compensation.

b. Alternatively, is the employee paid on a fee basis?

c. Or, is the employee one of those professionals – physicians, lawyers, teachers and film-making industry employees – excepted from the salary or fee basis test? (If yes, then the $455 minimum salary or fee also does not apply.)

❑ 2. Does the employee's "primary duty" consist of the performance of work that requires knowledge of an advanced type in a field of science or learning customarily acquired by a prolonged course of specialized intellectual instruction?

- The primary duty means the principal, main, major or most important duty that the employee performs.
- The employee must consistently exercise discretion and judgment – i.e., he or she must generally use his or her advanced knowledge to analyze, interpret or make deductions from varying facts or circumstances.
- The work must be predominantly intellectual in character.

Source: Daniel B. Abrahams, *Employer's Guide to the Fair Labor Standards Act* (Thompson Publishing Group).

Fig. 19-B
Checklist for "Learned" Professional Exemption "Highly Compensated Employee" Test

- ☐ 1. Is the employee's total annual non-discretionary compensation at least $100,000?

- ☐ 2. Is the employee paid on a salary or fee basis not less than $455 per week (or $380 per week, if employed in American Samoa by employers other than the federal government), exclusive of board, lodging or other facilities?
  - a. Is the employee paid on a salary basis? With certain limited exceptions, he or she must:
    - experience no reduction in salary for variations in the quality and quantity of work;
    - experience no deductions for partial-day absences; and
    - receive each pay period a pre-determined amount constituting all or part of his or her compensation.
  - b. Alternatively, is the employee paid on a fee basis?
  - c. Or, is the employee one of those professionals – physicians, lawyers, teachers and film-making industry employees – excepted from the salary or fee basis test? (If yes, then the $455 minimum salary or fee also does not apply.)

- ☐ 3. Does the employee regularly and customarily perform one or more exempt professional duties?

Source: Daniel B. Abrahams, *Employer's Guide to the Fair Labor Standards Act* (Thompson Publishing Group)

Fig. 19-C

Learned Professional Exemption Decision Chart

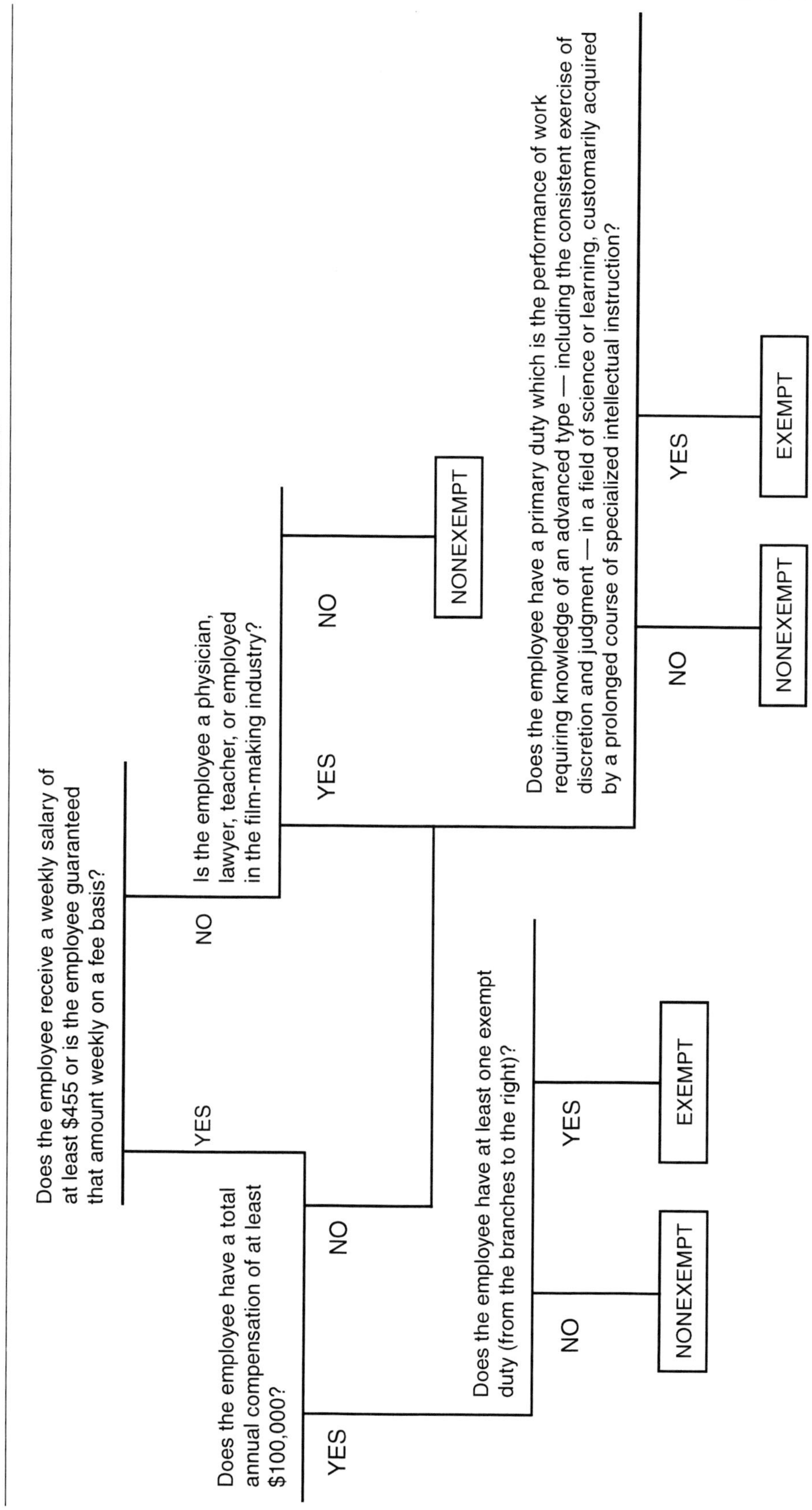

Source: Daniel B. Abrahams, *Employer's Guide to the Fair Labor Standards Act* (Thompson Publishing Group).

Fig. 19-D
Checklist for "Creative" Professional Exemption "Standard" Test

- ❑ 1. Is the employee paid on a salary or fee basis not less than $455 per week (or $380 per week, if employed in American Samoa by employers other than the federal government), exclusive of board, lodging or other facilities?
  - a. Is the employee paid on a salary basis? With certain limited exceptions, he or she must:
    - experience no reduction in salary for variations in the quality and quantity of work;
    - experience no deductions for partial-day absences; and
    - receive each pay period a predetermined amount constituting all or part of his or her compensation.
  - b. Alternatively, is the employee paid on a fee basis?
  - c. Or, is the employee one of those creative professionals in the film-making industry excepted from the salary basis test? (If yes, then the $455 minimum salary or fee also does not apply.)
- ❑ 2. Does the employee's "primary duty" consist of the performance of work that requires invention, imagination, originality or talent in a recognized field of artistic or creative endeavor?
  - The primary duty means the principal, main, major or most important duty that the employee performs.

Fig. 19-E
Checklist for "Creative" Professional Exemption "Highly Compensated Employee" Test

- ❑ 1. Is the employee's total annual non-discretionary compensation at least $100,000?
- ❑ 2. Is the employee paid on a salary or fee basis not less than $455 per week (or $380 per week, if employed in American Samoa by employers other than the federal government), exclusive of board, lodging or other facilities?
  - a. Is the employee paid on a salary basis? With certain limited exceptions, he or she must:
    - experience no reduction in salary for variations in the quality and quantity of work;
    - experience no deductions for partial-day absences; and
    - receive each pay period a predetermined amount constituting all or part of his or her compensation.
  - b. Alternatively, is the employee paid on a fee basis?
  - c. Or, is the employee one of those creative professionals in the film-making industry excepted from the salary or fee basis test? (If yes, then the $455 minimum salary or fee also does not apply.)
- ❑ 3. Does the employee regularly and customarily perform one or more exempt professional duties involving the performance of work that requires invention, imagination, originality or talent in a recognized field of artistic or creative endeavor?

Source: Daniel B. Abrahams, *Employer's Guide to the Fair Labor Standards Act* (Thompson Publishing Group)

Fig. 19-F
Creative Professional Exemption Decision Chart

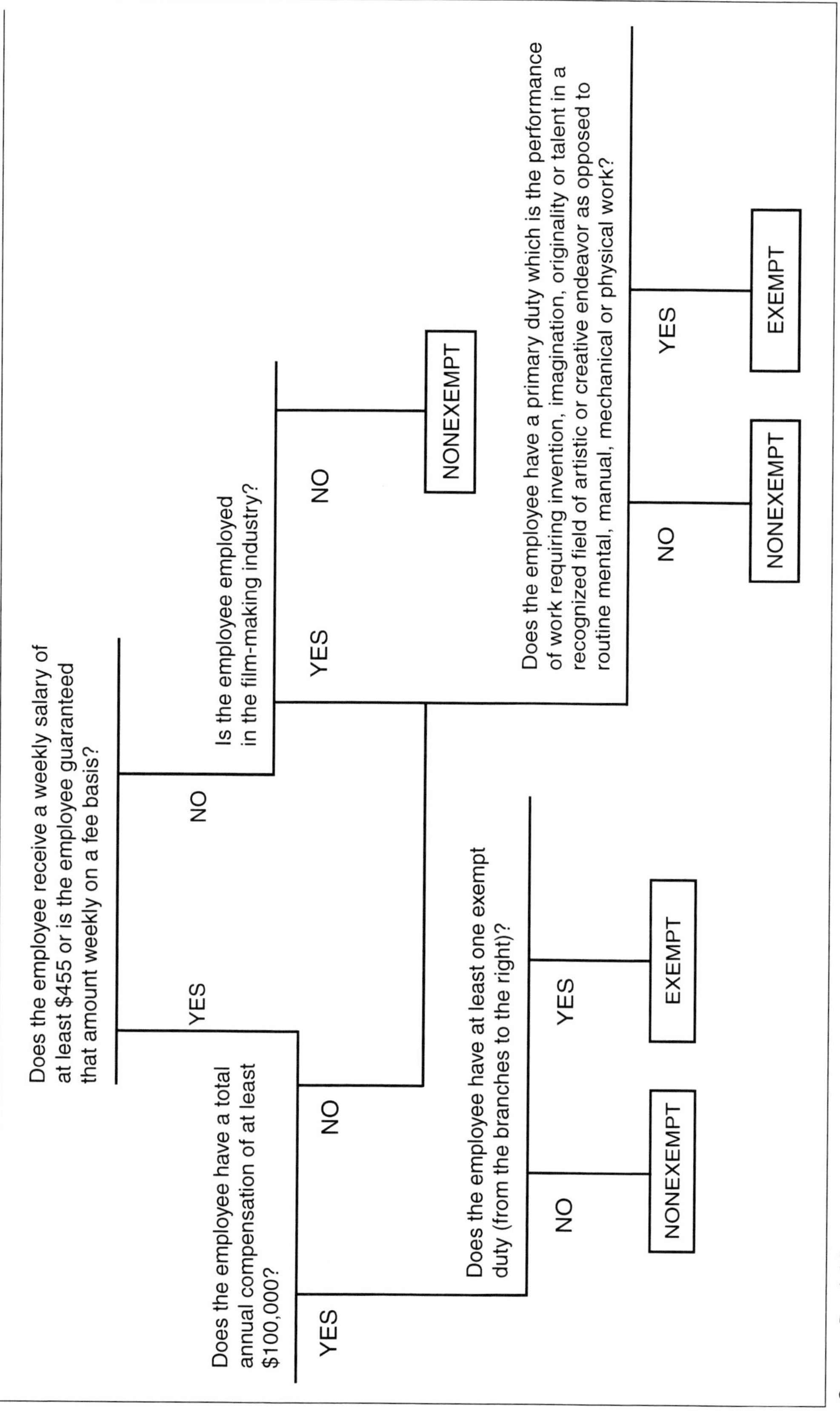

Source: Daniel B. Abrahams, *Employer's Guide to the Fair Labor Standards Act* (Thompson Publishing Group)

20. Q: How can I determine whether a computer employee is exempt?

A: To be classified as an exempt computer employee, the employee must:

- apply systems analysis techniques and procedures, including consulting with users, to determine hardware, software or system functional specifications;
- design, develop, document, analyze, create, test or modify computer systems or programs, including prototypes, based on and related to user or system design specifications;
- design, document, test, create or modify computer programs related to machine operating systems; or
- perform a combination of the aforementioned duties, the performance of which requires the same level of skills.

Note that an exempt computer employee may be paid on a salary basis (earning at least $455 per week) *or* he or she may be paid at least $27.63 for each hour worked, including any overtime hours.

Source: 29 C.F.R. §541.400(b).

21. Q: How can I determine whether an outside salesperson is exempt?

A: To be classified as an exempt outside salesperson, the employee must be one:

1. whose primary duty is:
   - making sales within the meaning of section 3(k) of the act; or
   - obtaining orders or contracts for services or for the use of facilities for which a consideration will be paid by the client or customer; and
2. who is customarily and regularly engaged away from the employer's place or places of business in performing that primary duty.

Outside sales employees are not required to be paid on a salary or fee basis to be exempt. They are not eligible for the act's "highly compensated employee" test. Outside sales employees may be paid on a salary, fee, commission, piece, bonus or any other basis, or combination of bases, with no minimum compensation required. Outside sales employees should not be confused with certain "inside" sales employees, who may be entitled to an overtime (but not a minimum wage) exemption under Section 207(i) of the FLSA.

Source: 29 C.F.R. §541.500(c).

Flexible Time

22. Q: Can I calculate overtime over our pay period (two weeks) rather than for the 40-hour week, to let employees control their hours better? Mine want more flexibility in arranging their work schedules but I don't want to pay any more overtime.

A: Yes. The Fair Labor Standards Act is based on a seven-day week and overtime is calculated on hours worked above 40 during that seven-day period. This limits but does not prevent flexibility. You can still monitor and control overtime. The flexibility just has to be within the single workweek. For example, four 10-hour days; days of varying length, adding up to 40 hours; and varying starting and quitting times.

Source: 29 U.S.C. §207.

23. Q: Are there any rules limiting the number of hours that can be worked in one day? We have a lot of employees on flextime.

A: Not under federal law, but many states have laws limiting or requiring such things as: the number of hours that may be worked in a day; the number of hours that may be worked without a break; the number of hours worked without a meal break; and overtime for more than eight hours worked in a day. You should consult your state laws regarding these matters.

Minimum Wage

24. Q: Do I have to pay the federal minimum wage, the state minimum wage, or whichever one is higher?

A: The FLSA creates a "floor," not a "ceiling." You must pay the highest of the minimum wages that apply in your jurisdiction. The chart, Fig. 24-A, includes the minimum wages in the 50 states and the District of Columbia. Please note, many of these minimums are frequently adjusted, some annually.

If your employees are working on a government contract, you should make sure they are not covered by one of the federal laws, such as the Davis-Bacon Act or the Service Contract Act, which impose a "wage determination" from the Labor Department on workers. The wage determination requires that employees be paid the "prevailing wage" in your community for people in their job categories. The prevailing wage, which includes an amount for benefits, is almost certainly above the minimum wage. You should know about the applicable prevailing wages before bidding on a government contract that imposes them on your workers.

FIG. 24-A
STATE MINIMUM WAGES

Current Federal Minimum Wage	**$5.85**
Alabama	NONE
Alaska	$7.15
Arizona	$6.75
Arkansas	$6.25
California[1]	$7.50
Colorado	$6.85
Connecticut	$7.65
Delaware[2]	$6.65
District of Columbia	$7.00
Florida	$6.67
Georgia	$5.15
Hawaii	$7.25
Idaho	$5.85
Illinois[3]	$7.50
Indiana	$5.85
Iowa[4]	$6.20
Kansas	$2.65
Kentucky	$5.85
Louisiana	NONE
Maine[5]	$6.75
Maryland	$6.15
Massachusetts[6]	$7.50
Michigan	$7.15
Minnesota[7]	$6.15
Mississippi	NONE
Missouri	$6.50
Montana[8]	$6.15
Nebraska	$5.15
Nevada	$6.33
New Hampshire[9]	$5.85
New Jersey	$7.15
New Mexico[10]	$5.15
New York	$7.15
North Carolina	$6.15
North Dakota	$5.85
Ohio[11]	$6.85
Oklahoma	$5.85

continued on next page

Fig. 24-A (cont.)

Oregon	$7.80
Pennsylvania	$7.15
Rhode Island	$7.40
South Carolina	NONE
South Dakota	$5.85
Tennessee	NONE
Texas	$5.85
Utah	$5.15
Vermont	$7.53
Virginia	$5.85
Washington	$7.93
West Virginia[12]	$6.55
Wisconsin	$6.50
Wyoming	$5.15

[1]Minimum wage will increase to $8.00 an hour on Jan. 1, 2008.

[2]Minimum wage will increase to $7.15 an hour on Jan. 1, 2008.

[3]Minimum wage will increase to $7.75 on July 1, 2008, to $8.00 on July 1, 2009, and to $8.25 on July 1, 2010. Minimum wage for workers who are 18 and older. Workers under the age of 18 can make no more than 50 cents less than the requisite wage for workers who are 18 and older. There are separate minimum wage requirements for "learners."

[4]Minimum wage will increase to $7.25 an hour on Jan. 1, 2008.

[5]Minimum wage will increase to $7.00 an hour on Oct. 1, 2007.

[6]Minimum wage will increase to $8.00 an hour on Jan. 1, 2008.

[7]$5.25 per hour if employer's annual gross sales volume is below $625,000.

[8]$4.00 if employer's annual gross sales are $110,000 or less.

[9]Minimum wage will increase to $6.50 an hour on Sept. 1, 2007.

[10]Minimum wage will increase to $6.50 an hour on Jan. 1, 2008.

[11]Interstate commerce and businesses grossing over $500,000 follow federal minimum wage.

[12]Minimum wage will increase to $7.25 an hour on June 30, 2008. Under state law, these increases do not apply to employers that have less than $500,000 in annual revenue, are engaged in interstate commerce, or employ fewer than six employees.

Overtime

25. Q: Headquarters just told me to pay overtime when an employee works more than 40 hours a week, but our normal workweek is 37.5 hours. What should I do?

A: The FLSA requires overtime pay for hours worked above 40. You can pay more than that, as you have, but you do not have to. It is all but certain that moving from a 37.5-hour to a 40-hour base for overtime will be perceived as a pay cut by those employees who received overtime pay based on your prior system.

Source: 29 U.S.C. §207.

26. Q: How do I calculate the "regular rate" when it isn't very regular? I know that I have to pay one-and-one-half times the regular rate for overtime – but what about employees who get a shift differential, hazardous duty pay, or bonus?

A: An employee's "regular rate" is the total of all compensation received for the workweek (except certain premium payments) divided by the total number of hours worked in the workweek. This includes most payments made by the employer to or on behalf of the employee. Certain types of payments are specifically excluded by the Fair Labor Standards Act.

The following are examples of types of compensation that must be included in an employee's regular rate of pay:

- bonuses promised for accuracy of work, good attendance, continuation of the employment relationship, incentive, production and quality of work;
- shift differentials, hazardous-duty pay and longevity pay; and
- contest prizes.

The following are examples of types of compensation that need not be included in an employee's regular rate of pay:

- absence pay for infrequent or unpredictable absences, such as vacation, illness, bereavement, disaster relief payments or jury leave;
- "discretionary" bonuses;
- holiday pay, if it is equivalent to regular earnings; and
- certain premium pay for time worked outside standard hours.

Source: 29 C.F.R. §207(e); 29 C.F.R. §778.109.

Docking/Deductions

27. Q: When my exempt engineers don't work a full 40-hour week, can I dock them for time not worked? I am a government contractor and I both bid and bill my projects by an hourly rate.

A: I am assuming that the engineers are exempt, either as administrative employees or learned professionals. In that case, you cannot dock them for not working a given number of hours. They should be salaried, and as salaried workers, they must receive a fixed payment for their work each week, not for hours worked.

Being a salaried employee is one of the basic tests of being exempt; this is called the "salary basis test." The salary basis test requires that:

- employees regularly receive, on a weekly or less frequent basis, a pre-determined amount of at least $455 per week that constitutes all or part of their compensation;
- the amount may not vary depending on the quality or quantity of their work;
- employees must not be paid hourly; and
- employees must receive their full salary for the week regardless of the number of days or hours worked, subject to a number of exceptions.

This is important: If you make improper deductions you may lose the exempt status of certain employees for certain time periods if the facts demonstrate that you did not intend to pay the employees on a salary basis. This will generally require that you have an actual practice of making improper deductions.

Sources: 29 C.F.R. §§541.600, .602 and .603(a).

28. Q: When can I make deductions that result in an exempt employee receiving less than a full salary for a given week?

A: Salary deductions are permitted when:

- the employee is absent from work for one or more full days for personal reasons, other than sickness or disability;
- the employee is absent for one or more full days because of sickness or disability (including work-related accidents) and the deduction is made in accordance with a bona-fide plan, policy or practice of providing compensation for loss of salary occasioned by such sickness and disability;
- the employer imposes penalties in good faith for infractions of safety rules of major significance;
- the employer imposes, in good faith, unpaid disciplinary suspensions of one or more full days for infractions of certain workplace conduct rules;

- the employee takes leave under the Family and Medical Leave Act; or
- the employee is absent the entire workweek or performs no work during an entire workweek.

Salary adjustments for hours worked also are allowable in the initial and terminal week of employment.

Source: 29 C.F.R. §541.600 *et seq.*

Training

29. Q: Do I have to pay employees for time they spend in training programs?

A: It depends on who wants the training – you or the employee.

For the most part, if you are requesting that the employee attend the training, it is "on the clock." Time employees spend in training programs need *not* be counted as compensable working time only if the following four requirements are met:

- attendance occurs outside the employee's regular work hours;
- attendance is voluntary;
- the employee does no productive work while attending the training; and
- the training program is not directly related to the employee's job.

Source: 29 C.F.R. §785.27.

Mistakes

30. Q: Have I "converted" an exempt employee into an hourly employee? I mistakenly docked him, but I corrected that right away.

A: No. Employers are given a "window of correction" under the rules. This window of correction provides that isolated or inadvertent salary deductions will *not* result in the loss of an exemption for any employees subject to the improper deductions if the employer reimburses the employees.

"Inadvertent" deductions are those made unintentionally, for example, as a result of a clerical or timekeeping error. The window of correction does not require reimbursement to be made within a specific time. You would be even safer if you had a policy to cover this circumstance. For that, see the next question.

Source: 29 C.F.R. §541.603(c).

31. Q: We are a new company with high turnover and I am concerned that payroll mistakes will erroneously convert exempt employees to nonexempt status. What should I do?

A: Relax. Under the applicable regulations, there is a "safe harbor" for inadvertent errors, although it is not available for everything.

The Fair Labor Standard Act's "safe harbor" rule will prevent the loss of an exemption for any employees, even if a manager has engaged in the actual practice of making improper deductions, *provided* the employer meets certain requirements. To qualify under the safe harbor provision, the employer must:

- have a clearly communicated policy that prohibits improper pay deductions and includes a complaint mechanism;
- reimburse employees for any improper pay deductions; and
- make a good faith commitment to comply in the future.

Furthermore, the "safe harbor" will *not* protect employers that willfully violate their policy by continuing to make improper deductions after receiving employee complaints. It also will not protect an employer who fails to reimburse an employee for any improper deduction.

If either is the case, the exemption will be lost for the time period in which the improper deductions were made for employees in the same job classification working for the same managers responsible for the actual improper deductions.

A copy of a sample policy with options you can choose from to fit your situation follows (Fig. 31-A).

Source: 29 C.F.R. §541.603(d).

Fig. 31-A
Expanded Sample Salary Basis Policy

It is the employer's policy to comply with applicable wage and hour laws and regulations. Accordingly, the employer intends that deductions be made from your pay only in circumstances permitted by the Fair Labor Standards Act and the U.S. Department of Labor's rules governing the salary basis of pay for exempt employees. The improper pay deductions specified in Title 29 of the Code of Federal Regulations §541.602(a) may not be made from the pay of employees who are subject to the salary basis test.

If you have any questions or concerns about your salaried status or you believe that any deduction has been made from your pay that is inconsistent with your salaried status, you should immediately raise the matter with your immediate supervisor. If you have raised the matter with your supervisor and it is not resolved within ten (10) business days, or if, for any reason, you are uncomfortable discussing the matter with your supervisor, you must submit your question, concern or complaint to [Name] in the [HR, Payroll, Other] Department at: [Insert at least two of the following: room number, telephone number, fax number, email address].

To ensure that the employer understands your concern or complaint (hereinafter, both referred to as "complaint") and is able to conduct a proper investigation, the employer requires that any complaint that seeks the payment of money or requests a change in policy be submitted in writing. No particular form is required, but each such complaint must include the employee's name, ID number and a brief description of the issue. You also must identify the pay period(s) to which the complaint relates. If you are unable for any reason to submit your complaint in writing, the employer representative named in the previous paragraph (or his/her representative) will take a statement from you. You then will be asked to review and sign the statement to ensure it accurately reflects your complaint.

The employer is committed to investigating and resolving all complaints as promptly, but also as accurately, as possible. Consistent with the U.S. Department of Labor's policy, any complaint will be resolved within a reasonable time given all the facts and circumstances. If an investigation reveals that you were subjected to an improper deduction from pay, you will be reimbursed and the employer will take whatever action it deems necessary to ensure compliance with the salary basis test in the future.

Public Sector

32. Q: What are the special salary test rules for public-sector employees?

A: Under the special salary test rules, *public-sector* employers may make certain deductions from salary that would otherwise defeat the white-collar exemptions if made by a private-sector employer.

A public-sector employee who otherwise meets the salary basis requirements may have his or her pay reduced or be placed on leave without pay "for absences for personal reasons or because of illness or injury of less than one work-day when accrued leave is not used by an employee because:

- permission for its use has not been sought or has been sought and denied;
- accrued leave has been exhausted; or
- the employee chooses to use leave without pay."

Pre- and Post-Work Time

33. Q: Do I have to pay my employees for the time they spend waiting to punch in on the time clock?

A: Generally, no.

Most pre- and post-work activities outside an employee's principal activities are not considered compensable. They are only compensable if there is a contract, custom or practice to pay for such time. Such activities would normally include checking in or out, or waiting in line to do so; changing clothes; washing up or showering; and waiting in line to receive pay checks, unless required by the nature of the job (see the question below).

Sources: 29 U.S.C. §254; 29 C.F.R. §790.7(g).

34. Q: Some of my employees have to get ready for the job before starting work and then clean up after work. Is this time "on the clock"?

A: Maybe. Such pre- and post-shift activities may or may not be "compensable" time (for which employees must be paid), depending on the circumstances.

Under the Fair Labor Standards Act's "Portal-to-Portal" rule provisions, certain pre- and post-shift activities are specifically *excluded* from compensable working time:

- walking, riding or traveling to and from the actual place where an employee's "principal activity" is performed; and
- activities that are required but occur either before an employee starts, or after an employee finishes, his or her "principal activity" in a given workday.

Ordinary home-to-work commuting is also generally not compensable, nor, typically, is walking from the front gate of a plant to a particular work station. The act also states that "preliminary" or "postliminary" activities, occurring before or after an employee's "principal" activities, are not compensable. But what kinds of activities fall into this category?

FLSA rules state that a categorical listing of pre- and post-shift activities is not possible, because an activity that is "preliminary" (and thus not compensable) in one situation may be "principal" (and thus compensable) in another.

Sources: 29 U.S.C. §254; 29 C.F.R. §790.7(f).

35. Q: What's the best way to handle the pre- and post-shift work issue? It's complicated and hard to keep track of.

A: First, you should establish a policy or rule against unauthorized work. That alone is not enough, however. You must enforce the rule, through disciplinary measures if necessary. Additional steps you can take include the following:

- *Adopting a clear time and attendance policy.* Clearly outline when employees are allowed to work and emphasize that the policy is the authoritative guide on working time. Send a clear message to employees not to work off the clock, even if a manager tells them to. Instruct employees not to arrive at work more than a few minutes before their shifts begin and not to stay more than a few minutes after their shifts end. Tell workers who must wait for transportation home to wait in a cafeteria or other public space. Make clear that any falsification of payroll records, through either under-reporting or over-reporting work time, is prohibited. Urge employees to report any person who tells them to falsify their timesheets, and make sure your policy explains how to correct falsified timesheets.

- *Requiring managers to review weekly time entries.* Even if the company uses an automated recordkeeping system, require your managers to review and approve each employee's weekly timesheet. Require employees to review and certify the accuracy of their timesheets.

- *Training all staff about timekeeping policies.* Train payroll staff to identify questionable timesheets by having the managers describe to them what type of work the employees perform and what hours they generally work. Managers who clearly communicate their timekeeping practices to payroll personnel will have a better defense in case of a lawsuit.

- *Uniformly addressing any policy violations by employees or supervisors.* Any disciplinary action taken against an employee for performing unauthorized work should be applied to all employees, regardless of their job position. Employers can more effectively defend against a lawsuit if they can prove that they made a sincere effort to prohibit their employees from working "off the clock" and if they are able to show uniform enforcement of their work time policies.

36. Q: Can I ignore timesheets when I calculate actual hours worked? I know everybody clocks in and then does things not related to work – getting coffee, chatting, etc.

A: Yes. The Fair Labor Standards Act (FLSA) requires employers to pay employees only for time actually worked. So, by virtue of the Portal-to-Portal Act, the FLSA specifically excludes from hours worked activities that are "preliminary and postliminary" to the main job duties. What you have described, however, doesn't even rise to that level; it is completely unrelated to work.

Further, under the FLSA, nonexempt workers need not necessarily be paid additional compensation when a workplace time clock indicates that the employees may have performed a few minutes of extra work. Rounding such recorded work time on a fair and even basis, up and down, is permitted by Labor Department regulations implementing the FLSA.

According to those regulations, "[i]t has been found that in some industries, particularly where time clocks are used, there has been the practice for many years of recording the employee's starting time and stopping time to the nearest five minutes, or to the nearest one-tenth or quarter of an hour. Presumably, this arrangement averages out so that the employees are fully compensated for all the time they actually work."

You should also note that, in some situations, other small amounts of work-related activities may not be considered compensable. Under what is commonly referred to as the "*de minimis* rule," courts and the Labor Department have recognized that insubstantial or insignificant periods of time outside of scheduled working hours may be disregarded as working time.

Generally, the long-established "*de minimis* rule" states that periods of time of less than 10 minutes are too small to be considered compensable working time. However, regularly scheduled work periods, no matter how small, ordinarily cannot be considered "*de minimis*."

Sources: 29 U.S.C. ¶254(a); 29 CFR §§785.47 and .48(b); *Anderson v. Mt. Clemens Pottery Co.,* 328 U.S. 680 (1946).

37. Q: Do I have to pay our repairmen for their commuting time? Ours drive company cars to work.

A: As you may have imagined, this is not entirely straightforward. First, the company car is not a factor in determining what is compensable time, but the use of the employer's vehicle must be by mutual agreement between the employer and the employee, and the employee should understand his obligations.

Second, if you are *only* talking about commuting, whether it is to the home office or directly from the employee's home to the first repair job, that is *not* considered compensable time, even if the employee is using a company car and even if the trip to the first work site is a longer trip than to the home office. It is well established that normal travel from home to work is not work time, no matter how long the commute.

However, if an employee is required to report to the home office or some other meeting place where he or she picks up materials, equipment or other employees, or receives instructions such as a work schedule or repair route before traveling to the first job, compensable time starts at the home office or meeting place no matter whose vehicle is being used.

You should be very clear about what you require, because if an employee leaves home on the way to a work site, but stops at the home office or shop for *his or her own convenience*, the time spent traveling from the office to the site is not compensable. That is considered the commute.

Sources: 29 CFR §785.35; *Marshall v. R&M Erectors Inc.*, 429 F. Supp. 771 (D. Del. 1977); *Saribekian v. Concrete Drilling & Sawing Co.*, 1990 WL 60779 (N.D. Ill. April 24, 1990).

Meal Breaks

38. Q: Do I have to give my employees time off for meal periods?

A: It depends. *Federal* law does not require meal periods, but many state laws do. For those employers who do provide meal periods, the Fair Labor Standards Act regulations define when such a period may or may not be excluded from compensable working time. For example, according to FLSA regulations, meal periods are *not* counted as hours worked – and thus not compensated – if the following conditions are met:

- The meal period generally is at least 30 minutes long.
- The employee is completely relieved from all duties during the period.
- The employee is free to leave the duty post.

Source: 29 C.F.R. §785.19.

Comp Time

39. Q: Can I start giving my employees comp time? They are clamoring for it.

A: It depends. If you are a public-sector employer, you can offer comp time. If you are a private-sector employer, comp time is not an available option. This is widely misunderstood.

Let's be clear about what we mean by "comp time." As usually defined, comp time is time off *in lieu of* overtime pay. That should not be confused with flex time or with controlling overtime.

Flex time is permitted and used in the private sector to permit employees to arrange and adjust their schedules to meet other needs in their lives. It can mean little more than fluctuating start and quit times. It can mean four 10-hour days a week or other variations on that theme. In every common variation, however, flex time respects the 40-hour week and pays overtime for hours worked above 40 to nonexempt employees.

Employers often ask if comp time can be awarded to exempt employees. Frankly, the question appears to misunderstand comp time and exempt. An exempt employee is not paid by the hour but for the quality of his or her work. So, there is no special term needed for telling an exempt employee to take a day off as a reward for a job well done or for working a grueling schedule to meet a deadline.

Recordkeeping

40. Q: What kind of payroll records do I have to keep?

A: First, this is what the Fair Labor Standards Act regulations state should be in a payroll record for each nonexempt employee:

- the hours worked each workday; and
- the total hours worked each workweek.

The regulations allow an employer that places employees on a fixed schedule to maintain records showing the schedule of daily and weekly hours the employee normally works and, in weeks in which the employee adheres to the schedule, indicate by check mark or other statement that such hours were in fact worked. In weeks during which an employee works more or less than his or her scheduled hours, the employer must show the exact number of hours actually worked.

Second, the FLSA requires that each employer preserve *for at least three years*:

1. payroll records;
2. certificates, collective bargaining agreements and individual contracts; and
3. sales and purchase records.

The FLSA also requires that employers preserve *for at least two years*:

1. basic employment and earnings records;
2. wage rate tables;
3. order, shipping and billing records; and
4. records of additions to or deductions from wages paid.

Other records are also required, depending on the exempt/nonexempt status of the worker.

Sources: 29 C.F.R. §§516.2(a)(7) and (c); 29 C.F.R. §516.5.

Compensation Plans

41. Q: Can I discipline employees for telling each other how much they make? We consider our salary information confidential.

A: No. The National Labor Relations Board, which most people believe deals only with unions and employees in unions, has ruled that all employees have a right to communicate about terms and conditions of employment, and pay is at the top of that list.

You may tell employees that the company regards their compensation as confidential and ask them to do the same. But you may not discipline someone for sharing that information.

> **Source:** 306 NLRB 1072 (1992).

42. Q: An employee lost an expensive cell phone – can I dock his wages to pay for it?

A: You face a number of problems here. First, if this is an hourly employee, you can't dock his or her wages so that the compensation falls below the applicable minimum wage in the week of the deduction. Second, a number of states have anti-garnishment laws that prevent any deductions from compensation, other than statutory ones, without a court order. Third, the Labor Department takes a dim view of any reductions in an exempt employee's salary other than those expressly permitted by law, and considers such docking a violation of the salary basis test.

Some employers, faced with the necessity of providing costly, often fragile, and easily lost equipment, have tried loan agreements and other forms of pledges to protect themselves, when permitted by state law. Others increase insurance coverage to avoid these problems entirely.

> **Source:** 29 C.F.R. §541.602 *et seq.*

Independent Contractors

43. Q: How do I determine if someone qualifies as an independent contractor?

A: This is not an easy question to answer. Frequently, employers assume that because the worker has signed a "Consultant's Agreement" he or she is not an employee. That is not always the case. There have been situations in which workers are working side by side doing the same job under the same conditions, but one of them is considered an employee and the other is not.

These non-employees have been called "perma-temps" and the employer was responsible for a great deal of back pay. That is not advised. The best way to analyze this question is to look at the actual work done by the employee.

The most commonly used test to establish whether a worker is an employee or an independent contractor is the "economic reality test." Various courts have phrased the test in different ways, but the federal Labor Department has stated that a number of factors should be considered, including the following:

- the extent to which services rendered are an integral part of the employer's business;
- the permanency of the relationship;
- the amount of the worker's individual investment in facilities and equipment;
- the opportunities for the worker to experience profit and loss; and
- the degree of initiative, judgment or foresight exercised by the individual who performs the services.

Based on the above factors, if the "economic reality" of the situation indicates that a worker is economically dependent on the business in question, the worker is probably not an independent contractor, but rather is an employee covered by the Fair Labor Standards Act's minimum wage and overtime protections.

Some employers have made sure that independent contractors work for a limited time or on a defined project and have tangible indications of their independence. The difference is similar to hiring a plumber to do *a* job who drives his own truck and uses his own tools and arrives when he chooses, as opposed to someone who shows up a fixed number of days as directed to use your tools to do plumbing work. The first plumber is an independent contractor; the second is not.

Source: Wage and Hour Opinion Letter, June 23, 1986.

44. Q: Can I just fire my employees and replace them with independent contractors? My benefits costs are killing me.

A: That may sound good in theory but it might wind up costing you more than it's worth in lower morale and reduced productivity, not to mention possible litigation. And even the theory depends on whether the people you hire are truly independent contractors and not employees.

Actual job duties determine if someone is an employee or independent contractor. The fact that you call them "independent contractors" or "consultants" is irrelevant if they, in fact, meet the legal definition of employees. Even if the workers sign consultant or independent contractor agreements and agree to these titles, they could still be considered employees, depending on the nature of their working relationship with your company.

For purposes of deciding whether your workers are employees who are entitled to be included in your benefit plans, or independent contractors, who are not, you need to look at the actual nature of the working relationship. Generally, the relationship of employer and employee exists when the person for whom services are performed has the right to control and direct the individual who performs the services – not only the result to be accomplished by the work, but the details and means by which that result is accomplished.

It is not necessary that your company actually direct or control the manner in which the services are performed; it is sufficient if you have the right to do so. The right to discharge is also an important factor indicating that the person possessing that right is an employer.

Other factors characteristic of an employer, but not necessarily present in every case, are the furnishing of tools and a place to work to the individual who performs the services. In general, if an individual is subject to the control or direction of another merely as to the result to be accomplished by the work and not as to the means and methods for accomplishing that result, he or she is not an employee.

A useful Independent Contractor Checklist to assist in making the determination about whether a worker is an employee or independent contractor follows (Fig. 44-A).

Source: 26 C.F.R. §§31.3401(c)-1(b).

Fig. 44-A
Independent Contractor Checklist

		YES	NO
1.	Not required to follow instructions on how to perform services?	☐	☐
2.	Possesses skills necessary to perform tasks and does not need additional training?	☐	☐
3.	Engaged in an occupation or business that is distinct from that of the Company and provides services that are different than those provided by the Company?	☐	☐
4.	Able to subcontract all or portion of project?	☐	☐
5.	Hires and supervises own employees?	☐	☐
6.	Works on one project and moves on, accepting additional projects when and if available?	☐	☐
7.	Sets own work schedule, working as necessary to accomplish end result?	☐	☐
8.	Works simultaneously for the principal and others, as long as end result is achieved?	☐	☐
9.	Able to choose where to perform some, if not all, of services?	☐	☐
10.	Controls the manner and method of performance?	☐	☐
11.	Is responsible for the end result and is not required to submit interim reports?	☐	☐
12.	Paid by project or job?	☐	☐
13.	Assumes burden of business expenses?	☐	☐
14.	Furnishes tools, equipment and materials necessary to perform services independently?	☐	☐
15.	Invests in tools, business equipment, publications, and supplies appropriate for business?	☐	☐
16.	Accepts benefits *and* risks of business transaction; has opportunity to profit from project price and risks a loss if the end result is unacceptable or costs exceed the project price?	☐	☐
17.	Works for more than one firm at a time?	☐	☐

HFINC

continued on next page

FIG. 44-A (CONT.)

		YES	NO
18.	Makes services available to general public?	☐	☐
19.	Company can terminate relationship only according to the terms of an agreement (or face potential exposure for breach of contract)?	☐	☐
20.	Obligated to complete work under contract (or face potential exposure for breach of contract)?	☐	☐
21.	Parties believe they are creating an independent contractor relationship?	☐	☐

Part-Time/Temporary Employees

45. Q: Do I have to provide fringe benefits to part-time employees who work more than a certain number of hours?

A: Federal law does not require that you provide any fringe benefits to employees, except Family and Medical Leave to covered employees (see Q.s 110-128). If you do provide benefits (a pension plan, for example), all that the law requires is that you treat similarly situated employees in the same way. If you have a plan that provides benefits to full-time employees, you must make sure that all full-time employees are offered those benefits.

You are not required to also offer benefits to part-time employees. If you do, however, you must ensure that all part-time employees are treated equally.

The definition of "full-time" is not always left to the employer. If you have a pension plan, you may require a person to reach age 21 to be eligible to participate in the plan and to have 12 months of service during which 1,000 hours of work are performed. In subsequent years, a "year" of credited service for vesting purposes is 1,000 hours.

Source: ERISA 203(a)(3).

Workplace Culture

3

Introduction

The term "workplace culture" is the way your company operates on a day-to-day basis as far as your employees are concerned. It is your company's "personality," the "way things are done." It affects what is expected of your workers – how they dress, are evaluated and disciplined, whether they can set their own schedules or telecommute.

Workplace culture includes the accommodations your company makes for persons with disabilities or religious needs. Part of it is your diversity and dress code and your tolerance for drugs or alcohol. It also includes whether you closely monitor your employees' use of telephones and computers, their off-duty conduct and whether you use polygraphs or non-competition agreements.

Your company's evaluation process, discipline procedures and retention policies are part of its culture. So are your safety and security measures, position on union organizing and work-life balance.

This chapter addresses many of the questions you probably have about all of these issues and more. Practical tips and sample policies, forms and checklists are included where appropriate.

Questions in This Chapter

Union Organizing

Telecommuting

Accommodations – Disability

46. Q: Are there limits to what I have to do to accommodate a disabled employee? The only accommodation that will help one of my employees is reassignment to a desk job, but there are better qualified employees who want that job.

A: Reassignment is the reasonable accommodation of last resort, but if there is nothing else that will enable your employee to keep working for you, you should consider it.

The Americans With Disabilities Act (ADA) specifically lists reassignment to a vacant position as a reasonable accommodation and most courts agree that it is, although a few have determined that if the employee cannot perform the essential functions of the job he or she was hired to do, the person is not a qualified individual with a disability and, therefore, not eligible for a reasonable accommodation (*Motley v. New Jersey State Police*, 196 F.3d 160 (3d Cir. 1999); *Foreman v. Babcock & Wilcox Co.*, 117 F.3d 800 (5th Cir. 1997)).

The Equal Employment Opportunity Commission (EEOC), which enforces the employment provisions of the ADA, views reassignment as a reasonable accommodation if the employee is qualified for the position in terms of training and skills. You may assign the employee to a lower-paying position if there is no equivalent position available. If the worker accepts the lower position, you may reduce his pay accordingly.

Your employee with a disability does not have to be the *best* qualified applicant for the job. The EEOC insists that if reassignment is the only reasonable accommodation available, the worker with the disability does not have to compete for it. Several courts agree, although at least one appeals court characterized reassignment without competition as "affirmative action with a vengeance" (*EEOC v. Humiston-Keeling*, 227 F.3d 1024 (7th Cir. 2000)).

Reassignment ordinarily is not reasonable if it would conflict with your seniority system, if you have one, even if that system is not part of a union collective bargaining agreement, the U.S. Supreme Court has ruled. But the Court noted that exceptions may be reasonable in certain circumstances. For example, if your seniority system is not uniformly and consistently enforced, a change to accommodate a worker with a disability probably would not make a difference.

Sources: 42 U.S.C. §12111(9)(B); *Eckles v. Consolidated Rail Corp.*, 94 F.3d 1041 (7th Cir. 1996), *cert. denied*, 520 U.S. 1146 (1997); *Cravens v. Blue Cross and Blue Shield of Kansas City*, 214 F.3d 1011 (8th Cir. 2000); *Davoll v. Webb*, 194 F.3d 1116 (10th Cir. 1999); *U.S. Airways v. Barnett*, 535 U.S. 391 (2002); EEOC Enforcement Guidance Reasonable Accommodation and Undue Hardship Under the ADA.

47. Q: Am I within my rights to terminate a disabled employee? I have tried for over six months to make this accommodation thing work for one employee, but she just can't do the job and I have no other job for her.

A: Probably. If you and your employee have really worked together to try to find a solution and you do not have another position available that she is qualified for, she is not a qualified individual with a disability protected by the Americans With Disabilities Act (ADA).

The Equal Employment Opportunity Commission (EEOC), which enforces the employment provisions of the ADA, as well as some courts, has adopted an "interactive process" for finding reasonable accommodations. What that means is that you and the employee are expected sit down together to discuss the employee's limitations and try to find workable solutions that do not cause an undue hardship on your business. The flowchart, Fig. 47-A, describes this process in detail.

You indicate that you have done that over the course of a number of months and nothing has worked. If that is so, you will not violate the ADA by letting the worker go. Even if your employee should sue you under the law, the fact that you earnestly attempted to find a reasonable accommodation will work in your favor to prevent the worker from being awarded any punitive damages and probably from even winning a discrimination claim.

Sources: 42 U.S.C. §1981A; EEOC Technical Assistance Manual on Title I §3.8.

Fig. 47-A
Flowchart of Reasonable Accommodation Process

This flow chart outlines the reasonable accommodation process, which as defined in the *EEOC Technical Assistance Manual on Title I*, consists of: (1) determining a job's essential functions; (2) consulting with the individual with a disability to determine his or her abilities and limitations; (3) identifying possible accommodations in consultation with the individual; and (4) selecting the best accommodation. This chart includes points made in the EEOC's discussion of the process and provides additional points to consider when trying to identify a reasonable accommodation.

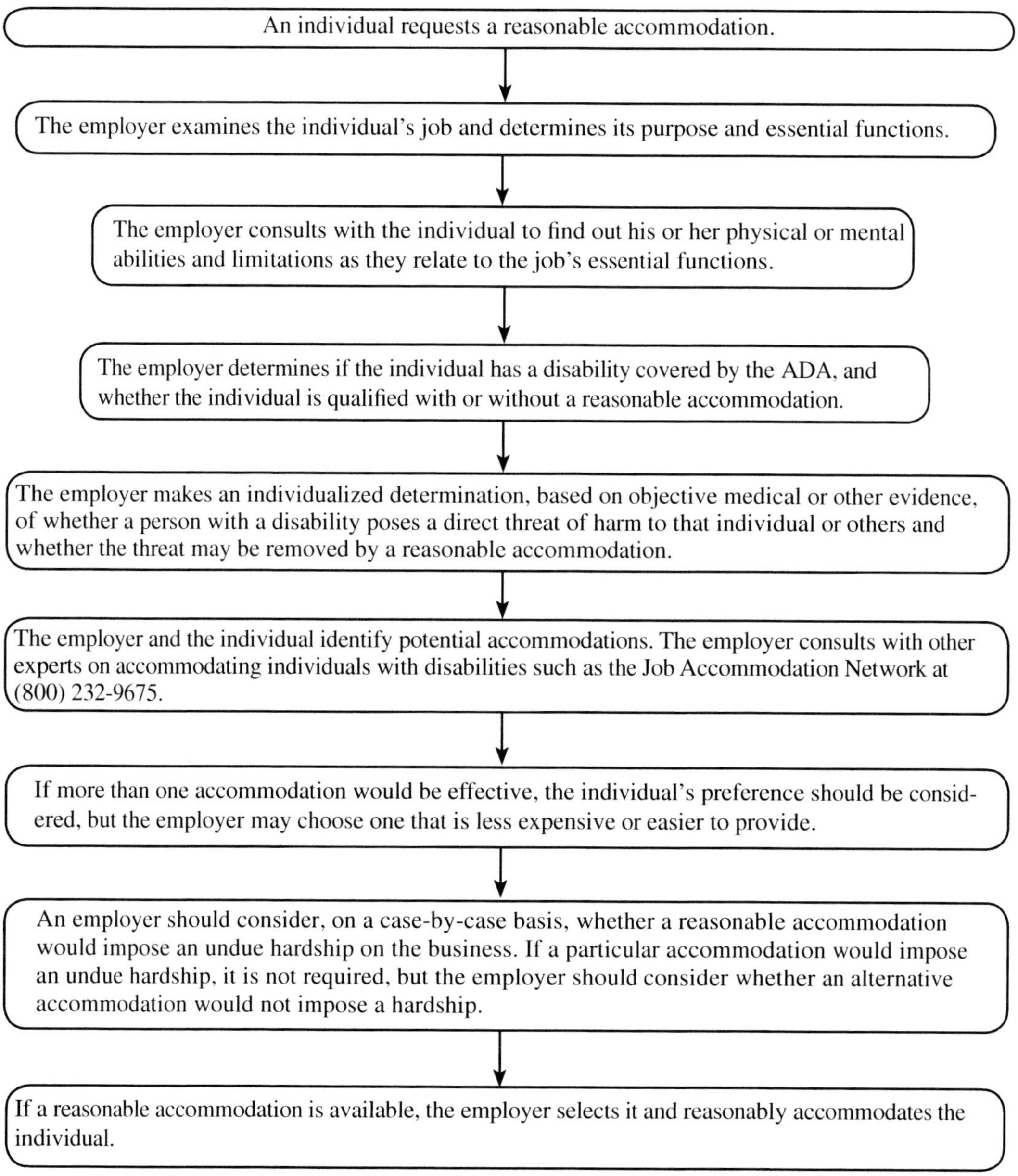

48. Q: What can I do to minimize the cost impact of a catastrophic illness? An employee's son, who is on our plan, has contracted AIDS. I'm afraid of a huge spike in our health insurance costs.

A: The Americans With Disabilities Act (ADA) is very specific on this. You may not discriminate with respect to employment or benefits against a qualified individual because of the disability of a person with whom that qualified individual has a relationship or association.

If your employee's son is qualified for coverage under your existing insurance plan, you cannot exclude him from coverage. Nor can you exclude the employee from health insurance coverage because of your fear of future illness.

If you truly believe you are facing fiscal disaster, you can stop providing health insurance to all of your employees, but that has its own consequences.

Sources: 42 U.S.C. § 12112 ((b)(3)(B)(4).

49. Q: Can I transfer an employee who has returned from cancer treatments – with a clean bill of health – to a lower-paying job for his own safety? He works on a very busy packaging line where we have had our share of injuries, and I don't want him to get hurt.

A: Probably not. Assuming that the employee is a qualified individual with a disability (not all courts agree that cancer is a disability), you would have to show that he poses a direct threat to the health or safety of himself or others.

A "direct threat" under the Americans With Disabilities Act (ADA) is defined as a significant risk that cannot be eliminated or reduced through reasonable accommodation. This criterion is stringent, and must be based on an individual assessment of the worker's present ability to safely perform essential job functions. The decision must be based on medical or other objective evidence, not opinion or speculation. To determine the risk, you must review:

- the risk's duration;
- the nature and severity of the potential harm;
- the likelihood that the potential harm will occur; and
- the imminence of the potential harm.

In your case, the employee has "a clean bill of health" now. Medically speaking, he does not pose any more risk of danger to himself or co-workers than he did before he underwent cancer treatments. Unless your employee does not meet some federal or state safety standard due to a physical impairment that resulted from his cancer or some other ailment or injury, he is not a direct threat in the workplace. Transferring him to a lower-paying job would be actionable discrimination under the ADA.

Sources: 42 U.S.C. §§12111(3), 12113; 29 C.F.R. §1630.2; *Chevron v. Echazabal*, 536 U.S. 73 (2002); *Albertsons v. Kirkingburg*, 527 U.S. 555 (1999).

50. Q: How far do I have to go in making an accommodation? A job applicant told me she needs a flexible work schedule because her child has cerebral palsy. I want to hire her, but we don't have flexible work schedules here.

A: Because it is the applicant's child, and not the applicant herself who has the disability, you probably would not violate the Americans With Disabilities Act (ADA) by not hiring her.

But it will be hard for you to prove that you did not discriminate against the applicant because of her son's condition. Moreover, flexible work schedules are a common business practice. Unless you can show that having one would be an undue hardship on your business, if the applicant chooses to sue you, a jury probably would not be very sympathetic to your position.

The ADA prohibits *discrimination* against a qualified individual who associates or has a relationship with an individual with a disability. That means you could not refuse to hire the applicant because of her son's disability. But there is nothing in the law that requires an *accommodation* because someone the employee has a relationship with has a disability. The accommodation is for the employee's disability to enable him or her to perform a job's essential functions because of a physical or mental limitation. In this case, the employee herself has no disability.

Nonetheless, you might want to re-think flexible work schedules. You might be able to hire a well qualified worker and avoid a lawsuit in the process.

Sources: EEOC Enforcement Guidance Reasonable Accommodation and Undue Hardship Under the ADA.

Accommodations – Religious

51. Q: I want to respect everybody's religion, but where can I draw the line? I let one employee, a Sikh, wear his turban at work. Now, I have people wanting to wear kinte cloths, kufi caps, even hijabs and veils.

A: Title VII of the 1964 Civil Rights Act and state anti-discrimination laws require you to "reasonably accommodate" an employee's sincerely held religious practices or beliefs on request, unless doing so would impose an "undue hardship" on your legitimate business interests.

- A reasonable religious accommodation is any adjustment to the work environment that will allow the employee to practice his or her religion, including the modification of grooming requirements or dress codes. The law puts a corresponding duty on the employee to cooperate with your good faith offer of a reasonable accommodation.
- You can show undue hardship if accommodating an employee's religious practices imposes more than a negligible cost (whether it be economic or non-economic), diminishes workplace efficiency, infringes on other employees' rights or benefits, impairs workplace safety, violates a collective bargaining agreement, or the proposed accommodation conflicts with another law or regulation.
- Along with other employers, you increasingly face the dilemma of deciding how far you must go to accommodate a religious employee's dress or personal appearance. Head coverings, robes, beards, face paints, religious insignias and symbols, and other outward tokens of faith may deviate not only from your dress codes but also from co-workers' expectations.

The critical question comes down to business needs. For example, an employer does not have to accommodate robes or long skirts in a manufacturing plant where loose garments might get caught in heavy machinery. Nor does the employer have to accommodate untrimmed beards, flowing hair or headdresses if those things are incompatible with the workplace environment, such as a restaurant or hospital.

Retailers whose employees routinely have contact with customers have the right to enforce personal appearance standards to appeal to customer preference and to promote a professional public image. However, in an office environment, employers have been sanctioned for forbidding religious dress or head coverings, long hair or beards for men, and religious insignias or symbols.

Following 9/11, the Equal Employment Opportunity Commission issued guidance on "The Workplace Rights of Muslims, Arabs, South Asians, and Sikhs," specifically addressing the needs of Sikh men to wear turbans and Muslim women to wear hijabs (head scarves).

In such cases, it is sometimes the employee's co-workers, rather than the employer, who object to the religious employee's appearance. The potential for workplace disruption, and loss of efficient working time, may be high when a religious employee's appearance offends co-workers.

The EEOC's guidelines make it clear that claiming co-workers might be upset or uncomfortable, or that a client objects, is not an undue hardship. Nor may an employer deny such a requested accommodation based on speculation that the other Sikh or Muslim employees may seek the same treatment.

The EEOC does recognize that if other employees subsequently request the same accommodation and granting it to all of the requesters would cause undue hardship, the employer may make an appropriate adjustment at that time. For example, if accommodating five employees would not cause an undue hardship but accommodating six would impose such hardship, the sixth request could be denied.

To make a long story short, employers may "draw the line" on religious attire by limiting accommodations to employees with sincerely held, generally recognized religious beliefs, when the requested clothing or insignia does not interfere with safety, efficiency, discipline or other appropriate business concerns. For example, retailers probably could show that permitting employees to completely cover their faces would pose an undue hardship on their businesses.

You should review your dress codes to ensure that your policy is reasonably related to your employees' jobs and that it is applied equally to all employees in your workplace.

The safest course of action is to document thoroughly the nature of each request and all attempted accommodations. Explore with each employee exactly what he or she feels is required by his or her religious beliefs, confirm these conversations in writing and ask any co-workers who object to put their concerns in writing as well.

Err on the side of granting such requests if possible. Courts are unlikely to be sympathetic to an employer that orders an employee not to display or wear an item of religious apparel absent concrete evidence that the employee's actions interfere with business operations.

Sources: 42 U.S.C. §2000e-2(a); EEOC Guidance: The Workplace Rights of Muslims, Arabs, South Asians, and Sikhs.

52. Q: Do I have to mess up everyone's schedule because of one employee's religious request? We're open six days a week, and one of my employees just told me his religion won't allow him to work on Saturdays, or even late on Fridays.

A: This multi-part question requires several answers.

- Work schedule changes and requests for time off for religious observances are two classic examples of reasonable accommodations that may be required under Title VII of the 1964 Civil Rights Act. The religious beliefs must be sincerely held, and based on an actually recognized religion, not just something the employee made up on his or her own. Of course, that is a very difficult thing for you or any other employer to determine.

- It is important to remember that religious accommodation requests necessitate individualized decisionmaking. Consequently, a solution that works in one situation may not work in another, and both time and energy must be expended in working with the employee, co-workers and supervisors to arrive at an appropriate accommodation. Rest assured, however, that defending against a charge of religious discrimination will be far more time consuming and expensive.

Employers are often hesitant to grant requests for employee schedule changes or time off not only because of fears or accusations of favoritism, but also because of the inconvenience of trying to rearrange work schedules. Fortunately, in many cases, accommodation may involve no more cost to the employer than posting a bulletin board notice asking for a volunteer employee to switch shifts on the date of the religious holiday. Other methods employers have found useful are flexible arrival and departure times and flexible work breaks, granting of optional or floating holidays, exchange of lunch time for early departure time and creation of a staggered work schedule.

- How far must you go? Schedule changes that infringe on the rights of co-workers, violate the seniority provisions of a collective bargaining agreement or result in more than a negligible cost to the employer constitute "undue hardship" and need not be granted.

- Probably the most difficult situation arises when the employer must pay overtime to other employees because of a religious employee's unavailability for work. The EEOC's guidelines instruct that infrequent or temporary payment of overtime or other premium wages will be treated as a negligible cost to the employer; not an "undue hardship."

- However, regular payment of wages, or payment when a large number of employees must all take off on the same day, most likely will be deemed an undue hardship, especially when the business enterprise is small or operating costs are high.

If the job in question requires that the employee be available for weekend work, or on-call outside regular work hours, consider including a question on the employment application or job description about whether the candidate is available to work any shift, including nights and/or weekends, or if there are any specific times when he or she is unavailable for work for any reason. This may help to avoid the "news to me" problem.

Sources: 42 U.S.C. §2000e-2(a); EEOC Guidance: The Workplace Rights of Muslims, Arabs, South Asians, and Sikhs; EEOC Guidance: Religious Accommodation Under Title VII.

53. Q: Do I have to pay a Muslim employee during prayer (he's not exempt), or can he stay late without collecting overtime? This employee says he has to pray three times a day at work. He can't always fit his prayers into normal lunch or break times, and if I give him the time off, everyone else will want the same.

A: You have a duty to reasonably accommodate the employee's need for breaks to pray during the workday, absent undue hardship, under Title VII of the 1964 Civil Rights Act. It is essential that you document your efforts to reasonably accommodate such requests, and err in favor of granting the accommodation.

In its guidelines on "The Workplace Rights of Muslims, Arabs, South Asians, and Sikhs," the Equal Employment Opportunity Commission specifically addresses requests by Muslim employees for time to pray at multiple times during the work day. While the guidelines encourage flexible scheduling when possible, they provide that if the employee cannot fit required prayers into normal lunch or break times, he or she can be required to make up the lost work time, at no additional monetary cost to the employer in additional salary, either regular or overtime.

In evaluating undue hardship, you may consider only whether you can accommodate the employee making the request. You cannot base your denial on speculation that other workers will request time off as well. Once again, reasonable accommodation requires individualized decisionmaking. If other employees subsequently request the same accommodation and granting it to all of the requesters would cause undue hardship, you can make an appropriate adjustment at that time, perhaps through staggered scheduling of prayer breaks.

Sources: 42 U.S.C. §2000e-2(a); EEOC Guidance: The Workplace Rights of Muslims, Arabs, South Asians, and Sikhs; EEOC Guidance: Religious Accommodation Under Title VII.

Diversity

54. Q: How should I handle the usage of racial epithets by minority employees when it's among themselves? At company-sponsored softball games and picnics, some of my black employees use the "N" word with each other. I'm pretty sure they are joking, but I wouldn't permit it at the workplace. I'm also afraid of what might happen if someone else uses the word – even in the same joking spirit. Can I ask them to cut it out?

A: Every company-sponsored event should be considered an extension of the workplace. Accordingly, behavior such as using the "N" word, particularly involving interactions between co-workers that is not acceptable in the office or the plant, is not acceptable at the company picnic (or holiday party).

Your failure to address the repeated use of racial epithets – regardless of the reason or to whom the comment is directed – at company-sponsored parties, sporting events, or other gatherings can lead to liability for racial harassment under Title VII of the 1964 Civil Rights Act and state anti-discrimination laws.

According to the Equal Employment Opportunity Commission (EEOC), racial harassment is unwelcome conduct that unreasonably interferes with an individual's work performance or creates an intimidating, hostile or offensive work environment. Examples of harassing conduct include: offensive jokes; slurs; epithets or name calling; physical assaults or threats; intimidation; ridicule or mockery; insults or put-downs; offensive objects or pictures; and interference with work performance.

An employer may be held liable for the harassing conduct of supervisors, co-workers, or non-employees such as customers or business associates over whom the employer has control. An isolated incident does not normally create a hostile work environment, unless it is extremely serious. The EEOC takes the position that even one use of the "N" word is extremely serious.

Here, while some minority employees may consider their use of the word a joke, their minority co-workers may not. The employees involved should be counseled in compliance with your established performance policies to stop making such remarks, whether at work or a company-sponsored event. They should be told that future incidents will lead to disciplinary action, up to and including termination.

The counseling should be documented, and a reminder circulated to all employees that appropriate workplace conduct standards will remain in force throughout all company-sponsored events, and that inappropriate behavior may result in disciplinary action. Where inappropriate remarks have been a problem, that issue should be specifically addressed, with reference to your workplace harassment and conduct policies.

Employees need to be educated about workplace harassment. Diversity training presents the perfect opportunity to do that. The EEOC emphasizes that the most important step for an employer in preventing harassment is clearly communicating to employees that harassment based on race, gender, disability or any other protected status will not be tolerated and that employees who violate the prohibition will be disciplined.

Other important steps include adopting effective and clearly communicated policies and procedures for addressing complaints of harassment, and training managers on how to identify and respond effectively. (See the sample Rules of Conduct, Fig. 54-A)

Fig. 54-A
Sample Employee Rules of Conduct

Your adherence to certain rules and regulations governing employee behavior is necessary for the efficient operation of the Company and for the benefit and safety of all employees. Conduct that interferes with operations, discredits the Company, is offensive to others or is not in the best interests of the Company will not be tolerated. Examples of conduct for which you may be subjected to disciplinary action, up to and including immediate dismissal, are listed below. **This list does not include all conduct for which you may be disciplined. Incidents requiring discipline will be handled on a case-by-case basis.**

- Being convicted of a crime bearing on your suitability as an employee, including but not limited to, theft or any other act of dishonesty.
- Dishonesty.
- Driving a Company vehicle under the influence of drugs or alcohol.
- Failing to abide by any Company policy set forth in this Employee Handbook.
- Failing to follow an order or request by any member of management.
- Failing to maintain a Company vehicle in a condition satisfactory to the Company.
- Falsifying an employment application or any other Company record.
- Fighting, horseplay or scuffling.
- Filling out another employee's timesheet.
- Gambling on Company property.
- Leaving the job without permission.
- Making statements that could result in a loss of Company goodwill or that are offensive to others.
- Negligence or improper conduct leading to damage of Company property.
- Other employment unless approved by management in advance.
- Possessing a weapon.
- Possession, use or distribution of alcohol or drugs during working hours.
- Possession or use of illegal substances on or off Company property.
- Reporting to work or working under the influence of alcohol or drugs.
- Sexually or otherwise harassing another employee.
- Sleeping on the job.
- Theft of Company property, failure to report any known theft of Company property or concealment of any theft of Company property.
- Threatening, intimidating, cursing or otherwise interfering with another employee.
- Unauthorized possession, use or removal of property belonging to the Company or another employee.
- Unsatisfactory work performance, whether or not deliberate.
- Unauthorized release or disclosure of Company, client or customer information.
- Unauthorized use of telephones, mail system or other Company equipment.
- Unauthorized absence from work station during the work day.
- Unsatisfactory attendance and punctuality or failing to give required notice of absence or lateness.
- Violating safety rules.
- Violating the Company dress code.
- Violating the Company safety policy.
- Violating the Company business expense reimbursement policy.

55. Q: If nearly all of my employees are minorities, do my supervisors have to be minorities too? My business is in an urban community, and just about everyone in service or data entry jobs is a minority, but very few managers are.

A: If your workforce mirrors the availability of qualified candidates in the surrounding geographic area, there is no basis for legal liability.

Accordingly, if census data shows that the majority of those qualified to hold service or data entry jobs within the local population are minority group members, there is no cause for concern. At all times, however, the goal of any employer's selection process should be to identify the best qualified candidate for the position, without regard to protected group status, even when underutilization exists. In fact, attempts to "balance out" the racial composition of an employer's workforce by favoring non-minority candidates over minority group members have led to Title VII liability for race discrimination.

That said, it is important to ensure that minority employees and women in entry-level jobs are provided opportunities to advance within the company through employer-sponsored training programs, job progressions and other forms of promotion to more responsible positions, depending on their abilities and qualifications. A "bottom heavy" workforce in which minority employees hold exclusively entry-level jobs may signify a "glass ceiling" problem.

Remember, too, that workplace diversity is not limited solely to gender and race. Diversity includes personality, education, lifestyle, sexual preference, national origin, age and background, among other things.

56. Q: How should I deal with a charge of reverse discrimination? I supply goods to some big companies, many of which say they prefer to deal with suppliers that have diverse workforces. So, when I had an executive slot open, I promoted a very able minority woman. Now the other candidate for the job, a more senior white guy, says he's been discriminated against. Did I do anything against the law?

A: Maybe. Promotion and hiring decisions should always be based on qualifications. If you hire or promote the person who is best qualified for the position, you always have a strong defense against any discrimination claim. If two candidates are *equally* qualified, race, gender or some other factor favoring diversity can be used as a plus factor, but only if the candidates are truly equal in qualifications.

In an effort to promote diversity, employers have at times elected to consider minority status and gender as factors in employment decisions, motivated by their affirmative action commitments and a desire to "do the right thing." However, recent court decisions and agency actions strongly suggest that employers now face the very real prospect of unanticipated liability for reverse discrimination when efforts to promote affirmative action and diversity go too far.

Driven by a growing wave of resentment against corporate diversity programs, non-minority employees are increasingly likely to bring reverse discrimination claims. A decision to promote a less qualified minority woman over a better qualified, more senior white male candidate may lead to liability under both Title VII of the 1964 Civil Rights Act and state anti-discrimination laws.

If your company policy dictates that promotions will be awarded based on seniority, you really have a problem. It is important to note that a desire to promote diversity does not constitute a legitimate, non-discriminatory reason sufficient to justify any employment selection decision.

Efforts to promote diversity and affirmative action are best directed at expansion of the applicant pool to include minority group members and women.

Dress Code

57. Q: Can I tell people how to dress at work without infringing on their rights? Last summer I saw a lot more skin around here than I wanted to.

A: Yes, if you do so carefully.

As even the Equal Employment Opportunity Commission (EEOC) recognizes, employers have the absolute right to impose and enforce nondiscriminatory dress and grooming standards, as long as they are consistently applied. Yet, many employers remain reluctant to take on dress and grooming issues, while others simply require workers to wear uniforms.

A well-drafted dress code should further a legitimate business purpose and comply with nondiscrimination standards and federal, state and/or local safety and health regulations. Examples of the latter are requiring protective clothing, headgear, goggles or masks.

All employees should be informed of the dress code's requirements and consequences for noncompliance. The key is that any standards must be consistently applied to preclude discrimination claims that the dress code has been applied disproportionately to any protected group, including women.

Even if no formal dress code or policy is in place, the employer remains free to address incidences of inappropriate workplace attire on a case-by-case basis, as long as similar concerns are handled in similar fashion. In fact, if only one or two employees are dressing inappropriately, it may be preferable to address the issue one-on-one rather than impose an across-the-board rule that could have unintended consequences.

When "too much skin" is being displayed, you have the right to impose standards requiring appropriate workplace attire. The EEOC has recognized specifically that the antidiscrimination laws do not prohibit employers from imposing restrictions on skimpy clothing. Of course, what is "appropriate" for an office environment differs greatly from what employers can reasonably expect employees to wear in a warehouse or factory environment where no one wears a suit or tie, but protective clothing may be required by applicable law.

> Sample Personal Appearance Policy
>
> Dress and grooming standards contribute to the morale of all employees and affect the business image ABC Company presents to the community.
>
> During business hours, employees are expected to present a clean and neat appearance and to dress according to the requirements of their positions. Employees who appear for work inappropriately dressed will be sent home and directed to return to work in proper attire. Under such circumstances, nonexempt employees will not be compensated for the time they are away from work.
>
> Please consult your supervisor, department head or human resources if you have any questions as to what constitutes appropriate attire.

At the same time, you must reasonably accommodate the sincerely held religious beliefs of your employees. An employee may ask for an exception to a dress code to wear religious attire and you may deny the request only if permitting it would pose an undue hardship on the day-to-day operation of your business.

For example, if wearing a hijab (head scarf) would pose a genuine safety risk of getting caught in factory machinery or conflict with safety standards requiring protective headgear, you could deny the request. Employers need not compromise legitimate safety concerns to accommodate religious beliefs. However, no accommodation request may be denied based solely on an employer's or customer's preference. The EEOC and many state agencies have been quite aggressive in pursuing such claims to litigation.

In fashioning a dress code policy, you should identify legitimate business-related reasons for the policy and ensure that it is flexible enough to accommodate religious practices and is sensitive to racial and ethnic concerns. Generally, a broad policy is preferable to enable you to deal with specific issues as they arise.

Drugs and Alcohol

58. Q: How can I maintain a drug-free workplace without worrying about discrimination and lawsuits? A friend of mine was sued because he tested an employee for drugs at his business – I can't afford that kind of trouble.

A: It appears that you are referring to a situation in which a minority employee was asked to take a drug test when the employer did not have a proper foundation for doing so, or under circumstances in which it was claimed a non-minority employee would not have been tested. Problems such as that can be avoided by having a policy that clearly sets out the criteria for drug and alcohol testing.

Many employers have pre-employment drug-testing requirements and, if they are uniformly and consistently applied and you use a reputable lab, these are rarely a cause for legal problems. For employees (as opposed to applicants), "for cause" drug testing policies are common. These policies require testing after an accident, when the employee appears to be "under the influence," and other similar workplace incidents.

The circumstances that can lead to testing should be stated in the policy and your supervisors should be trained about the criteria. Random drug testing policies are still widespread, but they are prohibited in some jurisdictions and are almost always unavailable for public-sector employees. When you have a random testing policy, you must take steps to insure that it is truly random, or you will open yourself to the same sort of charges your friend suffered in your question.

If you have a unionized workforce, drug testing is a subject that must be negotiated. Obviously, drug testing should never be used to discipline or harass an employee. A sample Drug and Alcohol Policy follows (Fig. 58-A).

You should also make sure that the lab that does your testing is reputable and has procedures you approve. To protect you and the employee, the exchange of information about prescription drugs used and similar health-related information should take place at the lab. You should be given only the results of the drug test. The lab should also have strict procedures regarding the confidentiality of its files.

Fig. 58-A

ALCOHOL AND CONTROLLED-SUBSTANCES

POLICIES AND PROCEDURES

THE POLICIES AND PROCEDURES CONTAINED HEREIN ARE NOT TO BE CONSIDERED CONTRACTUAL OBLIGATIONS OF THE COMPANY ("THE COMPANY") TO ANY EMPLOYEE, NOR ARE THEY DEEMED TO ABROGATE IN ANY FASHION THE AGREEMENT THAT ANY EMPLOYMENT CAN BE TERMINATED, WITH OR WITHOUT CAUSE OR NOTICE, AT ANY TIME BY EITHER THE EMPLOYEE OR THE COMPANY. SUBJECT TO APPLICABLE STATE AND FEDERAL LAW, THE COMPANY RETAINS THE RIGHT TO INTERPRET, REVISE, AMEND AND ABOLISH THE POLICIES AND PROCEDURES CONTAINED HEREIN AT ANY TIME.

PURPOSE AND SCOPE

The purpose of this policy is to provide a safe work environment and to prevent accidents and casualties caused by employees under the influence of controlled-substances or alcohol. The Company ("THE COMPANY") is concerned with the safety and health of its employees, the inhabitants of the properties it manages, and the general public. As such, THE COMPANY respects and honors the letter and spirit of the Drug Free Workplace Act, 41 U.S.C. § 701 et seq., as amended. THE COMPANY intends to maintain the quality of its services and to provide its employees who have controlled-substance or alcohol problems with encouragement in obtaining proper professional assistance. Any employee seeking assistance concerning his or her use of alcohol or controlled-substances should notify the Personnel Office. Every effort will be made to keep this information confidential. The employee may be referred to the Employee Assistance Program conducted by or on behalf of THE COMPANY. Questions regarding this policy should be directed to the Personnel Office.
THE COMPANY

HFSFT001

continued on next page

Fig. 58-A (cont.)

POLICIES AND PROCEDURES

TITLE: ALCOHOL AND CONTROLLED-SUBSTANCE TESTING

DATE: June ___, 20--

This provision sets out THE COMPANY's alcohol and controlled-substance testing policy and procedures. **Any termination of an employee as it relates to this policy will be without severance pay.**

I. Current Employees

A. Testing.

1. Random Testing. THE COMPANY, in its sole discretion, shall have the right to routinely, periodically or intermittently request that any current employee take an alcohol or controlled-substance test, which shall occur at a testing facility of THE COMPANY's choosing. The employee shall sign a Consent form such as the one accompanying this policy before taking the test. A refusal to take a drug screen will result in disciplinary action, up to an including termination.

2. Post Accident Testing. THE COMPANY is particularly concerned with promoting health and safety. As a result, if an employee sustains an injury for which any professional medical attention is required, the employee will be subject to a drug screen, to be taken as soon after the accident and possible. The employee shall sign a Consent form such as the one accompanying this policy before taking the test. A refusal to take a drug screen will result in disciplinary action, up to an including termination.

If an employee is thought to be involved in causing an accident, but is not injured, he or she will also be subject to a drug screen. The employee shall sign a Consent form such as the one accompanying this policy before taking the test. A refusal to take a drug screen will result in disciplinary action, up to an including termination.

3. Erratic or Unusual Behavior. All employees shall be asked to take a drug screen when an incident of erratic and unusual behavior has been documented based on the employee's appearance, behavior, and/or performance. The employee shall sign a Consent form such as the one accompanying this policy before taking the test. A refusal to take a drug screen will result in disciplinary action, up to an including termination.

2

continued on next page

FIG. 58-A (CONT.)

B. Procedures

The testing, at a laboratory contracted by THE COMPANY, shall consist of urinalysis (or, if because of an accident or any condition preventing the ability of the employee to provide a urine sample, a blood test) and the urine (or other) specimen shall be separated into two parts prior to the testing. The first part shall be used to conduct the initial test. The second part shall be used to conduct a confirmatory test if the first test is involving a current employee is positive. A second test shall be conducted in all cases where a first test involving a current employee is positive. Every reasonable effort shall be made to keep all test results confidential among THE COMPANY, the employee, and the testing facility.

Any employee's refusal to (1) sign a Consent to the test (i.e., alcohol or controlled-substances test), such as the one attached to this policy; and/or (2) take the requested test, shall constitute a willful and deliberate violation of THE COMPANY's employment Policies and Procedures and as such, may result in that employee's immediate termination.

While awaiting the results of the drug tests (24-48 hours for a negative; 48-72 hours for a positive), the employee may, in THE COMPANY's sole discretion, be permitted to return to the job site/office or may be put on administrative leave with pay.

C. Positive Test. For purposes of this policy, a "positive" test means that any level of alcohol or of a controlled substance has been detected by the test. In addition, anomalous results, such as those caused by drugs designed to mask the presence of controlled-substances can be regarded as a "positive test" for purposes of this Policy, or may be the basis for an additional test. Controlled-substances include, but are not limited to, amphetamines, barbiturates, other hypnotics, cocaine, narcotics (opiates such as heroin, morphine, codeine and methadone), PCP and other hallucinogens, marijuana and any other cannabinoid, and any drugs identified in the Controlled Substances Act, 21 U.S.C. § 812, as amended.

D. Consequences. If the employee's initial and confirmatory tests are positive, as defined herein, that shall constitute a willful and deliberate violation of THE COMPANY's employment Policies and Procedures and as such, THE COMPANY, in its sole discretion may

(1) take appropriate disciplinary action against the employee, up to and including termination of employment, or

(2) refer the employee to the company-paid Employee Assistance Program or to another appropriately qualified health care professional for evaluation and diagnosis of his or her problem and treatment recommendations. Such an employee may be required to participate in, and successfully complete, a treatment program as a further condition of employment. The employee may be required to provide a release of information to the referring individual (e.g., the department manager, Chairman or President) so that participation and progress in the treatment program can be monitored. Failure to comply with any of the recommended treatment conditions shall constitute a willful and deliberate violation of THE COMPANY's employment Policies and Procedures and as such may result in immediate termination.

E. Prescription Drugs. "Controlled-Substance", as that phrase is used in this policy, includes not only illegal substances, including marijuana, but also prescription drugs. If an

3

continued on next page

FIG. 58-A (CONT.)

employee tests positive, but he or she contends that the positive result was caused by his or her taking, in proper doses, a drug prescribed by a physician for that employee, then it shall be the employee's burden to prove to THE COMPANY's satisfaction, (1) that the positive result was caused by the prescribed drug, and (2) that taking proper doses of the prescribed drug caused the drug level detected by the test. THE COMPANY will hire a physician to evaluate the proof submitted by the employee, which may consist of a statement by the employee's physician. If the physician hired by THE COMPANY agrees with the proof provided by the employee, then THE COMPANY may choose, in its sole discretion, not to terminate the employee, but rather to take such other disciplinary or other measures as it deems appropriate.

II. Applicants.

THE COMPANY has the right to request that an applicant take a controlled-substance test. If that test is positive, the applicant shall not receive an offer of employment. In the event an offer of employment has already been made, a positive test result may result in the withdrawal of that offer of employment. If the applicant refuses to take the test, his or her application for employment shall be deemed withdrawn.

An applicant who tests positive may reapply for employment with THE COMPANY after one year.

III. The Possession, Sale, Use or Transfer of a Controlled Substance or the Use of Alcohol.

A. Controlled-substances. The observed possession, sale, use, effects of such use, or transfer of a controlled substance by any employee shall constitute a willful and deliberate violation of THE COMPANY's employment Policies and Procedures and as such, may result in immediate termination. Additionally, THE COMPANY may contact the appropriate authorities to take further action. These sanctions shall not apply to the possession or use, in appropriate prescribed doses, by the employee of a drug prescribed for the employee by his physician.

B. Alcohol. The observed use of alcohol, or effects of such use, by any employee during normal business hours shall constitute a willful and deliberate violation of THE COMPANY's employment Policies and Procedures and as such, may result in immediate termination. Moreover, the observed use of alcohol, or effects of such use, by any employee while "on call" evenings or weekends (e.g., Maintenance Engineers, Maintenance Mechanics, or Property Patrols), shall constitute a willful and deliberate violation of THE COMPANY's employment Policies and Procedures and as such, may result in immediate termination. This shall not apply to the use of alcohol at company-sponsored events with the prior approval of THE COMPANY.

4

continued on next page

FIG. 58-A (CONT.)

SAMPLE

CONSENT

Subject to The COMPANY's Policies and Procedures, I hereby agree to have a urine test (or blood test, if necessary) to detect alcohol or controlled-substances. I also agree that the report of any test may be released to The Company. I understand that if the test detects the presence of alcohol, controlled-substances, or masking drugs, then that shall constitute a willful and deliberate violation of THE COMPANY's Employment Policies and Procedures by myself, and The COMPANY may take such disciplinary or other measures which, in its sole discretion, it deems appropriate, one of which may be the termination of my employment, without severance pay.

____________________ Witness

____________________ Signature

____________________ Date

____________________ Time

5

59. Q: If we serve alcohol at company events, are we undercutting our own policy prohibiting the use of drugs and alcohol at work?

A: There is no easy answer to this question. Alcohol is America's drug of choice; there's no doubt about that. But alcohol in the workplace is a problem and, yes, you are undercutting your own policy by serving alcohol at company functions. But that is not the whole story.

It is not only possible, but commonplace for a distinction to be made between "drinking on the job" or coming to work inebriated, and being offered a beer at a company function. Most employers rely on the idea that an employee is not going to over-do it in front of his or her employer. That *may* be right. However, you should be aware that serving alcohol at work does have the potential for problems.

You already know that for some people, alcohol can reduce inhibitions. You may not be aware, however, that you may be found liable for damages if someone who is found to have had too much to drink gets into an automobile accident on the way home from the wine and cheese party. Those employers that deal with this problem usually do so only for holiday parties, when they buy "tapster's insurance" or similar additional liability coverage.

Maybe the best choice is to upgrade the food and eliminate the alcohol. Your policy provides you with the rationale for not serving drinks at work. Let's hope that your employees don't need alcohol to enjoy each other's company and the drive home will be a lot safer.

60. Q: Can I just impose a drug testing policy out of the blue? I just became a sub-contractor on a government contract. The prime contractor told me I have to have a drug-testing policy. I have never had a problem with employee drug use, and I'm concerned my employees will think I no longer trust them.

A: Yes. In many situations, a sub-contractor is going to be asked to adopt workplace conduct policies that mirror those of the prime contractor while working on the contract site, especially in a government contract situation.

This is particularly true with respect to drugs, because government contractors are required to ascribe to a "drug-free workplace" policy. Although that policy does not require drug testing, the prime contractor here has made that decision for you. Because of your workplace history, you should not have a drug problem going forward, but you should ask the prime contractor for its drug-testing policy to see if it is one you can adopt or adapt. To keep the contract, you must abide by the contractor's requirements.

Identity Theft

61. Q: Why has identity theft become an issue for HR? I thought that has to do with an individual's credit cards and bank accounts, not their employment.

A: There are many kinds of identity theft, and some of them may give HR managers a great deal to worry about. Just imagine how much important personal information you have about your employees: full names, family members' names, birth dates, home addresses, home phone numbers, Social Security numbers, bank account numbers (for direct deposit) pension account numbers, health information, a number of company passwords that are probably used on personal accounts as well, and so on. And you are responsible for protecting that information.

Your question seems based on the belief that ID theft could only happen to a single individual as the result of a personal computer glitch or a bank error. However, the recent notorious cases involving ING and the Department of Veterans Affairs, just to name two, indicate that it is as likely that carelessness or dishonest conduct at the workplace will lead to ID theft of many people all at once, and that is a great deal to worry about.

First, your business may have liability to each employee for losses as a result of alleged negligence in protecting personal information. Second, your business will almost certainly grind to a halt as properly concerned employees seek assistance in clearing their credit, securing their savings, getting new Social Security cards, new credit cards, even new driver's licenses. Third, you will have to devote significant resources to fixing the problems and making sure breaches of security do not recur.

There are steps you can take to reduce the threat of ID theft at the workplace. The U.S. Government Accountability Office provided suggestions on ways federal government agencies could prevent and respond to improper disclosure of personal information. That same information is applicable to the private-sector workplace.

Two key ways to reduce the likelihood that personal information will be compromised are conducting a privacy impact assessment and ensuring that a robust security program is in place. A "privacy impact assessment" includes identifying the specific instances when personal information is collected and maintained, and assessing how the information is being protected.

Elements of a robust security program include:

- periodically assessing the risk of a breach and the magnitude of harm that could result from the unauthorized use of information;
- having policies and procedures that cost-effectively reduce risks to an acceptable level and ensure that security is addressed throughout the life cycle of each information system;
- providing security awareness training for users of information systems that contain personal data;

- periodically testing and evaluating the effectiveness of information security policies;
- having a process for planning, implementing, evaluating and documenting remedial action to address any deficiencies through plans of action and milestones; and
- having procedures for detecting, reporting and responding to security incidents.

After a breach, immediately notify everyone who might have been affected. This may not only reduce your liability, it is the first step in re-establishing credibility with the affected employees.

62. Q: What I can do to prevent theft of business plans and sensitive personal information in electronic form? Many of our employees have these files on their laptops and PDAs.

A: You are right to be concerned, and there are steps you can take.

The first concern must be security. You must ask yourself what security processes are in place to protect sensitive information. As recent examples have demonstrated, there is a difference between routinely taking information home, including laptops, and accessing information at home. Providing remote access to a company server is one way to enhance security, because all information resides on the server and nothing is taken to another location where it could be lost or stolen.

But even that may not be enough. We learn everyday how exposed our electronic communications devices are to hackers and thieves. Two ways to address that problem are to password protect files and then encrypt sensitive data to protect against the loss of information. Many commercially available encryption products are available and provide at least some additional layers of protection.

Finally, train your employees in the proper practices of working off site. With so many employees working remotely, you can never keep all the electronic devices on the premises, but you can help your employees develop a sense of ownership not merely of the computer or PDA, but also of the company and its information. Reminding employees that some of the information they are protecting is their own is a good place to start to develop the right attitude.

Personnel Surveillance

63. Q: Can I monitor my employees' time on non-work Web sites? Can I discipline them or dock them for wasted time? I don't want to be a spy, but I've got to cut down on time lost to Web surfing and blogs.

A: Yes, you can – but there are several things to consider before you do so, including employees' expectations of privacy and whether you really want to limit all Internet and e-mail use to strictly business needs. Some leeway, within definite guidelines, may be more appropriate for non-work time such as lunch breaks.

Moreover, you should be careful about disciplining employees before you have a policy in place that they have been given. Some state courts are weighing the employer's property rights against the employees' reasonable expectation of privacy. Employees have sometimes won when the employer failed to notify them about potential monitoring. Further, some states have laws against intercepting telephone or electronic communications without the consent of one of the parties to the message. (For example, Colorado, Connecticut, Florida, Georgia, Nebraska, Ohio, Wisconsin and Wyoming all have laws concerning interception of electronic communications.)

Many employees simply do not understand that "deleted" messages can be retrieved and that e-mail messages cannot be withdrawn once they are sent. The use of passwords or access codes may lead employees to assume that their workplace e-mail, voice mail and Internet communications are private, personal and not their employer's business.

But electronic communications are company property. In addition to lost productivity, inappropriate e-mails to or about co-workers or customers and logons to sexually explicit, politically or racially inflammatory Web sites or chat-rooms create a significant risk to you of liability for sexual harassment, discrimination and defamation. Policies and practices to enforce them are also essential to protect your company's trade secrets and proprietary information, and to guard against copyright infringement by Web surfers.

Accordingly, many companies make some effort to monitor their employees' communications, including Internet surfing. You can adopt a comprehensive e-mail, voice mail and Internet policy. You need to consistently enforce any policy prohibiting the use of the Internet and e-mail for personal, non-job-related searches or messages. You also should advise employees that e-mail messages may be accessed by supervisors and computer use (including "web-surfing") will be monitored.

At a minimum, your policy should establish guidelines for computer usage. Procedures for electronic monitoring of communications and e-mail retention guidelines should be included. The best practice is to distribute copies of the policy to all current employees after its implementation, in addition to all new hires. You can even send it via e-mail. Each employee should sign an acknowledgment documenting that they have read and understand the policy's terms, and that any failure to comply may result in discipline, up to and including termination of employment.

In addition, the policy should incorporate the employer's workplace harassment and anti-discrimination policies, emphasizing in no uncertain terms that neither discrimination nor harassment over computerized communication systems will be tolerated, and doing either will lead to discipline. As with other types of workplace harassment or discrimination, employees should be encouraged to report all incidents of apparent harassment and discrimination on the Internet or through e-mail as quickly as possible.

Finally, to guard against the unauthorized disclosure of confidential or proprietary information, the policy should state that no such material should be forwarded through e-mail or posted on the Internet without management's approval. Confidential or proprietary information should be password protected and computer access to that information should be limited to those with a "need to know." Any e-mails containing such material should be marked "confidential."

Given the potential for copyright and trademark infringement by employees who "cut and paste" materials from the Internet, for which you may be liable, employees should be discouraged from downloading information from the Internet absent prior approval, and never for commercial use without written authorization.

An effective Internet and e-mail policy is only the first step, however. It is essential to implement an effective, workable means of enforcement, through the adoption of software that blocks or filters access to certain types of Web sites and allows access to employee e-mail accounts and tracking logons to Internet sites. Because the Internet is both a valuable resource and a distraction, such products can be tailored to your business needs, allowing access to useful sites while blocking access to others.

For a sample electronic technology policies, see Fig. 63-A – Fig. 63-F.

Fig. 63-A
Sample Use Policies
Policy 1 – Broad Computer and Electronic Communications Systems Policy

This policy applies to all electronic communications systems owned, licensed or operated by the Company, including e-mail, connections to the Internet and similar networks. This policy applies to all employees.

General Use of Systems

The Company's computer network is equipped with e-mail capability and employees are urged to use e-mail to communicate with others when it is appropriate to do so. Use of e-mail messages is not, however, intended to be a substitute for communication through speaking with another employee, client, or party or sending a written memorandum when such communication is needed to properly service clients or carry out the Company's business. Each person should access his or her e-mail several times per day to ensure prompt receipt of any messages.

Electronic communications are considered part of the Company's business records and may be subject to disclosure to third parties for use in litigation. It is important to compose messages in the same professional manner in which any other written communication or memorandum would be composed. Sarcasm and derogatory language must be avoided.

Prohibited Use of Systems

The Company's electronic communications systems are for the purpose of conducting the Company's business. Personal or other nonbusiness use is prohibited during working time. In addition, any use of the Company's electronic communications systems connected with the sale of any goods or services for profit is strictly prohibited at any time. Nonemployees are strictly prohibited from utilizing the Company's electronic communications systems at any time.

Electronic communications systems must not be used in a manner that is contrary to the Company's policies and procedures, as expressed in this handbook or elsewhere. Thus, employees are prohibited from engaging in the inappropriate use of the e-mail systems and are prohibited from transmitting any material that could be construed as illegal harassment in violation of the Company's Equal Employment Opportunity Policy and/or Harassment Policy. Any offensive or otherwise inappropriate material received by an employee must be immediately reported to a supervisor and should not be transmitted further through the system. Employees may not use the Internet to gain access to Internet sites that contain content that may be perceived as discriminatory, harassing or offensive to others. Use of the Company's access to the Internet for purposes of gaining access to sites containing pornography or other material embarrassing to the Company is strictly prohibited.

Employees shall refrain from transmitting or accessing the personal information of others, false or otherwise. This includes medical records, salary information, disciplinary action or any other material that a reasonable person would deem confidential.

Employees may not download any program onto the Company's computer equipment or diskettes without prior approval from the appropriate personnel.

No Right of Privacy

All employees should be aware that, because the electronic communications systems are designed for business use to serve the Company's clients or customers and conduct other Company business, the Company may from time to time access and review e-mail messages. In addition, because of the nature of the computer system's technology, the e-mail system stores e-mail messages sent and all messages likewise are maintained on tape backup. For this reason,

continued on next page

Fig. 63-A (cont.)

e-mail messages cannot be considered private by the employee. Employees using any Company electronic communication systems for personal purposes do so at their own risk and expressly consent to Company monitoring, recording, transcribing, copying or storing of communications in a separate location.

Security

In using all electronic communications systems, employees are required to protect the integrity of confidential, sensitive and privileged information. Employees utilizing the Company's electronic communications systems to send materials or messages outside of the Company must exercise great care to protect sensitive, privileged or confidential information from being intercepted. Information sent through the Internet can be monitored by external systems. If necessary, sensitive, confidential or privileged information can be transmitted through the Internet only when the sender and recipient can use encryption.

Acknowledgment:

Through his or her signature below, the employee acknowledges that he or she fully understands the policies set forth above and, as a condition of access, hereby consents to the monitoring of e-mail and electronic transmissions sent through the Company's computer system.

________________________ ____________________

Employee's Signature Date

Fig. 63-B
Sample Use Policies
Policy 2 – E-Mail, Voice Mail and Internet Usage

Electronic and voice mail communications are the property of the Company and should be used for business purposes only. They are not to be used for personal communications (e.g., political messages, charitable announcements or solicitations, for sale ads, recipe exchange, or personal or vulgar remarks/criticisms relating to the Company or its employees). The misuse of Company time, equipment, facilities or telephones for personal purposes, including personal gain, is a violation of Company policy and may result in disciplinary action.

Electronic mail, voice mail and Internet communications are subject to the same confidentiality and ethical conduct rules that apply to any other form of Company communication. All Company communications, including electronic mail, facsimiles, voice mail and Internet communications, shall be made with due regard to the interests of the Company, its employees and customers. Expressly prohibited are false and/or malicious communications, and communications of a sexually or racially offensive nature. In that regard, the Company's policies against harassment, including sexual harassment, apply to electronic communications as well as any other form of communication.

E-mail should not be considered a private method of communication and messages may be monitored without prior notice, to prevent personal use of these systems as well as to monitor the quality of our services. Therefore, employees should not have an expectation of privacy with regard to e-mail messages or computer files that they use at work and should refrain from using the e-mail system or computer files for any messages that they consider private or confidential.

Employees having questions concerning the application of the foregoing principles should speak with their supervisor or any officer of the Company.

Fig. 63-C
Sample Use Policies
Policy 3 – Computer Use

Computer equipment and computer software provided by the Company is for business use only. Use of the computer equipment or computer software for personal reasons is prohibited unless such use is approved by a supervisor.

The Company has the capability to access, review, copy or delete information prepared on, stored on, or in any other manner or status maintained on computer equipment, computer software or computer discs, notwithstanding the use of passwords, "fire walls" or other measures intended to protect the security or confidentiality of the information. The Company reserves the right to access, review, copy or delete all such information, including such information to any third party (inside or outside the Company) it deems appropriate. **Accordingly, an employee cannot have an expectation of privacy in any such information. Deleting information from computer equipment, computer software or computer discs does not guarantee that it has been erased or is not capable of being accessed.**

Should an employee make approved use of the Company's computer equipment, computer software or computer discs to prepare, store or otherwise maintain personal information, such information will be treated no differently from other information. That is, the Company reserves the right to access, review, copy, delete or disclose it for any purpose.

Also, the copying of computer software of the Company, or the installation of computer software on the computer equipment of the Company, may violate copyright laws, otherwise be illegal, or result in the introduction of computer viruses or other defects in the computer systems of the Company. Accordingly, employees are absolutely prohibited from copying software of the Company for any reason, or installing personal software of any kind in a computer of the Company, without the prior written approval of the President of the Company, or his or her designee.

Computer software purchased by the Company is purchased for specific uses and machines. Unauthorized copying of computer software for installation on other machines of the Company also is expressly prohibited. Before any software is installed into a computer of the Company, or any computer disc that has not been in the exclusive use, custody and control of the Company is placed in a computer of the Company, appropriate measures must be taken to ensure that said computer software or disc does not contain a "computer virus" or other defect.

If you have any questions or concerns regarding the Company's computers and computer software, or this policy, please contact either your supervisor or the Company system administrator.

Fig. 63-D
Sample Use Policies
Policy 4 – E-Mail Use

The Company maintains an e-mail system that is intended solely for the conduct of Company business. The Company treats all messages (or records of such messages) prepared, transmitted, received or stored in the Company e-mail system as business messages of the Company.

The Company has the capability to access, review, copy or delete messages (or records of such messages) prepared, transmitted, received or stored on these communications systems. It reserves the right to access, review, copy or delete all such messages (or records of such messages), including messages of a personal nature, for any purpose and to disclose them to any third party (inside or outside the Company) it deems appropriate, without notification to or permission from the employee who prepared, transmitted, received or stored the messages (or records of such messages).

Accordingly, employees have no right or expectation of privacy in any electronic communication and deleting a message (or record of such message) from an electronic communication system does not guarantee that it has been erased from the system. **As a condition of continued employment, all employees consent to the access, review, copying, deletion or disclosure of electronic communication messages (or records of such messages).**

The use of the Company's e-mail systems for personal matters is strictly discouraged. No e-mail communication, personal or otherwise, should include the following:

A. Offensive communications, such as those involving defamatory, obscene, racial or sexual messages, or messages that disclose personal information about other individuals without authorization; and

B. Any references to outside business ventures, political campaigns or similar nonbusiness related activity.

Should employees make incidental use of the Company e-mail system to prepare, transmit, receive or store personal messages, such messages (or records of such messages) will be treated no differently from other messages. That is, the Company reserves the right to access, review, copy, delete or disclose them for any purpose.

In addition, Company records are subject to disclosure to law enforcement and other governmental agencies, as well as third parties, through subpoena or other process. Moreover, any electronic communication is subject to being intercepted by third parties. Consequently, employees always should ensure that the business information contained in electronic messages is accurate, appropriate and lawful. When the certainty of confidentiality is important, other means of communication should be used.

Any violation of this policy, or any abuse of the Company's communications systems will result in disciplinary action, up to and including discharge.

Fig. 63-E
Sample Use Policies
Policy 5 – E-Mail Systems

Policy

E-mail is provided by the Company to assist employees as they conduct daily Company business. The e-mail system, its contents and passwords are the property of the Company. This policy outlines the following:

A. appropriate and inappropriate use of e-mail;

B. management's rights and responsibilities; and

C. employee responsibilities.

Procedure

1. E-mail may be used for Company business only. Appropriate use of e-mail includes sending:
   A. work-related correspondence;
   B. approved Company announcements; and
   C. meeting schedules and announcements.
2. Inappropriate use of the e-mail system includes sending:
   A. messages that contain trade secrets or other confidential information;
   B. personnel information (e.g., discussions of performance reviews, disciplinary actions, Employee Relations inquiries, etc.);
   C. Company financial records;
   D. copyrighted software or copyrighted documents as e-mail attachments;
   E. any form of solicitation for commercial ventures, religious or political causes or nonbusiness related messages;
   F. e-mail that contains ethnic slurs, racial epithets, or anything that may be construed as harassment or disparagement of others based on their race, national origin, gender, sexual orientation, age, disability, or religious or political beliefs;
   G. sexually explicit images, messages or cartoons; and
   H. messages that are disruptive, excessive, offensive to others or harmful to morale.

Management's Rights and Responsibilities

1. E-mail is not private and messages are considered Company records. E-mail, under the appropriate circumstances, may be accessed and read by designated Company employees or outside individuals for business purposes. The Company reserves the right to enter an employee's e-mail files whenever there is a business need to do so, including the following:
   A. when the Company has a business need to access the employee's mailbox or computer because the employee is absent and the supervisor has reason to believe needed information is located in the employee's e-mail;
   B. when the Company receives a legal request from law enforcement officials to disclose e-mail messages or in ongoing legal proceedings;
   C. when the Company has reason to believe that the employee is using e-mail in violation of Company policy; or

continued on next page

Fig. 63-E (cont.)

D. during periodic audits of the e-mail system.

2. Managers are responsible for communicating, monitoring, and enforcing this policy.

Employee Responsibilities

1. Employees are required to use the e-mail system in a responsible and productive manner. Employees will be held accountable for the content of all text, audio or visual images that they place, or transmit, via the Company's e-mail system.
2. Employees should immediately delete inappropriate e-mail or attachments that are sent to them. Such messages should not be printed or forwarded. In addition, employees receiving inappropriate e-mail or attachments shall notify their immediate supervisor.
3. Misuse of the e-mail system is a serious offense that may expose the Company and employee to criminal and/or civil liability. Violations of this policy will result in disciplinary action up to and including termination.

Fig. 63-F
Sample Use Policies
Policy 6 – Sample Release

I, ____________________, having read the above policy, understand that the Company's computer systems, including e-mail and Internet access, is provided for business use only, and is not to be used for personal reasons. I understand that all files are deemed to be Company property and that the Company can, and on occasion will, exercise the right to review, transmit, intercept and generally access any and all files, including e-mails that are found on the Company's system. I understand that this access can take place at any time and without further notice.

By my signature, I acknowledge that I have read the Company policy regarding computer use. I further acknowledge that I have been given notice that computer files and personal e-mails may be accessed at any time by the appropriate Company representative. I hereby release and hold harmless the Company and its employees and agents from any liability whatsoever arising from a request for access and any decisions made concerning my continued employment based on the results of such access. I also understand that in certain circumstances law enforcement officials may be notified.

________________________________ ________________________________

Employee's Signature Date

64. Q: Can I search employees' desks for illegal drugs? I smelled marijuana in the men's room, which is not open to the public and key-entry only. This is a drug-free workplace and I know our owner would have a fit if he found out about it.

A: It depends on whether your state recognizes an employee's right to privacy (more than half the states do) and what that right entails, and on whether you have a union contract with provisions that deal with searches.

Obviously, suspected illegal activity or other workplace misconduct must be investigated. Situations involving potential employee drug use routinely raise the prospect of searching desks, lockers or cubicles for contraband. How can needed information be obtained through a search without creating liability for violating what an employee most likely perceives as his or her right to privacy?

Although the U.S. Constitution prohibits unreasonable searches, these protections don't extend to private employers. However, most states have laws that give workers certain privacy rights – for example, the right not to have surveillance cameras in restrooms or to be spied on through a secret one-way mirror. In many states, however, no law explicitly says what is and isn't allowed when it comes to searches in the workplace. Accordingly, the answer to this question involves balancing two competing concerns.

First, you must have a valid, work-related justification for performing the search. Here, it may not be appropriate to search every male employee's desk on an entire floor, unless they all have access to the men's room in question and there are no other men's restroom facilities available.

The better approach might be to narrow the scope of the search through a preliminary factual investigation. When was the marijuana odor first noticed? Who was in the office on that date and time? Were any particular employees observed that day with symptoms of drug use? On the other hand, if only five employees work on the floor and use only that private men's room, there is a stronger basis for a wholesale search that is more likely to withstand a legal challenge.

Second, you must consider the employees' reasonable expectations of privacy. Depending on your company policy, past practices and common sense, employees are entitled to a higher expectation of privacy in particular areas within the workplace, such as a changing room locker or desk drawer, particularly if you have not warned workers that these areas might be subject to search.

The key to accomplishing lawful workplace searches when business needs require such an investigation is to take steps in advance to diminish the affected workers' expectations of privacy by, for example, implementing a policy notifying them that certain seemingly private areas such as desks or lockers constitute company property, which you have a right to access. Here are some additional guidelines:

- **Search only if necessary.** Make sure there is a documented, legitimate business reason for any search. Suspected workplace drug use certainly qualifies.

- **Verify first, if possible.** Before conducting a search, attempt to narrow the scope to only those employees who really are viable suspects.
- **Implement a policy** to reduce employees' expectations of privacy. Inform employees of your right to conduct searches, at any time for any reason, with or without notice, and reinforce that no employee should have any expectation of privacy in his or her office, desk, filing cabinet, computer, electronic communications, lockers or even personal property while on company or client premises, including the employee's car.
- **Avoid random searches.** Such searches, absent a reason to suspect wrongdoing, often lead to liability, even if the employer's policy puts employees on notice that they may occur.
- **Never conduct a physical search of an employee's body.** Consider calling the police instead.
- **Restrooms and changing rooms are generally off limits to employer surveillance.** Most workers legitimately expect that they will not be monitored while using the toilet or changing their clothes. Some state laws specifically prohibit such surveillance, even if employees are warned in advance.
- **Consider the worker's privacy expectations.** Before searching, think about whether an average worker would consider a particular space private in your workplace. Do the employees routinely lock their desk drawers? If so, they might have higher privacy expectations. In contrast, if workers routinely use each other's desks or desks are not assigned to particular individuals, an unlocked drawer is not as private.
- **Don't hold employees against their will.** Some employers detain workers in connection with a search to keep the worker out of the area being searched or to pressure an employee into consenting to the search or even confessing to the misconduct in question. That can lead to liability for false imprisonment if you lead the employee to believe that he or she is not free to leave.

65. Q: Can I install a hidden video surveillance camera? We've experienced a lot of theft lately.

A: Video surveillance in the workplace is permissible, under certain circumstances, depending on the applicable state law.

In general, your business needs must be balanced against your employees' legitimate expectations of privacy. For example, although security cameras in stairwells and parking garages are clearly justified for safety reasons, employers sometimes install cameras in areas that are absolutely not appropriate, such as dressing rooms, bathrooms and locker rooms.

Given a series of related thefts, installation of a hidden camera in an open, public work area such as a stockroom most likely would withstand any legal challenge as an extension of a manager's ability to supervise a wider area. However, if you target a camera on something such as a single employee's workstation, a court may find the use of the selective surveillance to be overly invasive.

Many states have provisions that limit or prohibit video surveillance. Before implementing this practice, you should research privacy provisions in your state. Employers of union workers may be required to bargain with the union to implement video surveillance. When considering the use of video surveillance, you should:

- Keep any videotape machinery and materials in a safe and confidential place. Store the materials under lock and key and only for a reasonable period of time.
- In some areas there is a heightened expectation of privacy that cannot be lowered by posting a notice. These areas include bathrooms, locker rooms and dressing rooms. Surveillance of any kind should be avoided there.
- Many states do not allow the use of accompanying audio with video surveillance.
- Require all employees to sign a written acknowledgment that they understand and agree they may be subjected to video surveillance in work areas.
- Remember, because unnecessary monitoring can lead to poor employee morale and potential liability, it should be used only to protect legitimate business interests, and employees should be so informed. It you target only certain employees or groups of employees for monitoring, you may face liability for discrimination.
- After you've caught the thief, post a notice that video monitoring is in use in all areas where videotaping is allowed. This will lower employee expectations of privacy and serve as a deterrent to future incidents.

Polygraphs

66. Q: Can I make employees take a lie detector test? We just "lost" a couple thousand dollars. Only two employees had access and opportunity, and I don't want to fire them both.

A: Yes, if your suspicion about these two employees is reasonable, if you carefully follow certain procedures and if you generally confine the lie detector test to information about this incident. In other words, test as a last resort and be very careful if you do so.

Virtually all private-sector employers are covered by a federal law called the Employee Polygraph Protection Act (EPPA). The law does not apply to employees of state or local governments. The EPPA generally prohibits employers from requiring a job applicant or an employee to take a lie detector test.

It also prohibits employers from refusing to hire an applicant because that applicant refuses to take a lie detector test, and an employer may not discipline or fire an employee for refusing to take a lie detector test. Moreover, an employer cannot use the results of a lie detector test given to an applicant or employee as a basis for not hiring the applicant or for disciplining or terminating the employee.

Employers must post a notice in the workplace advising employees of their rights under the EPPA. You can download a copy of the poster from the Department of Labor's Web site: http://www.dol.gov/esa/regs/compliance/posters/eppa.htm.

But there are certain situations in which you can require an employee to take a lie detector test. The law permits an employer to administer a lie detector test if:

- the test is part of an ongoing investigation involving economic loss or injury to the employer's business, such as theft, embezzlement, misappropriation or an act of unlawful industrial espionage or sabotage;
- the employee had access to the property that is the subject of the investigation; and
- the employer has a reasonable suspicion that the employee was involved in the incident or activity under investigation.

In those cases, the employer must give the employee a statement, before the test, that explains in detail the specific incident or activity being investigated and the basis for testing particular employees. The statement must be signed by someone who is authorized to legally bind the employer (other than a polygraph examiner) and it must be retained by the employer for at least three years.

The statement must include an identification of the specific economic loss or injury to the business, language indicating that the employee had access to the property that is the subject of the investigation and a statement describing the basis for your reasonable suspicion that the employee was involved in the incident or activity under investigation.

You also must give the employee written notice regarding the test, inform the employee of the right to consult with legal counsel and provide detailed information about the instrument being used and the employee's rights under the law.

You must follow certain procedures regarding the administration of the test itself. For example, the person being examined must be permitted to terminate the test at any time. He or she may not be asked any question concerning religious beliefs or affiliations, opinions regarding racial matters, political beliefs or affiliations, any matter relating to sexual behavior, or beliefs or affiliations concerning labor unions.

Before taking any adverse employment action, you must further interview the employee on the basis of the results of the test and provide him or her with a written copy of any opinion or conclusion rendered as a result of the test and a copy of the questions asked during the test, along with the corresponding charted responses.

Even assuming you meet all of these requirements, you cannot take action against the employee based solely on the results of the lie detector test; you must have additional evidence supporting your action.

If you report a theft or other incident involving economic loss to the police and the police, during the normal course of their investigation, administer a lie detector test to your employees, you will not be considered in violation of the EPPA. And if the police ask you to cooperate with their investigation by making employees available for a lie detector test during working hours, that would not be a violation on your part either.

But you are prohibited from using the results of a lie detector test administered by the police. If your employees' union requests that you offer a lie detector test to discharged employees as a means of clearing their names, you are allowed to administer that test.

If you violate the EPPA by requiring an employee to take a lie detector test when doing so is not warranted, or if you fail to follow the proper procedures when a test is warranted, the U.S. Department of Labor can bring an action against your company for civil money penalties, an injunction against violating the EPPA and an order requiring you to promote or reinstate the employee, and to provide back wages and benefits. The employee also has a right to bring his or her own action against your company. These same rights apply to job applicants.

Sources: 29 U.S.C. §§ 2001, *et seq.*, specifically §2007; 29 C.F.R. §801, *et seq.*; *Mennen v. Easter* Stores, 951 F. Supp. 838 (N.D. Iowa 1997); *Watson v. Drummond Co., Inc.*, 436 F.3d 1310 (11th Cir. 2006).

Non-competition Agreements

67. Q: Can I require current employees to sign a covenant-not-to-compete?

A: The short answer is "yes," but only where state law permits non-competes to start with (California, for example, does not).

The caveat is that a covenant-not-to-compete is a contract and, as with any other contract, there has to be something of value (called "consideration") given in exchange for the employee's signature on the non-compete agreement. Some courts have ruled that continued employment is adequate "consideration"; others have not. For that reason, the safest course is to give employees these agreements at the same time they receive pay raises or bonuses.

You need to remember that covenants-not-to-compete are looked at skeptically by courts because they are a restriction on an individual's right to earn a living. Many judges say that an employer will get all the protection it needs, *not* all the protection it wants.

For that reason, to be enforceable, these agreements need to be reasonable. To be reasonable, they should be limited in time, scope and geographical area. You cannot, for example, expect to keep an employee from competing with everything your business does for the rest of his or her life everywhere in the country, or even everywhere in the state.

You probably can enforce an agreement that for a period of two years an employee will not open a business within your town or county that produces the same product or offers the same service as you do. On the other hand, if it reflects the nature of your business and the employee's job, you can have a broader, even national geographical scope but you should shorten the time period of the covenant. Think of striking a balance.

Some states will allow courts to rewrite parts of agreements to make them acceptable if a former employee sues, but some states require that the entire agreement be declared void and unenforceable if any provision is deemed illicit. It is advisable to have a lawyer prepare or at least review any non-compete agreement for enforceability.

For a sample covenant not to compete, see Fig. 67-A.

Sources: Covenants-not-to-compete are governed by state law, primarily by judicial decisions. If you plan to have your employees sign these agreements, it is a good idea to get some advice from your lawyer.

Fig. 67-A

COVENANT NOT TO COMPETE AND NOT TO SOLICIT

[The presumption is that this covenant is in a Hiring Agreement; if it is in a Termination Agreement, some additional modifications regarding consideration will have to be made. Post-employment 'Restrictive Covenants' are not enforceable in every jurisdiction.]

A. For a period of one year following the termination of Employee's employment, Employee will not participate, personally or financially, directly or indirectly, in competition with Employer in the business of **[please include a description of the kind of work at issue]** for any competitor within **[100 miles of Employer's place of business] [within 50 miles of any of Employer's places of business] [within the United States of America] [wherever Employer does business anywhere in the world]**.[1] Employee acknowledges that Employer's business is nationwide and that Employee is expected to market Employer's services throughout the United States.

B. For a period of one year following the termination of Employee's employment, Employee will not solicit business from Employer's existing customers or existing sources of business or in any other way induce Employer's existing customers and existing sources of business to cease doing business with Employer.

C. During the term of his employment and for one year following the termination of Employee's employment, Employee will not solicit any of Employer's employees to leave the employ of the Employer and/or to be employed by any other person or entity.

D. Employee acknowledges that the provisions of this Article are of particular importance for the protection and promotion of Employer's existing and future interests and that in the event of any breach of this Article, a claim for monetary damages may not constitute an adequate remedy. Employee therefore agrees that, in the event of a breach or a threatened breach by Employee of this Article, the Employer may apply to any court of competent jurisdiction for injunctive or other relief, and Employee will not object to the form of the action to the form of relief sought in any such action. Should Employer be required to enforce the provisions of this Article in any judicial proceeding, the Employee will be responsible for the payment of all of Employer's costs, including attorney's fees, should the Employer prevail.

E. If any portion of this Article is found by a court of competent jurisdiction to be unenforceable, the parties to the consent to the enforcement of the provisions of this Article to the maximum extent permitted by law.

F. The provisions of this Article will survive the termination of Employee's employment by Employer.

1 Please note that the longer and broader the restriction, the more difficult it will be to enforce.

HFHRT011

68. Q: How should I enforce the non-solicitation clause in our covenant-not-to-compete? Two employees just quit to work for a former supervisor I let go six months ago. The supervisor has a clause in his covenant-not-to-compete that bars him from soliciting my employees for 18 months.

A: This is a matter of state law, so the answer can vary, depending on your location. The general rule applied by the courts is that limitations on an individual's freedom to work where he or she wants to are closely reviewed and face a stiff challenge. In this case, you can try to ask a court to stop your supervisor from "raiding" your employees. When raiding (sometimes called "pirating") is overt and repeated, courts often are willing to step in.

The problem you face is that the two employees who left to join the supervisor want to work with him. It is likely they will testify that they are the ones who initiated the solicitation and asked to join the new company. If that is the case, very few, if any, courts will get involved.

You mentioned that the supervisor had a covenant-not-to-compete, but you did not indicate that was true of the lower-level employees. What happened to you demonstrates that it makes sense to have carefully drafted non-compete agreements for all employees whose competing efforts would damage your business. As you know, such provisions prevent employees from working for a competitor for a fixed period, usually in a stated geographic area.

You didn't mention whether the employees that left had employment contracts. Those contracts could have penalty or damages clauses on which you can act. Were you to do so, it would serve as an object lesson to others.

69. Q: My boss just told me "to secure our intellectual property." What should I do?

A: In this information age, even companies that do not describe themselves as "dot. coms" have intellectual property (IP). So let's start there.

The most obvious intellectual property a company may have would be anything invented or designed. This can be tangible, such as a product, your company name or a corporate logo. But often, IP is something intangible, such as a manufacturing process, a computer program or an algorithm. However, it needn't be so sophisticated. In the broadest terms, intellectual property can be confidential information about how your company runs, its customer lists, its price lists, your training manual and things of that kind.

When your boss asks you to "secure" the intellectual property, she or he is most likely talking about making sure that your rights to your IP are protected. For many people, IP itself means the *rights* to the ideas or information, rather than the stuff itself.

Depending on the nature of the IP, you can secure it by a variety of means. There are stringent legal protections such as patents, copyrights and trademarks, but the information or material must qualify for those protections. In most cases, to qualify for that level of protection, the information or material must be unique or original. It is very likely that IP of that kind has already been secured by the inventor, designer or writer as well as by the company. But there is a lot of information that may be considered a trade secret or even proprietary business information that should also be secured.

Securing more mundane types of information is less structured, and perhaps more difficult as a result. First, if there is information your company regards as a trade secret, you should look at the Uniform Trades Secrets Act and find out if your state has enacted such a law. If so, make sure what you are trying to protect meets the legal definition of a trade secret. If it does, you will learn what obligations you have and what protections you can have.

Even if your material or information is not a trade secret under a law, it can still be confidential, proprietary business information, and you can secure it. One way to begin is to treat it as if it were confidential. That means the information is not on your Web site; it is not in your sales brochures, marketing materials, recruiting documents or other similar documents. If such information is electronically stored, limit access to it by means of a password or other "key."

Make sure that your employment contracts or offer letters include or attach provisions directly addressing your employees' obligation to keep your IP (including proprietary business information) confidential. Fig. 69-A is an example of such a policy.

Fig. 69-A

THOMPSON

Thompson HR Forms
http://forms.thompson.com

Employee Confidentiality and Invention Assignment Agreement

This Confidentiality And Invention Assignment Agreement (this "Agreement") is entered into on __________ ____, 200_, between __________ (the "Company"), and __________ (the "Employee").

The Employee acknowledges that the Company operates in a competitive environment and that it enhances its opportunities to succeed by establishing certain policies, including those included in this Agreement. This Agreement is designed to make clear that (a) the Employee will maintain the confidentiality of the Company's trade secrets; (b) the Employee will use those trade secrets for the exclusive benefit of the Company; (c) inventions that the Employee creates will be owned by the Company; (d) the Employee's prior and continuing activities separate from the Company will not conflict with the Company's development of its proprietary rights; and (e) when and if the Employee's employment with the Company terminates, he or she will not use his or her prior position with the Company to the detriment of the Company.

In consideration of **(check one or more boxes)**

❑ the commencement of Employee's employment
❑ Employee's promotion

and the compensation paid to Employee, Employee acknowledges and agrees with the Company as follows:

1. **Effectiveness.** This Agreement shall become effective on the earlier of (1) commencement of Employee's employment with the Company, or (2) the date and time at which any Confidential Information (as defined below) was or is first disclosed to Employee.

2. **Protection of the Company's Confidential Information.**

a. **Confidential Information.** The Company has and will develop, compile and own certain proprietary and confidential information that has great value in its business ("Confidential Information"). Confidential Information includes all information which is not generally known to the Company's competitors and the public, and which has or could have commercial value to the Company's business. It includes not only information disclosed by the Company (or its customers, affiliates or vendors) to Employee during the course of his or her employment with the Company, but also information developed or learned by the Employee himself or herself during the course of his or her employment with the Company, such as Inventions, as defined below. Confidential Information includes, but is not limited to, the following categories of information: [*tailor or replace following to fit Company's information:* information regarding the Company's technology, computer programs, products, product specifications, techniques, inventions, discoveries, improvements, research, test results, or know-how; information regarding the Company's customers' and vendors' identities, characteristics, performance and agreements; information regarding the Company's affiliates', sub-affiliates' and

HFHRT015

1

continued on next page

FIG. 69-A (CONT.)

employees' characteristics, performance and agreements; and information regarding the Company's marketing, sales and business plans, strategies, forecasts, unpublished financial information, budgets, projections, and efforts.] Employee acknowledges that such information is secret, valuable and owned by the Company, and that the Company has exercised substantial efforts to preserve the information's secrecy.

b. Protection of Confidential Information. During and after his or her employment, Employee agrees to keep confidential, and not to disclose to any third party or to make any use of Confidential Information of the Company, except for the benefit of the Company and in the course of his or her employment with the Company. Employee also agrees not to remove or otherwise transmit Confidential Information or Inventions (as defined below) from the premises or possession of the Company without the express prior written consent of an authorized representative of the Company. Employee also agrees to not publish the results of his or her work through literature or speeches, without submitting such literature or speeches to the President of the Company at least ten (10) days before dissemination of such information for a determination of whether such disclosure may destroy trade secret status or be prejudicial to the interests of the Company or whether disclosure may constitute an invasion of its privacy. Employee agrees not to publish, disclose or otherwise disseminate such information without prior written approval of the President. Employee acknowledges that he or she is aware that the unauthorized disclosure of Confidential Information of the Company may be highly prejudicial to its interests, an invasion of privacy, and an improper disclosure of trade secrets. Whenever the approval, designation, specification or other act of the President is required under this Agreement, the President may, by written designation, authorize an agent of the Company to perform such act.

c. Exclusive Employment and Non-Solicitation of Customers, Affiliates, Sub-Affiliates or Employees. Employee acknowledges the highly confidential nature of information regarding the Company's customers, affiliates, sub-affiliates, employees, agents, independent contractors, suppliers, and consultants. The Employee will not during his or her employment or within one year after it ends, without the Company's express written consent, directly or indirectly (i) hire, solicit, recruit, or induce to leave the employ of the Company any employee, agent, independent contractor or consultant of the Company; (ii) use the Company's Confidential Information to solicit the business of any clients or customers of the Company (other than on behalf of the Company); or (iii) encourage to terminate or alter any relationship between (a) the Company, and (b) any customer, affiliate, sub-affiliate, employee, agent, independent contractor, supplier, consultant, or any other person or company. During the Employee's employment with the Company, he or she will not do anything to compete with the Company's present or contemplated business, nor will he or she plan or organize any competitive business activity. The Employee will not enter into any agreement that conflicts with his or her duties or obligations to the Company. The Employee agrees that such activities would necessarily and inevitably involve disclosure or use of Confidential Information in violation of this Agreement.

d. Prior Knowledge and Inventions. Except as disclosed on Exhibit A to this Agreement, Employee does not know anything about the Company's Confidential Information, other than that which he or she learned from the Company. Employee also has disclosed on Exhibit A a complete list of all Inventions and information proprietary to Employee and which Employee wants to exclude from the application of this Agreement.

2

continued on next page

FIG. 69-A (CONT.)

e. Proprietary Information or Trade Secrets of Others. Employee will not disclose to the Company, or use, or induce the Company to use, any proprietary information or trade secrets of others. Employee represents and warrants that he or she has returned all property and confidential information belonging to all prior employers. Employee further represents and warrants that he or she has no other agreements, relationships or commitments to any other person or entity that conflict with Employee's obligations to the Company under this Agreement.

3. Inventions.

a. Disclosure of Inventions. Employee promptly will disclose in writing to the Company all discoveries, developments, designs, ideas, improvements, inventions, formulas, processes, techniques, know-how, and data (whether or not patentable or registrable under copyright or similar statutes) made, conceived, reduced to practice, or learned by Employee (either alone or jointly with others) during the period of his or her employment, that are related to or useful in the business of the Company, or which result from tasks assigned to Employee by the Company, or from the use of premises owned, leased, or otherwise acquired by the Company. For the purposes of this Agreement, all of the foregoing are referred to as Inventions.

b. Assignment/Ownership of Inventions. Employee acknowledges and agrees that all Inventions other than those listed in Exhibit A belong to and shall be the sole property of the Company and shall be Inventions of the Company subject to the provisions of this Agreement. Employee assigns to the Company all right, title, and interest Employee may have or may acquire in and to all Inventions. Employee agrees to sign and deliver to the Company (either during or subsequent to his or her employment) such other documents as the Company considers desirable to evidence the assignment of all rights of Employee, if any, in any Inventions to the Company and the Company's ownership of such Inventions. Any provision in this Agreement requiring Employee to assign rights to an Invention does not apply to any invention that qualifies under California Labor Code § 2870, which section is reproduced in the attached Written Notification to Employee (Exhibit B).

c. Power of Attorney. In the event the Company is unable to secure Employee's signature on any document necessary to apply for, prosecute, obtain, or enforce any patent, copyright, or other right to protection relating to any Invention, whether due to mental or physical incapacity or any other cause, Employee hereby irrevocably designates and appoints the Company and each of its duly authorized officers and agents as his or her agent and attorney-in-fact, to act for and in his or her behalf and stead to execute and file any such document and to do all other lawfully permitted acts to further the prosecution, issuance, and enforcement of patents, copyrights, or other rights or protections with the same force and effect as if executed and delivered by the Employee.

4. Termination of Employment.

a. Delivery of Documents and Data Upon Termination of Employment. In the event of termination (voluntary or otherwise) of Employee's employment with the Company, Employee agrees, promptly and without request, to deliver to and inform the Company of all documents and data pertaining to his or her employment and the Confidential Information and Inventions of the Company, whether prepared by Employee or otherwise coming into his or her possession or control, and to sign Exhibit C to this Agreement. Employee will not retain any written or

3

continued on next page

FIG. 69-A (CONT.)

other tangible material containing any information concerning or disclosing any of the Confidential Information or Inventions of the Company. Employee recognizes that the unauthorized taking of any of the Company's trade secrets is a crime under California Penal Code § 499(c) and is punishable by imprisonment in state prison or in a county jail for a time not exceeding one year, or by a fine not exceeding five thousand dollars ($5,000), or by both such fine and such imprisonment. Employee further recognizes that such unauthorized taking of the Company's trade secrets also could result in civil liability under California's Uniform Trade Secrets Act (Civil Code §§ 3426-3426.11), and that willful misappropriation may result in an award against Employee for triple the amount of the Company's damages and the Company's attorneys' fees in collecting such damages.

b. Obligations of Employee After Termination of Employment. In the event of termination (voluntary or otherwise) of Employee's employment with the Company, Employee agrees that he or she will protect the value of the Confidential Information and Inventions of the Company and will prevent their misappropriation or disclosure. Employee will not disclose or use to his or her benefit (or the benefit of any third party) or to the detriment of the Company any Confidential Information or Invention.

5. Injunctive Relief. Because Employee's breach of this Agreement may cause the Company irreparable harm for which money is inadequate compensation, Employee agrees that the Company will be entitled to injunctive relief to enforce this Agreement, in addition to damages and other available remedies.

6. Attorneys' Fees. [*Optional*] If any action is necessary to enforce this Agreement, the prevailing party shall be entitled to recover its attorneys' fees.

7. Understanding. Employee acknowledges and agrees that the protections set forth in this Agreement are a material condition to his or her employment with compensation by the Company.

8. Amendment and Binding Effect. This Agreement may not be amended except by an instrument in writing signed by both parties. This Agreement shall be binding on the heirs, executors, administrators, and other legal representatives and assigns of Employee, and is for the benefit of the Company and its successors and assigns.

9. Governing Law. This Agreement shall be governed by the laws of the State of California.

10. Entire Understanding. This Agreement expresses the entire understanding of the parties about the described subject matter, superseding all prior or contemporaneous agreements and understanding (whether oral or written) between the parties with respect to the subject matter.

11. Cumulative Remedies. Each and all of the several rights and remedies provided for in this Agreement shall be cumulative. No one right or remedy shall be exclusive of the others or of any right or remedy allowed in law or in equity. No waiver or indulgence by the Company of any failure by Employee to keep or perform any promise or condition of this Agreement shall be a waiver of any preceding or succeeding breach of the same or any other promise or condition. No waiver by the Company of any right shall be construed as a waiver of any other right. Any waiver by the Company or

4

continued on next page

Fig. 69-A (cont.)

by the Employee must be in writing and signed by either the Employee, if he or she is seeking to waive any of his or her rights under this Agreement, or by an officer of the Company (other than the Employee) or some other person duly authorized by the Company. The Company shall not be required to give notice to enforce strict adherence to the terms of this Agreement.

12. Severability. If a court finds any provision of this Agreement invalid or unenforceable as applied to any circumstance, the remainder of this Agreement and the application of such provision to other persons or circumstances shall be interpreted so as best to effect the intent of the parties hereto. The parties further agree to replace any such void or unenforceable provision of this Agreement with a valid and enforceable provision that will achieve, to the extent possible, the economic, business, and other purposes of the void or unenforceable provision.

13. Employment at Will. This Agreement is not an employment agreement. I understand that my employment and compensation can be terminated, with or without cause, and with or without notice, at any time. Nothing contained in this Agreement shall limit or otherwise alter the foregoing.

Employee has read this Agreement and understands its terms. Employee has completely filled out Exhibit A to this Agreement and has signed and received a copy of Exhibit B, the written notification to Employee setting forth California Labor Code § 2870.

Dated:____________________ ____________________________

[Employee's Typed Name]

Dated:____________________ ____________________________

[Typed Name of Company Official]

5

Performance Evaluations

70. Q: How can I get more consistency in my evaluation process? The evaluations of a new supervisor are consistently lower than those given by other supervisors. He happens to supervise a female-dominated group and many employees are complaining about discrimination.

A: You begin with the new supervisor. Disproportionately low performance ratings from one new supervisor normally do not warrant major changes to an otherwise effective, consistent and business-related evaluation process that has been functioning without incident.

Moreover, because evaluations are inherently subjective and thus unique to the particular manager, it is fairly unlikely that the evaluation process is to blame. Instead, you should take the following steps to assess whether the lower ratings are an isolated circumstance that should be addressed with the supervisor individually or evidence of a systemic problem:

- First, review the new supervisor's evaluations of female employees as compared to any similarly situated male employees within the admittedly female-dominated group to determine whether the women receive disproportionately lower ratings as compared to their male counterparts.

- Next, examine the content of the evaluations. Are the ratings supported by legitimate, business-related concerns with the female employees' performance that have been documented by narrative comments on the form and/or prior notices, memos, warnings or other direction given to the employee concerning those issues?

- Review how the female employees were rated previously by the prior supervisor. Were similar problems noted? Had the employees received less than positive evaluations in the recent past for the same or similar reasons? Is the new supervisor's treatment of similar issues and performance levels consistent with his predecessor's?

- Compare the substance of the new supervisor's evaluations with those completed by experienced supervisors managing subordinates performing the same or similar jobs, both male and female, to determine whether similar performance has been rated in similar (not identical) fashion, without regard to gender.

If this review indicates that women reporting to the new supervisor received disproportionately lower ratings than their similarly situated male counterparts and those ratings were not justified by legitimate, documented business considerations, the matter should be addressed directly with the new supervisor. In addition there are several options that might help to reduce future problems of this type with any manager:

- Ensure that all new supervisors and managers receive appropriate training on how to evaluate employees under your policies and procedures, including instruction on appropriate counseling, documentation and discipline.

- Ensure that all new supervisors and managers receive appropriate EEO training emphasizing your policy that all employment decisions, including evaluation, counseling and discipline are to be made based on legitimate, nondiscriminatory business-related reasons in compliance with applicable policies and procedures, and without regard to race, sex, national origin, age or any other protected category.

- Assign an experienced HR representative to work with the new supervisor during the first several rounds of evaluations, to ensure that he or she understands the process, and to identify any potential problems early on.

- Have an experienced second-level manager review all performance evaluations from supervisors managing employees performing the same or similar jobs, to ensure consistency in application of the evaluation process without regard to race, sex or other protected status.

- Assign an experienced HR representative to each department or organizational unit to review all major employment actions: annual performance evaluations; promotions; performance management issues; and discipline, including, of course, all proposed terminations. This not only helps to identify potential problems at an early stage, but also bolsters the legitimacy of the action because it was reviewed independently by a trained professional prior to its implementation. And it minimizes the individual manager's role as the sole decisionmaker.

- Implement a process whereby employees can respond in writing to their written performance evaluations. Once again, this not only helps to identify potential problems, but also establishes a record of legitimate, nondiscriminatory decisionmaking within the company.

- Hold supervisors and managers accountable for the performance management process, including the completion of evaluations. Specifically, rate their effectiveness at evaluating subordinates in their own performance reviews. Evaluating managers on the quality and the consistency with which they complete performance appraisals not only motivates them to take the process seriously, it sends the message that evaluations are valued by the company.

71. Q: How should I manage the transition to new, higher standards for performance? Our new president is insisting on more productivity and higher quality, and wants employee evaluations to reflect those goals.

A: There are three key components to effective performance evaluation:

- clearly communicating the employer's expectations to employees;

- documenting performance issues when they arise for all employees, not just a few; and

- consistently applying and enforcing performance standards, once established.

Leadership changes often result in altered expectations for employee performance. The new regime expects more work of higher quality for less money, in a shorter time. Changed expectations must be communicated in a clearly understandable fashion to affected employees before they can be held accountable for compliance with them.

Your company's HR professionals and legal department should work closely with the new president to develop a list of expectations, based on the CEO's goals for the company. The group should also develop a plan for communication and implementation of those goals. The goals must be linked to key measures of success for the employer, such as customer satisfaction or increased sales.

If changes to performance standards as applied in the performance evaluation process are required, the process and evaluation forms need to be changed prospectively and communicated to employees prior to their adoption. Supervisors need to be trained on any changes to the evaluation standards and/or process before they can be expected to apply the new rules. In addition, the accountabilities for each job need to be reviewed and revised, if needed, to accurately reflect management's newly established goals.

In short, you need to inform your employees of how they are expected to perform and determine when they are not. The application of new, more stringent performance standards to employees' performance without first informing the workforce of what is now expected of them will lead not only to legal liability, but to morale problems and unrest that may reduce, not increase, productivity, quality and/or efficiency – exactly the opposite of your company new president's intended goal.

72. Q: What kind of documentation should be included in the evaluation process?

A: At a minimum, a basic performance evaluation process includes the following types of documentation:

- A performance management policy and procedure, describing how the quality of employees performance is to be evaluated, how often, by whom and on what basis. Reviews should be formalized at least once a year, if not more frequently, with less formal "interim" reviews conducted periodically.

- A performance evaluation form and rating system. (See the sample Performance Evaluation Form, Fig. 72-A.)

- Current, accurate job descriptions for all positions to be evaluated, identifying the core duties, responsibilities and tasks associated with each job. (See the sample job descriptions, Fig. 12-A.)

- Goals and accountabilities for each position to be evaluated and specific factors on which each employee is to be evaluated. These should be based on the expectations outlined in the job description and any specifically established goals for the time period in question (for example, sales targets or budgetary limitations).

- A policy and procedure for handling counseling and discipline of behavioral issues not tied to performance of a particular position (for example: absenteeism, insubordination, harassment, workplace misconduct such as theft, etc.) It should define the standards of conduct with which employees are expected to comply, and a summary of the types of misconduct that will result in discipline, up to and including termination from employment.

- A policy and procedure allowing for the implementation and monitoring of performance improvement plans (PIPs) to address chronic performance issues. The PIP should list specific performance goals that the employee needs to meet to retain his or her job. (See the sample Performance Improvement Plan, Fig. 72-B.)

- Contemporaneous written documentation of performance deficiencies and incidents occurring within each review period, in the form of e-mails, memoranda, warnings, counseling, and/or notes from the supervisor that can be used to support the ratings given.

- Support for above average ratings granted superior performers, to defend against challenges, including discrimination claims, from co-workers who receive less favorable evaluations and lower pay increases or other tangible benefits as a result.

Fig. 72-A

Performance Evaluation – EMPLOYEE

EMPLOYEE NAME:	MANAGER NAME:
JOB TITLE:	DEPARTMENT:
REVIEW PERIOD – FROM:	TO:
REVIEW DATE:	

This performance evaluation is to document how effectively you have performed over the stated period of time. You and your manager should discuss, evaluate and summarize your performance based upon your responsibilities, results and other performance factors. You should also clarify expectations, set specific objectives, and identify future actions to help you maintain or increase your effectiveness.

ESSENTIAL FUNCTIONS: (Summarize essential functions.)

RESULTS: (Describe specific accomplishments during the evaluation period.)

1

HFGNR008

continued on next page

Fig. 72-A (cont.)

PERFORMANCE FACTORS FOR EMPLOYEES: (Describe specific factors impacting employee results.)

TECHNICAL SKILL AND COMPETENCY: Demonstrates the skills needed to perform the job. Understands the work environment, the job requirements and the customer needs. Completes tasks with minimum direction.

CUSTOMER SATISFACTION: Responds actively and sensitively to the needs of internal and external customers.

QUALITY: Demonstrates a commitment to quality and the quality process.

PRODUCTIVITY: Plans and organizes work activities to improve results. Uses resources efficiently and effectively.

TEAMWORK: Establishes and maintains cooperative and productive working relationships.

DEPENDABILITY: Meets schedules and other time commitments.

2

continued on next page

Fig. 72-A (cont.)

PERFORMANCE SUMMARY: (Summarize the employee's overall performance, considering responsibilities, results and performance factors, and processes used. Indicate a rating based on the employee's sustained performance compared to that of other employees doing similar work.)

_______ Performance Consistently Far Exceeds Expectations

_______ Performance Consistently Exceeds Expectations

_______ Performance Consistently Meets and Sometimes Exceeds Expectations

_______ Performance Usually Meets Expectations

_______ Performance is Below Expectations

GOALS AND OBJECTIVES FOR THE NEXT REVIEW PERIOD: (Establish goals and objectives for the coming year that will provide the basis for the next performance evaluation.)

3

continued on next page

Fig. 72-A (cont.)

EMPLOYEE COMMENTS: (Optional)

SIGNATURES:

I prepared this performance review and believe that it fairly evaluates this employee's work performance for this period.

Manager's Signature: ______________________ Date: ______________

My signature indicates that my manager and I discussed this performance review.

Employee's Signature: ______________________ Date: ______________

I acknowledge the performance review and employee comments (if any) as documented.

Next Level Manager's Signature: ______________________ Date: ______________

4

Fig. 72-B

HR CONFIDENTIAL

TO: [Employee's name]
FROM: [Manager's name]
DATE: ___________
RE: **Performance Improvement Plan**
CC: HR Rep., Supervisor/Manager's Manager, [Employee's name] Personnel File

The purpose of this memo is to summarize your current job performance problems and to provide you a performance improvement plan.

I. Performance Problems

Your performance in the following areas is unsatisfactory and therefore you must make immediate and sustained improvements in each of these areas:

[Manager should briefly explain each performance item and give recent examples illustrating the performance problem.]

Initiative
Communication
Judgment
Productivity
Quality of work
Relationships with co-workers/management/customers
Attendance/Tardiness

II. Performance Objectives

To assist you in improving your performance in these areas, I am providing the following performance objectives that shall be effective immediately. You need to fully achieve each of these objectives to my satisfaction:

[List SMART (Specific, Measurable, Achievable, Relevant, Time Bound) goals here. Include milestone dates, where applicable. As some employees are able to rally for short periods of time, it is recommended that you include several objectives over a sufficient period of time to ascertain if the employee's improvement can be sustained. Depending on the department, the employee's specific job functions and other factors, this time frame may vary significantly.]

[It is suggested that manager(s) add the following three items, but it is in the manager's discretion whether to do so:

1 HFGNR009

continued on next page

FIG. 72-B (CONT.)

1. Until further notice, we will have weekly one-on-one meetings every [WEEKDAY] at [TIME]. The purpose of these meetings will be to review your performance and provide you with performance feedback. Come prepared to discuss and review the week's objectives and your performance toward meeting these objectives. You are expected to bring your [STATUS REPORTS OR OTHER DOCUMENTATION] with you to these meetings.

2. It will be your responsibility to communicate the status of your projects to me as needed between these one-on-one sessions.

3. You must complete all other job responsibilities as assigned in a timely and satisfactory manner.

If you do not fully meet your performance objectives and demonstrate sustained improved performance to my satisfaction, your employment with the Company will be terminated. Nothing in this memo creates any guarantee of employment with the Company for a specific period of time or in any way modifies your at-will employment relationship with the Company. Both you and the Company continue to have the right to terminate your employment at any time, for any reason, with or without cause.

____
Manager's Signature

I have received and read this Performance Improvement Plan.

______________________________ ______________________________
Signature of Employee Date

2

73. Q: Are there any laws governing what is appropriate discipline?

A: Although public-sector employers and those with collective bargaining agreements may be required to satisfy a "just cause" standard to support the imposition of discipline, there are no federal or state laws specifying what constitutes appropriate discipline for private-sector employers.

Of course, both federal and state law require that adverse employment actions, including virtually all forms of discipline, be applied in a nondiscriminatory fashion, without regard to race, sex, age, national origin, disability or other protected status.

Some states enforce laws prohibiting termination from employment for particular reasons, such as jury service, filing a worker's compensation or wage claims. In addition, some states have created the following exceptions to the employment-at-will doctrine, limiting the employer's right to terminate employees based on:

- Public policy exceptions, prohibiting termination for whistleblowing, for example.
- Implied contract exceptions (for failure to follow promises documented in an employee policy or handbook or for implied promises made verbally during an interview that require just cause to terminate).
- Implied covenants of good faith and fair dealing (such as terminating long-term employees just before they're due to receive some anticipated financial benefit).

Simply stated, employers may impose discipline for any legitimate, nondiscriminatory business reason. That reason may be entirely subjective in nature. However, once established, the employer must comply with its own policies and/or procedures concerning discipline and performance management, or face liability. Basically, "appropriate" discipline follows two principles of "industrial due process":

- employees deserve the opportunity to understand what their employer expects of them with respect to job performance and workplace conduct, and how he or she has failed to meet these expectations (i.e., what he or she has done wrong); and
- employees deserve an opportunity to explain and to change their behavior or performance through corrective action.

To accomplish these goals, discipline generally should be progressive; a failure to improve triggers increasingly severe consequences (from verbal counseling to final warning), culminating in termination from employment. Of course, there are certain types of misconduct that are so severe that they warrant immediate termination (e.g., theft, insubordination).

If employees covered under a collective bargaining agreement believe that meeting with a supervisor or being questioned during an investigation may result in disciplinary action against them, they have the right to union representation (the "Weingarten Rule"). Of course, any employer that is a signatory to a collective bargaining agreement must comply with its provisions governing discipline and discharge.

74. Q: How can I be consistent when disciplining employees? Every instance of misconduct seems to be unique.

A: Discipline needs to be consistent with respect to *types* of misconduct (e.g., theft, sexual harassment, insubordination or fighting). But as you have noticed, specific incidents rarely, if ever, reoccur.

For example, there are many ways that an employee might engage in personal business on company time, using company resources. Using the computer to perform personal Internet searches, sending personal correspondence through the company mail room at company expense and using a company car to run personal errands are some of the ways employees do this. All of these disparate factual incidents are the same *type* of misconduct and warrant similar discipline based on the offender's prior disciplinary record and job performance.

Similarly situated employees (similar position, responsibilities, salary, seniority, quality of performance) who engage in similar types of misconduct or have similar performance problems should receive similar treatment. "Similar" does not mean "identical."

75. Q: How detailed should the discipline section of my employee handbook be? There is no way I can list everything that might result in discipline.

A: The employee handbook should present the philosophy of the organization, strategic plan, employee information and the working environment. The purpose of the handbook is to clearly communicate information that is relevant and important to employees.

Not all HR policies need to be included, just those that employees need to know to understand working conditions, performance expectations, standards of conduct, compensation, benefits and their rights and responsibilities.

The handbook should not be a set of rules. Instead, it should provide guidelines to employees that are subject to change by the company at any time, with or without notice, as the needs of the business require. A disclaimer to this effect should be included at the beginning of any employee handbook.

With respect to grounds for discipline, your Discipline and Discharge Policy should state that any listing of offenses is intended to provide only examples, not an exhaustive list of the grounds for discipline and discharge. The policy should emphasize that termination may occur for other reasons.

See Fig. 75-A for a sample listing of Employee Handbook topics.

Fig. **75**-A
Employee Handbook Contents

Standard Employment Practices
- At-Will Employment
- Equal Opportunity Employment
- Sexual and Other Unlawful Harassment
- Immigration Law Compliance
- Criminal Convictions
- Evaluation Period
- Standards of Conduct
- Personnel File

General Policies & Procedures
- Orientation
- Reporting Changes
- Job Classifications (Exempt, Nonexempt)
- Pay Periods
- Hours of Work
- Breaks
- Time Keeping
- Overtime
- Salary Increases
- Payroll
- Performance Reviews
- Bonus Structure
- Expense Reimbursement
- Attendance & Punctuality
- Availability for Work
- Mandatory Meetings
- Telecommuting
- Job Sharing
- Holidays
- Vacations
- Drugs & Alcohol
- Violence & Weapons
- Smoking
- Food & Beverage
- Recycling
- Visitors
- Workplace Attire
- Telephone Use
- Voice Mail & Electronic Mail
- Use of Company Vehicles
- Use of Company Property
- Postage, Shipping & Office Supplies
- Personal Property
- Personal Safety
- Office Security
- Monitoring & Searches
- Inventions & Creative Works
- Confidential Information
- Conflicts of Interest
- Non-Solicitation
- Competing Employment
- Employment of Relatives

Leave Policies
- General Policies
- Sick Leave
- Short-Term Disability Leave
- Family & Medical Leave
- Personal Leave of Absence
- Jury Duty
- Military Duty
- Funeral Leave
- Emergency Closings & Severe Weather

Employment Benefits
- Benefits Eligibility
- Medical Insurance
- 401K
- Stock Options
- Employee Discounts
- Tuition Reimbursement
- Worker's Compensation
- COBRA

Disciplinary Policies
- Problem Resolutions
- Discipline
- Corrective Action

Separation Policies
- Job Abandonment
- Termination
- Termination Process
- Employment References

76. Q: How should I handle this situation: I have a minority employee who is very upset at a less than satisfactory performance evaluation. She is particularly angry because she heard a supervisor – not hers – use some racial slurs. But this supervisor had no role in preparing her evaluation and he was disciplined for his remarks. The employee says she's going to sue.

A: Should the employee challenge her less-than-satisfactory performance rating as discriminatory, your liability will depend on whether she received a comparable rating to that accorded similarly situated non-minority employees in the same position and reporting to the same supervisor, and whether better performing minority co-workers received higher ratings.

Isolated racial comments by an uninvolved supervisor, standing alone, normally will not constitute evidence of discrimination. Accordingly, if the employee did receive an evaluation comparable to those her non-minority counterparts received, your company's exercise of subjective business judgment in rating the relative performance of its workers should be respected and you will not be held liable for bias.

With respect to any hostile environment claim the employee might advance based on the racial slurs to which she was subjected, such isolated incidents generally will not be considered sufficiently severe or pervasive to have altered the terms and conditions of her employment. Moreover, you took appropriate remedial action to discipline the offending supervisor, so the claim should be dismissed.

Be advised, however, that the Equal Employment Opportunity Commission takes the position that even a single use of the "N" word can create an actionable environment of racial harassment. Your employee handbook should include a policy on harassment and your employees, especially supervisors, should be trained on what conduct is prohibited.

77. Q: How can I weed out employees who we know are poor performers, without getting sued? I have to make some cuts, and my problem is that our evaluation system doesn't help me identify poor performers – nearly everyone gets a "Satisfactory" or "Meets Expectations."

A: This is a tough question. Your performance evaluations obviously have not been doing the job they were intended to do, which is reward those employees who do a good job and notify those who do not about their shortcomings. They provide needed documentation.

Performance evaluations that are done right can provide a defense against lawsuits by disgruntled workers who claim they were discharged for discriminatory reasons. Actually, if evaluations are done correctly, there should be no surprises. Employees should be told about both good and bad performance throughout the year, not just during annual reviews. An employee who is not performing as well as expected should be aware of that fact long before a yearly evaluation is done.

Employees should be given clear, achievable goals and objectives. And it should be easy to tell when those goals and objectives had been met. Most important, evaluations based on those annual goals and objectives should be honest and backed up by specific examples.

But that doesn't help you now. The best you can do is make sure your reduction-in-force process is free of all types of discrimination and based only on business necessity. If possible, an outside source should be brought in to make the selection of those workers to be cut. With no information about gender, age, race, national origin, religion or disability, an outsider can make a more neutral choice based on the job and how well it is being done.

After this crisis has passed, review your performance evaluation system and make it more meaningful. Don't forget to train your supervisors so they know what is expected and understand that the purpose of an evaluation is to document performance, both good and bad. (See the sample Performance Evaluation Form, Fig. 72-A.)

Safety and Security

OSHA

78. Q: Do I have to bother with OSHA requirements? I've been in business for 36 years and have never seen or heard from OSHA.

A: Yes, you do. Private-sector employers with one or more employees are covered by the Occupational Safety and Health Act, which is enforced by the Occupational Safety and Health Administration (OSHA) of the U.S. Department of Labor.

If a state has an OSHA-approved state plan that protects private-sector employees' safety and health to at least as great an extent as the federal law, OSHA will defer to that state plan. State and local government employers are not covered by the federal law, but they are covered to the extent that applicable state laws cover government employers.

Because of the huge number of businesses covered by OSHA, it is possible that the agency will never come to inspect your workplace. But you should not count on that. And if an employee complains about a possible safety or health violation, OSHA or a state agency will investigate the complaint. You can be subject to civil fines if you violate an OSHA standard.

The Occupational Safety and Health Act has what is referred to as a "General Duty Clause," which is applicable to all private-sector employers. It provides: "Each employer shall furnish to each of his employees employment and a place of employment which are free from recognized hazards that are causing or are likely to cause death or serious physical harm to his employees" (29 U.S.C. § 654(a)(1)).

In addition, OSHA has issued a large number of safety and health standards. Standards are grouped into four major categories:

- general industry (29 CFR 1910);
- construction (29 CFR 1926);
- maritime (shipyards, marine terminals, long shoring) (29 CFR 1915-19); and
- agriculture (29 CFR 1928).

While some standards are specific to just one category, others apply across industries. Among the standards with similar requirements for all sectors of industry are those that address access to medical and exposure records, personal protective equipment and hazard communication.

Source: 29 U.S.C. Sec. 654(a)(1).
You should also consult OSHA's Web site to learn what standards are applicable to your company. See www.osha.gov.

79. Q: If an employee gets injured on the job, do I have to keep any records about the injury?

A: Yes, you do. If your company had more than 10 employees at any time during the last calendar year, OSHA requires that you keep injury and illness records, unless your establishment is classified in a specific low-hazard retail, service, finance, insurance or real estate industry. However, all employers must report to OSHA any workplace incident that results in a fatality or the hospitalization of three or more employees

Generally, employers are required to record each fatality, injury and illness that is work-related and meets one or more of the recording criteria specified by OSHA. This means that you must record an injury if it results in any of the following:

- death;
- days away from work;
- restricted work or transfer to another job;
- medical treatment beyond first aid; or
- loss of consciousness.

You must also consider a case to meet the general recording criteria if it involves a significant injury or illness diagnosed by a physician or other licensed health care professional, even if it does not result in death, days away from work, restricted work or job transfer, medical treatment beyond first aid, or loss of consciousness.

In addition, there are specific recording requirements related to the following:

- needle stick and sharps injuries;
- situations in which an employee is required to be medically removed under the medical surveillance requirements of an OSHA standard;
- situations in which the employee experiences work-related hearing loss; or
- when an employee has been exposed to tuberculosis on the job.

You should record the pertinent information on the OSHA Form 300, the Log of Work-related Injuries and Illnesses, within seven calendar days after you receive information that a recordable workplace injury or illness has occurred. You must keep the form on file for five years.

You should note that some employers may be subject to additional recordkeeping and reporting requirements. Many specific OSHA standards and regulations have additional requirements for the maintenance and retention of records for medical surveillance, exposure monitoring, inspections and other activities and incidents relevant to occupational safety and health, and for the reporting of certain information to employees and to OSHA.

Source: 29 C.F.R. Part 1904.

Evacuation Plans

80. Q: Do we have to have an evacuation plan? It seems very unlikely that a terrorist attack or other catastrophe would ever happen in our area.

A: Yes. All employees should know the best way out of your building in case of an emergency. It is the law.

The Occupational Safety and Health Administration (OSHA) of the U.S. Department of Labor requires that every employer meet certain minimum requirements for exit routes that must be provided in the workplace so employees can evacuate safely during an emergency. OSHA also sets minimum requirements for emergency action plans and fire prevention plans. You can meet legal requirements also by complying with National Fire Protection Association's Standard 101, Life Safety Code 2000 Edition (NFPA101-2000).

Provisions for People With Disabilities

When creating an evacuation plan, employers need to provide for employees and visitors to the workplace who have mobility or other impairments that would make it difficult for them to evacuate. This can be done in a number of ways, including having other workers volunteer to make sure the individual with a disability is notified of the need to evacuate and is safely removed from the building. Devices such as evacuation chairs are available to assist the evacuation of employees with mobility impairments.

Sources: 29 C.F.R. §§1910.34 through 1910.39; NFPA 101-2000, Life Safety Code, available on NFPA's Web site, www.nfpa.org.

Pandemic

81. Q: What, if anything, should we be doing to prepare for an avian flu outbreak or natural disaster?

A: Let's start with the understanding that a lot more than HR is involved in responding to a disaster. In fact, every facet of your company's management will have to be involved. But for now, let's leave matters such as supply chain, serving customers, preserving credit and repairs to those who are responsible, and focus on the role of HR.

Although your question is broader than avian flu, if a pandemic breaks out, there are some health-based responses that are all but unique to that situation. You may be asked to devise health and hygiene practices for the workplace. You may have to learn how to detect signs of illness and be responsible to getting people off site. You may have to arrange for vaccinations and treatment at work. There might be a quarantine or travel restrictions.

The federal government has been working on this issue with unusual intensity. The fruit of some of its learning is at http://www.pandemicflu.gov. That site also includes a number of employment-related suggestions.

As we have all learned, it is difficult to prepare even for a foreseeable disaster. One place to start is your policies. Regardless of the nature of the disaster (fire, hurricane, tornado, earthquake or flood), you will need policies, even contingent or emergency policies that provide you with maximum flexibility: flexible work hours, incentives for overtime and expanded leave opportunities.

You can also prepare contingency plans to address the possible displacement of your workforce by means of increasing cross training and distributing vital processes across regionally dispersed offices (if possible). Although it may sound extreme, you should consider locating an alternate workforce in another region or country, including, particularly, the HR staff.

You can also review all of your benefit programs, because it is certain that there will be an extraordinary reliance on support programs in the wake of a disaster. Many benefit/support programs are jointly funded by the employer and the employee. What plans do you have if the business is closed for a significant period of time? Both parties will be short of cash. You should discuss these issues with your insurers and providers now.

Any planning you do must include your Internet technology managers. First, constant communication with the employees is a necessity. Effective and continuous communication within the company and among the employees is among the most important benefits that can be provided during and after a disaster.

Second, expanding your capability to work from remote locales may be what keeps the business functioning. Expanding teleconferencing and video conferencing capabilities now would be an important step. You should even consider establishing virtual offices designed to work cooperatively to maintain critical services.

On a slightly different plane, you should work with IT to effectively identify, collect, maintain and protect all essential corporate knowledge. No matter how your information is stored – either paper or electronically – make sure it is off-site in a different area. It serves no purpose to have both locales affected by the same disaster.

There is an old saying: “the shoemaker’s children go barefoot.” Don’t let that happen to you and the HR staff. If disaster strikes, you will be called on in more ways than you can imagine and asked for more assistance than you can contemplate – or provide. It is a heavy burden, but you can begin training your staff now to take on these responsibilities. Those new duties will include family support, counseling and even planning memorials.

The checklist, Fig. 81-A, provides a valuable guide to the many steps you can and should take to prepare for a pandemic or other disaster.

Fig. 81-A
Checklist of Pandemic Preparedness Actions for HR Departments

The following checklist of HR-related actions will help you prepare your organization and your workforce to cope with an influenza or other pandemic. In addition, you should work with your systems operations department and technology service providers to make sure the appropriate technology is in place to support your HR-related pandemic initiatives.

I. Infection Control Ethic

__ Collect and disseminate to staff members reliable pandemic information from the Centers for Disease Control and Prevention, local public health departments, emergency management officials and other sources. Include information about family preparedness and at-home health care services.

__ Encourage employees to get annual flu vaccinations, or arrange for vaccinations to be given at work.

__ Track employees who receive vaccinations.

__ If an avian flu vaccine or antidote becomes available, arrange for employees to receive it.

__ Establish policies and procedures for preventing the spread of influenza at the workplace:

- Devise guidelines for modifying the frequency and type of face-to-face contact during a pandemic (for example, refraining from handshaking, adjusting office layout, minimizing meetings and avoiding shared workstations).
- Set up hand-sanitation stations in the lunchroom area and restrooms.
- Stock areas where customers are served with hand-sanitation fluid dispensers or "wipes" and receptacles for their disposal.
- Remind employees not to touch their mouths or eyes with their hands.
- Urge employees to seek medical attention for flu-like symptoms and not to come to work when feeling ill.
- Educate employees about healthy habits, such as the benefits of adequate rest and good nutrition. These messages may be conveyed via posters, items in the employee newsletter or intranet messages.

__ Work with the maintenance/janitorial department to implement special sanitation measures for computer keyboards, telephone receivers, doorknobs, stair rails, restrooms and eating areas.

II. Contingency Systems and HR Policies

__ Identify essential employees required to maintain basic services by location and function.

__ Identify employees with special needs (those with disabilities or compromised immune systems, for example) and incorporate their requirements in the pandemic response plan.

__ Appoint a pandemic coordinator and/or team and define their roles and responsibilities for preparedness planning. The team should include at least one representative from rank-and-file employees.

__ Work with temporary employment agencies to identify workers who could fill in for staffing shortfalls if needed.

__ Consider alerting your organization's own retired employees that their services may be needed in an emergency. Create a list of "the willing" and their contact information.

__ Train ancillary workers regarding current procedures for accessing information on the organization's computer systems. This will require secure, emergency log-on capabilities.

continued on next page

Fig. 81-A (cont.)

__ Establish an emergency communications plan consisting of platforms (hotlines, dedicated Web sites), key contacts and backup contacts, and a chain of communications to convey information about employees' whereabouts and health status.

__ Devise special policies for employee compensation and sick leave during a pandemic (for example, non-punitive, liberal leave policies).

__ Devise a policy requiring immediate mandatory sick leave for employees who have been exposed to the virus, are suspected of being ill or become ill at the workplace.

__ Devise guidelines for when employees may return to work after illness or exposure (based on Centers for Disease Control and Prevention guidelines).

__ Establish policies for restricting travel to affected geographic areas (based on Centers for Disease Control and Prevention travel recommendations).

__ Evaluate the local availability of health care services during a pandemic, and improve access when possible.

__ Anticipate fear and anxiety among employees. Evaluate employee access to, and availability of, mental health and social services during a pandemic (considering corporate, community and faith-based resources).

__ Identify medical consultation professionals who can assist in the organization's response to a pandemic.

__ Identify sources for obtaining flu countermeasures (for example, vaccines and antiviral medications).

III. Remote Work

__ Forecast (as best you can) employee absenteeism during a pandemic because of personal illness, family-member illness, community containment measures, school and/or business closures and public transportation closures.

__ Establish policies for flexible work hours specifically for a pandemic situation.

__ Consider acquiring laptop computers for key (or all) employees who do not have them, and set up remote links that may be activated in an emergency. (Laptops may be purchased through shared buying programs.)

__ Enhance your telecommuting program to accommodate emergencies when employees cannot get to work.

__ Make sure you have adequate technology to permit telephone conferencing, wireless communications, and other means for managers and other key employees to stay in communication.

IV. Partnerships

__ Collaborate with your organization's health plan and major health care facilities in the local and regional areas to share and coordinate pandemic plans.

__ Participate in community response planning by coordinating with federal, state and local public health agencies and emergency responders.

__ Share best practices with other businesses, chambers of commerce and trade associations.

__ Work with nearby businesses to develop cooperative arrangements, such as employee sharing, in the event a pandemic forces closure of one or more critical service providers in the community.

Union Organizing

82. Q: What can I do to discourage union organizing activity?

A: Most private-sector employers are covered by the National Labor Relations Act, which protects the right of employees to form a union. You are entitled to express your opinions about the union organizing effort, as long as you do not engage in any of the following actions:

- threaten employees with loss of jobs, pay or benefits if they join or vote for a union;
- threaten to close the plant if employees select a union to represent them;
- question employees about their union sympathies or activities in circumstances that tent to interfere with their right to form or join a union;
- promise benefits, including pay raises, to employees to discourage their union support; or
- transfer, terminate or assign more difficult work to an employee because of his or her union support.

Source: 29 U.S.C. § 158.

Telecommuting

83. Q: Can I limit working outside of the office just to the employees who must travel? I have some employees who want to telecommute.

A: Yes. You can have different standards for different jobs as long as you do not discriminate on the basis of gender, race, disability or some other protected quality. But telecommuting may be a reasonable accommodation for an employee with a disability, so you may have to make an exception beyond your traveling employees.

Although telecommuting does not necessarily mean working from home, it does mean working out of the office. Whether telecommuting will work for you depends on the type of jobs your employees do. Working on a manufacturing line at a plant, for example, would most likely not be a job that could be done remotely. Bookkeeping or accounting, on the other hand, probably could be done somewhere other than at the company offices. If you "out-source" any administrative jobs, you already understand what work does not need to be done at the workplace.

The most difficult part of telecommuting for most employers is figuring out how to evaluate productivity. For a worker who processes invoices of insurance claims, the measure can be the number of "units" done in a day. For professional office employees, however, work usually cannot be measured in "units." Those telecommuters must be measured on results and the attainment of established goals. There is also a problem in assessing any employee who is non-exempt. Is being "logged on" the same as being "on the job"?

In the end, there has to be a certain amount of trust between the supervisor and the telecommuter. It will become clear whether the job is getting done.

If you decide to venture into telework, you should develop a clear policy that specifies:

- the number of days per week employees will be permitted to work remotely;
- whether the work will be done at home, at a telework center or elsewhere;
- a work schedule;
- the manner and frequency of communication between the telecommuter and supervisor or co-workers;
- the type of equipment, such as a computer with Internet access, the employee needs;
- an available means of phone communication;
- how long an employee needs to be with the company before telecommuting is permitted; and
- anything else you are concerned about, such as workers' compensation issues.

It is advisable to have a trial period. Some people just do not do well telecommuting. Sometimes there are unforeseen difficulties, such as when several people need to work together on a project. A key question is whether an employee's physical presence on the job is an essential part of predictable job performance.

In addition, telecommuters report that the lack of physical presence in the workplace can result in lost promotional opportunities and limit professional growth and skill development.

When it works, many employees find they get more work done telecommuting than at the office because there are fewer interruptions, less stress and no commute. You may find productivity increases.

84. Q: If I let a worker telecommute as part of an accommodation for a disability, do I have to let everyone telecommute?

A: No. Although a policy may need to be modified as a reasonable accommodation for an employee with a disability, it may continue in effect in its original form for all other workers, according to the Equal Employment Opportunity Commission (EEOC), the federal agency that enforces the employment provisions of the Americans With Disabilities Act.

The EEOC considers telework a reasonable accommodation that employers should consider for some employees with disabilities. Several federal courts have agreed, although some caution that telecommuting is a reasonable accommodation only in those instances when jobs can be performed at home without any substantial reduction in performance. For example, if teamwork is an essential job function, telecommuting may not be a reasonable accommodation.

Sources: EEOC Enforcement Guidance: Reasonable Accommodation and Undue Hardship Under the ADA; EEOC Fact Sheet: Work at Home/Telework as a Reasonable Accommodation; *Humphrey v. Memorial Hospitals Assoc.,* 239 F.3d 1128 (9th Cir. 2001); *Waggoner v. Olin Corp.*, 169 F.3d 481 (7th Cir. 1999) (telecommuting was not feasible for worker in case before the court); *Smith v. Ameritech*, 129 F.3d 857 (6th Cir. 1997); *Vande Zande v. Wisconsin Dept. of Administration*, 44 F.3d 538 (7th Cir. 1995).

Employee Conduct

4

Introduction

Many if not most of the problems human resources professionals have involve the conduct of their employees. Sometimes it involves poor performance or attendance, which is relatively easy to handle if the worker's supervisor or manager has done proper documentation.

The really hard questions involve conduct that affects work but is not directly related to it. How to handle the harassment of a disabled co-worker, for example. And the sexual harassment of an employee by a vice president can keep an HR specialist up at night. Just how far can an employer go in getting rid of a worker who causes morale problems, or worse, puts the company in legal jeopardy?

Then there are the issues of off-duty conduct, especially involving alcohol or an arrest. And just what are your employees' free speech rights? Do you really have to keep a whistleblower on the payroll after an investigation shows there was no violation of whatever law he or she complained about? Sometimes an employer does everything right, but dislike for an employee or the employee's behavior leads to retaliation, which results in a hefty penalty, even though the worker's underlying claim is shown to have no merit.

All of this can be complicated, because when dealing with employee conduct you most often are dealing with personalities, and that is never easy. This chapter provides some guidance on the questions you have about when to step in and when to leave well enough alone so that your company stays out of court while you keep your workforce humming along efficiently.

Questions in This Chapter

Discrimination/Harassment Disability

Gender

National Origin

Age

Discrimination/Harassment

Disability

85. Q: At what point should I intervene in a potential harassment situation? One of our disabled employees complained that his co-workers are giving him a hard time, mainly dumb nicknames and embarrassing jokes. The supervisor knows about this but hasn't done anything because honestly, it doesn't amount to much. Should I step in and threaten discipline?

A: Yes, you should step in immediately and take whatever action is necessary to stop the harassment.

The Americans With Disabilities Act (ADA) prohibits harassment because of a disability in the same way that the Civil Rights Act of 1964 prohibits harassment because of race and gender. The Equal Employment Opportunity Commission (EEOC), which enforces the employment provisions of the ADA, has stated that one in five ADA claims brought by individuals with developmental disabilities allege harassment.

Your best defense to a harassment charge is to promptly correct any situation as soon as you become aware of it. A good anti-harassment policy that is enforced can be a valid defense to a claim. The best policies include:

- a clear explanation of the prohibited conduct;
- assurance that the employees who complain or provide information will be protected from retaliation;
- a clearly described complaint process that provides more than one person who can receive complaints;
- procedures for a prompt, thorough and impartial investigation of a complaint; and
- assurance of prompt, appropriate corrective action if harassment is found.

You should see to it that the policy is distributed to new employees when they are hired and all employees at least annually. Employees should sign an acknowledgment of receipt of the policy and managers and supervisors should be provided training.

Sources: EEOC's Questions & Answers About Persons With Intellectual Disabilities in the Workforce and the ADA; *Pendleton v. Jefferson Local School Dist. Bd. of Education*, 958 F.2d 372 (6th Cir. 1992).

86. Q: Can I fire an employee because of his appearance? One of my employees was in a fire. He came back to work and the poor guy looks just horrible. Both his co-workers and our customers have trouble dealing with or even looking at him. It has become a real problem for this small business. Can I just let him go?

A: No. One of the purposes of the Americans With Disabilities Act (ADA) was to prevent discrimination against individuals who are regarded as disabled because of their appearance.

You may not discriminate against an employee or job applicant because of a condition that others have an adverse reaction to, such as a burn, limp or lisp, even if that condition would not otherwise be a disability.

By the way, you mentioned you were a "small business." If you have fewer than 15 employees, you are not covered by the ADA. However, you may be covered by a state human rights act that has a lower threshold for coverage. You should find out.

Sources: 42 U.S.C. §12102(C); 29 C.F.R. §1630.2.

87. Q: What's the ADA's impact on promotion decisions? I am in the process of making an important promotion that will require a lot of third-world travel. I have been going through the personnel files of the candidates and I noticed from the insurance records that one of them has diabetes that looks pretty serious, judging from the number of claims. I don't want to put this employee at risk by sending him to places where he might not be able to get treatment. On the other hand, I wonder whether he would have an ADA claim if I passed him over. Any thoughts?

A: If you based a promotion decision on his disability, perceived or otherwise, with no more information than you now have, the employee would have an Americans With Disabilities Act (ADA) claim.

A federal appeals court recently dealt with a similar case in which the State Department refused to hire an applicant with HIV infection because some of the foreign countries he would be sent to lacked proper medical facilities. The court found that the agency's arguments against hiring the individual could be a pretext for disability discrimination. Reasonable accommodation could include permitting the employee to take accumulated leave to travel to get periodic health checkups, the court said.

Before refusing to promote your diabetic employee, you must determine whether there really is a direct threat to his health that some reasonable accommodation cannot reduce to an acceptable level. You need to discuss the matter with the employee and determine what, if any, accommodation he might need. In this case, the employee is in the best position to decide if the new job is one he could safely handle.

By the way, the ADA and other federal laws such as the Health Insurance Portability and Accountability Act (HIPAA) are supposed to keep employee health records confidential and out of the employment decision process. You did not explain how you had access to the employee's health records and insurance claims. By reviewing them as part of an employment decision process, you may have violated the ADA already. You should make sure that health records and related insurance documents are filed separately from all employees' personnel files and kept that way.

> **Sources:** *Taylor v. Rice*, 452 F.3d 256 (D.C. Cir. 2006).

Gender

88. Q: Do I have to follow our standard investigation procedures in each and every case of potential harassment? I just got a sex harassment complaint about a senior vice president. We have procedures for conducting an investigation, but this guy intimidates everyone. What are my options?

A: If you want to minimize your company's potentially very expensive liability for sexual harassment, you have no choice but to investigate the complaint. Your company is wise to have procedures for conducting an investigation, but unless you apply the procedures consistently – even in difficult situations such as this one – the company may face serious liability.

The U.S. Supreme Court has held that an employer can defend against liability for sexual harassment committed by supervisors if it can show that it took steps to prevent harassment and promptly corrected any harassment that occurred.

This may be a situation in which you would want to engage someone from outside your company to conduct the investigation. That would help insulate your in-house staff from feeling intimidated by the senior vice president and help ensure that the investigation is thorough and fair.

> **Sources:** Title VII of the Civil Rights Act of 1964, as amended, 42 U.S.C. §2000e, *et seq.*; *Faragher v. City of Boca Raton*, 524 U.S. 775 (1998); *Burlington Industries, Inc. v. Ellerth*, 524 U.S. 742 (1998).

89. Q: Am I legally obligated to investigate every report of harassment? A young woman executive just talked to me about being sexually harassed, but asked me not to say anything and to let her handle it. She's afraid that if this became public it could ruin her career.

A: To protect your company against liability for sexual harassment, you need to follow procedures for investigating complaints. The fact that the young executive asked you not to say anything could be construed as a choice on her part not to take advantage of your company's complaint procedure, and that fact could be raised as a defense by the company if she later decided to bring a suit against the company.

But you should not take that chance. Because you are part of the company's management or personnel structure, a court could very well decide that by failing to follow your company's complaint procedures, you exposed it to liability for any damages the woman might suffer.

You would be wise to tell the young woman that you are required to ensure that the situation is investigated. You should also ensure her that the law – and company policy – protect her against retaliation for reporting the sexual harassment.

90. Q: I just completed a difficult harassment investigation. We did everything "by the book" and were at the point of disciplining the harasser when the victim quit and filed a discrimination charge. How can I prevent this from happening again?

A: It sounds as though you may have done all you can to protect the company from legal liability. If you followed your investigative procedures and took all reasonable action to prevent the harassment from occurring in the future, a court will probably rule in your company's favor.

The one thing that employers sometimes neglect to do is keep the alleged victim informed about the investigation. Because investigations typically take some time to complete, complainants who are left in the dark may feel they were not taken seriously and that nothing is being done, especially if they must continue to work with the supposed harasser. Frequent updates can show the complainant that you are being supportive.

91. Q: How do I tell the harassment claims that have real merit from the ones that don't? For example, a woman just complained about harassment at a company picnic at a local park, miles from our workplace. Everyone had a few beers; everyone was dressed casually. Do I have to take this seriously?

A: Yes, you do.

Even though the alleged harassment did not occur at the workplace, it occurred at a company-sponsored function, and that means the company can be held responsible. It is important that you take the complaint seriously and that you investigate the complaint under the company's established procedures.

The type of dress and the casual situation would not be an excuse for harassment of any kind. Proper behavior should be expected of your employees at all company functions, and that fact should be made clear in your personnel manual and your company policies.

National Origin

92. Q: Can I require all employees to speak English? A group of Spanish-speaking employees – who can all speak English – speak Spanish to each other while on the job. The supervisor and the other workers don't like it because they don't know what's being said.

A: Maybe. It depends on the circumstances.

The Equal Employment Opportunity Commission (EEOC), the federal agency that enforces the Civil Rights Act of 1964, has issued a guideline for employers regarding English-only policies. It provides that:

> a rule requiring employees to speak only English at all times in the workplace is a burdensome term and condition of employment. The primary language of an individual is often an essential national origin characteristic. Prohibiting employees at all times, in the workplace, from speaking their primary language or the language they speak most comfortably, disadvantages an individual's employment opportunities on the basis of national origin. It may also create an atmosphere of inferiority, isolation and intimidation based on national origin which could result in a discriminatory working environment. Therefore, the Commission will presume that such a rule violates Title VII and will closely scrutinize it.

But the guideline also states that an employer is allowed to have a rule requiring that employees speak only in English at certain times when the employer can show that the rule is justified by business necessity. So, you might be able to establish a policy that requires employees to speak English to their English-speaking supervisors, if this can be justified as a business necessity. It may also be possible to require employees to communicate in English to their fellow workers who only speak English, when it is necessary to communicate with each other to get the job done.

If you believe you have a business necessity for adopting a requirement that English be spoken at certain times and in certain situations, the EEOC also requires that you put this rule in writing and notify employees of the consequences of violations. Otherwise, you may be considered to have engaged in discrimination on the basis of national origin.

Source: 29 C.F.R. §1607.7.

Age

93. Q: Will I be in for trouble if I terminate most of my older, higher-paid employees? I have to reduce my payroll costs or face the possibility of going into the red. The only thing that makes sense for me is to let some of the most highly paid workers go, but they are all over 40.

A: You'll probably get sued if you do this. Under the Age Discrimination in Employment Act (ADEA), it is illegal to terminate an employee on the basis of his or her age.

Employees over 40 years old are protected from all forms of employment discrimination by this statute. The ADEA and the Equal Employment Opportunity Commission's regulations do permit differentiations among employees that are based on factors other than age, even if the differing treatment has a disproportionate effect on employees who are over 40. But the regulations are clear that a decision that is based on the average cost of employing older employees *as a group* is unlawful, except with respect to employee benefit plans that qualify for special treatment under the law.

This does not mean, however, that you cannot do anything to cut costs. You can make *individualized* decisions based on the wages or salaries of individual workers – not the average cost of older workers as a group. That could qualify as a decision based on a factor other than age. But if every single one of the employees chosen for termination is over age 40, you would have a difficult time supporting your decision in court.

Sources: 29 US.C. §621, *et seq.*; 29 C.F.R. §1625.7; *Hazen Paper Co. v. Biggins,* 507 U.S. 504 (1993).

94. Q: Can I take age into consideration when making a hiring decision? I just got an application for a low-level job from a guy with years and years of experience. He says he'll take the pay cut, but he'd be 20 years older than his colleagues.

A: No. Unless it is a bona fide requirement of the job, such as a child to play a part in a movie, age should never be a consideration in employment.

Assuming he is over 40 and, therefore, protected by the Age Discrimination in Employment Act, it would be a violation of federal law to take this applicant's age into consideration, or the fact that he would be 20 years older than his colleagues. The only criteria you should use in making hiring decisions are the requirements and essential functions of the job and the applicants' qualifications and skills to meet and perform them.

Sources: 29 US.C. §621, *et seq.*; 29 C.F.R. §1625.7.

95. Q: Is there a way to replace an older worker with a younger one without having to worry about a discrimination claim? My current IT manager has been adequate, but I am not sure he is the right guy for the future. The person I am looking at is considerably younger than my current guy, who is well over 40. Is there a problem if I bring the new guy on as the head of IT?

A: There could be. You need to be careful here because you could be violating the Age Discrimination in Employment Act.

If the older worker has been performing satisfactorily and has been able to keep up with changes in technology, you should not decide to replace him with a new, younger employee based only on your generalized feeling that, because of his age, the younger worker is more "in tune" with the new technology.

If you have documented that the incumbent's performance has not been up to par and can show that his skills are not what you need for the job, that is a different matter. An employee can be held to job standards regardless of age.

Military

96. Q: How much "free speech" do I have to tolerate? I have a son who is career military. I'm a veteran myself. One of my employees is vocally anti-military, even at work. I am over trying to ignore it. Can I tell him to shut up or get out?

A: Yes, if you are a private employer and your state has no law on the subject.

In general, if you are a public employer (a federal, state or local agency), your employee would have First Amendment rights that might be infringed if you took action against him. But if yours is a private company, there is no prohibition against asking your employee to keep his views about the military to himself, or even to terminate him if he refuses to do so. The First Amendment restricts the government, not private citizens, from infringing on freedom of speech, but this is a delicate subject.

Retaliation

97. Q: How much leeway do I have in this situation? We have a minority employee who received a less than great evaluation. Frankly, I thought it was deserved and not even that bad. Anyway, this employee has not stopped complaining about it. He even wrote to the president of the company, claiming there was discrimination, that his supervisor is biased, and that he can no longer have any faith in management. The problem is, he is an important guy – we expect him to help us secure new work, meet with clients and participate in planning meetings in which we discuss new products and pricing. I am very reluctant to include him in these meetings because I no longer have any confidence in his loyalty to this business. I've been told that if I change his job responsibilities he could claim I was retaliating against him. If that's so, how can I protect my business?

A: This is a difficult situation and you need to be careful. Some courts would hold that changing this employee's job responsibilities, even if you do not change his pay or position, would be illegal retaliation against him for lodging a discrimination complaint.

Retaliation is any adverse employment action that occurs because of protected activity. "Protected activity" is usually interpreted broadly and can include:

- filing a discrimination complaint;
- testifying on another complainant's behalf;
- protesting an allegedly discriminatory practice; or
- participating in an investigation under a federal or state law.

However, if you have a solid reason to believe that the employee is making derogatory comments about the company to clients or potential clients, you would be justified in limiting his opportunities to make such comments. Documentation could be a key element in your defense against a claim of retaliation. There should have been documentation for his performance evaluation and you should keep a record of any negative comments or behavior after he was given the evaluation.

When taking adverse action against an employee, including a change of job duties, you should always ask yourself the following questions:

- Has the employee engaged in protected activity?
- Did the activity occur recently?
- Is there sufficient documentation to prove a legitimate business reason for the action you want to take?

98. Q: Do mothers of newborns have special rights? We are about to put our regular shift change into place so that "undesirable" shifts are shared by all the line employees. One of my employees is accusing me of retaliation. About eight months ago she complained about pregnancy discrimination, but once we got the paperwork straightened out and got her supervisor square with the timing, she had her

maternity leave. But now she says she can't change shifts because of her childcare arrangements and forcing her to do so is discrimination. We've been changing shifts like this for years. Am I risking a retaliation lawsuit if I change her shift?

A: You cannot stop the employee from suing you, but you would probably win in this circumstance.

If the employee sued, it is likely that the court would hold that the shift change occurred too long after the employee's pregnancy discrimination complaint to raise an inference of retaliation for making the complaint. The fact that you have been changing shifts in this manner for years would support your company's argument that the shift change in this case had nothing to do with the fact that the employee had claimed pregnancy discrimination.

And if she claims that you have to accommodate her childcare arrangement, you should know that neither the Pregnancy Discrimination Act nor the Family and Medical Leave Act requires you to take childcare arrangements into account when making business decisions.

99. Q: Does a two-year-old complaint give an employee lifetime job insurance? One of our employees lodged a sex harassment complaint about two years ago. We investigated and concluded that she had been harassed and we disciplined her boss. He quit soon after. It was a very hard decision because it was a close call; he was a productive manager, and she was and is a marginal employee. Here's my problem. If she gets another poor evaluation (which seems pretty certain), she is going to be let go. I am sure she will claim that this is retaliation for her harassment complaint. It's not, but with this history, I am not sure what to do.

A: For the timing of an employee's termination to support an inference of retaliatory motive on the part of your company, the termination must have occurred fairly soon after the employee filed her sexual harassment complaint.

It is unlikely that a court would find that a complaint lodged two years earlier was the cause of the employee's termination, assuming, of course, that you have a valid reason for terminating her at this time that is not related to her earlier complaint. The key to showing that is, of course, documentation by her supervisor of her poor performance.

100. Q: Can I fire an employee for falsely accusing a manager? One of my longest serving and most respected managers was accused of racism. We investigated and even brought in outsiders to do it. He was completely cleared. However, he is so angry with the accuser that he is demanding we fire him on the grounds that the accusation was false and designed to delay or avoid discipline. I agree with the manager on the facts, but am concerned that any action against the accuser will be considered retaliation. Are there any guidelines for this situation?

A: You are right to be concerned. Many employers that were cleared of discrimination have been found guilty of retaliation for taking an adverse employment action against the complaining employee. And yes, there are some guidelines.

The key question here is whether the accusations of racism against the manager were job related. Was the manager accused of favoring non-minority employees over minority co-workers, or of making inflammatory racial remarks or jokes at work?

Assuming that is the case, as long as the accuser complained about these work-related matters based on a reasonable, good faith belief that his accusations of racism were justified at the time they were made, and the manner in which he made the accusations was reasonable, he is immune from discipline or any other adverse employment action under Title VII of the 1964 Civil Rights Act and applicable state anti-discrimination laws.

The Equal Employment Opportunity Commission's guidelines provide the following examples of protected "opposition to a practice believed to be unlawful discrimination":

- complaining to anyone about alleged discrimination against oneself or others;
- threatening to file a charge of discrimination;
- picketing in opposition to discrimination; or
- refusing to obey an order reasonably believed to be discriminatory.

Examples of activities that are *not* protected opposition include:

- actions that interfere with job performance so as to render the employee ineffective; or
- unlawful activities such as acts or threats of violence.

If there is hard evidence that the accuser manufactured the racism charges simply to delay or avoid discipline for prior misconduct or pre-existing performance problems, or the accusations were made in a particularly offensive, threatening, criminal or violent manner, you may have an argument for discipline. But this course of action appears risky at best.

Sources: EEOC Guidance on Retaliation, http://www.eeoc.gov; EEOC Compliance Manual §8, Ch. II, Part D.

Off-Duty Conduct

101. Q: Can I fire an employee for getting arrested? I just learned that one of my employees got charged with [domestic violence][drug possession][assault] over the weekend. This company has strong feelings about that kind of conduct. Can I discipline or fire him without getting sued?

A: It depends, and you are right to be cautious when considering termination or lesser discipline based on an employee's off-duty conduct. Some states prohibit adverse employment action on the basis of an *arrest* as opposed to *conviction* for an offense.

But after-work activities may affect job performance, damage morale or sully the company's image, especially in a small town where word gets around fast. So there is no easy answer. When deciding whether to terminate employees for an arrest, the critical determining factor is the effect of the off-duty behavior on the employee's job performance, the workplace or the company's image. The more the off-duty behavior negatively affects work performance or the business as a whole, the more valid termination becomes as an option.

Termination is justified when off-duty conduct is antithetical to an employer's mission, products, services or public image. For example, a bank teller arrested for embezzlement may be treated more harshly than a teller arrested for domestic violence. Similarly, if an employee arrested for drug possession is responsible for transporting passengers as a bus driver or driving the employer's trucks, discipline up to and including termination appears legally defensible. Regrettably, however, there is no guarantee that the employer will not face a lawsuit. Regardless of the merits, litigation can be expensive.

If, given the nature of your business, you have particularly strong feelings about off-duty misconduct, such as drug use or possession, theft or violence, then you should list such off-duty misconduct as a ground for termination in your discipline and discharge policy.

At the same time, a policy of disciplining employees arrested for certain types of crimes may result in an adverse impact on minority or ethnic groups, and thus the potential for a discrimination claim under Title VII of the 1964 Civil Rights Act and state anti-discrimination laws.

Once again, the key to a successful defense against such a claim is to limit discipline to circumstances that are related to the way you conduct your business operations, a "reasonable belief" that the employee in fact engaged in the alleged off-duty misconduct and consistent application of the policy without regard to minority status. You are not required to satisfy the stringent "beyond a reasonable doubt" standard applicable to criminal charges to justify discipline.

Of course, an employee who fails to report for work can be terminated in compliance with your established attendance and/or call-in policies. The fact that he or she happens to be in jail makes no difference. In the event of a conviction, termination is an easy call as well. Even seemingly unrelated crimes become job-related if they involve dishonesty or violence.

102. Q: Can I fire an employee for writing bad things about the company on his blog? One of our employees posts a daily gossip column about the company on his blog, including critical comments about both the company's products and his supervisors. He's free to have his opinions, but do I have to tolerate this while he's on my payroll?

A: The answer depends in part on where you are located. Private employers may discipline employees for off-duty blogging without fear of an actionable free speech claim based on the First Amendment or applicable state constitution, because the constitutional protection applies to governmental action. However, a few state constitutions – not surprisingly, including California's – do apply free speech rights to private as well as public employers. Employers in those states must consider the state's constitutional equivalent to the First Amendment in assessing employee rights.

Several states, including New York and Colorado, enforce off-duty protection statutes prohibiting employers from taking adverse action based on an employee's off-duty political, union or recreational activities, including hobbies, and use of consumer goods that may apply to off-duty blogging. Other states protect only political expression.

While the employee-author of the critical gossip column is not a political blogger, he may be free to criticize your company's products and even the company itself as a "hobby" in some states. To the extent that he is accusing your company of discriminatory actions against its workforce, the employee may also be engaging in "protected activity" under the anti-retaliation provisions of Title VII of the 1964 Civil Rights Act and other state and federal anti-discrimination laws. He may thus be immunized from discipline for expressing his opinion that you engage in employment discrimination.

In addition, the National Labor Relations Act prohibits adverse employment actions against workers who engage in protected, concerted activity, even in a non-union environment. If the employee complains about terms and conditions of employment that affect him and his co-workers, not just expressing individual complaints, he may be immune from discipline for this reason as well. State and federal whistleblower protections may also apply.

Even if off-duty blogging is not protected by a federal or state statute, it may be protected by a state's common law, creating a public policy exception to the presumption of employment-at-will that may apply to speech outside the workplace. Of course, your right to terminate him will be restricted by any applicable employment contract or collective bargaining agreement

What does all this mean? At a minimum, you must be able to show that the employee's off-duty expressions of opinion have at least the potential to damage your reputation or profitability. Clearly, negative comments about your company that are publicized on the Internet can adversely affect how potential customers and/or clients view your operations.

Prior notice to employees of restrictions on off-duty blogging will strengthen your position. However, it is important to consider whether disciplining complaining employees would result in more adverse publicity than the initial blogging did. Finally, your location and the scope of the blogging may determine the result.

Free Speech

103. Q: Can I ban political material from the workplace? During campaigns, some employees put campaign materials on their office or cubicle walls and doors. It is often distracting and always leads to time-consuming discussions.

A: Yes. The First Amendment right to freedom of speech applies to government action, not that of a private employer, so you are completely within your rights to ask workers not to display political or any other material that might be offensive to or cause divisiveness among co-workers.

If you are a public employer (a federal, state or local governmental agency), your employees have First Amendment rights. But when you are dealing with political campaigns, the federal Hatch Act restricts certain federal and state employees from putting up campaign materials at the workplace.

Source: 5 U.S.C. §§1501-1508 and 7321-7326.

104. Q: What are the limits of religious rights in the workplace? One of my employees is devoutly religious, and believes she is morally bound to bring her religion to others. Even though she rarely uses work time, she does use our e-mail. Also, other employees have complained about the proselytizing in the lunchroom. Can I tell her to stop without violating the First Amendment?

A: Yes. This is a form of harassment of co-workers who do not believe as she does.

If you are a public-sector employer, you must be mindful of your employees' rights to freedom of speech and freedom of religion. This employee may be able to argue that you are violating her rights if you ask her to stop proselytizing in the workplace, but that has to be weighed against the rights of the other employees not to be harassed, so you are on firm ground.

Because the First Amendment only applies to government action, if you are a private-sector employer, you may impose rules about the use of the Internet and the lunchroom for religious purposes. You must be careful, however, to treat all religions equally. If you favor or disfavor certain religions, you could be in violation of Title VII of the 1964 Civil Rights Act, which prohibits employers from discriminating on the basis of religion.

Source: 42 U.S.C. §2000e, *et seq.*

105. Q: Do employees have the right to display whatever photos they want – short of indecent, of course? We have a policy that permits family photos (including pets) but prohibits provocative posters or sexual pictures at work. One guy has a picture of his wife from their recent vacation to some beach and, let's just say, it's very sexy. I feel odd asking someone to remove a spouse's picture, but I don't want to get into which relatives you can show wearing what. Does he have a right to display that photo?

A: No. You have a right to determine whether something is potentially disruptive to your workforce, and a picture that could make other employees uncomfortable would certainly be disruptive. The issue is not that the picture is of a family member, but rather that it could be considered offensive by some people.

Moreover, you have a duty to protect your employees from sexual harassment, and pictures of women in skimpy outfits could be determined by some courts to create a sexually hostile work environment. Because some of your employees, customers or clients might find the picture offensive, you are on solid ground requiring the removal of the offending photo. Just make sure that you enforce your policies consistently and without regard to gender, race, age, national origin or disability.

Sources: 42 U.S.C. 2000e *et seq.;* EEOC Guidance on Sexual Harassment.

106. Q: Where should I draw the line on charitable fundraising in the workplace? Our owner is a well-known philanthropist in our community and we encourage everyone to follow his example. However, in the past few years, we've seen an upsurge in charitable solicitation at work, whether it's buying wrapping paper for some school or sponsoring someone in a charity race. Once we've permitted it, can we stop or limit it without violating someone's rights?

A: You are permitted to prohibit all charitable solicitations in the workplace. If you decide, instead, to merely limit solicitations, you will need to make sure that the way in which you pick or choose is not based on race, color, sex, religion, national origin or the like.

You should not, for example, permit solicitations on behalf of certain religious organizations, but not others, or permit solicitations only on behalf of organizations that benefit particular ethnic groups. This is often quite difficult and, as a result, a number of employers prohibit all solicitations in the workplace.

Whistleblowing

107. Q: Can I fire an employee for bringing down an OSHA inspection out of spite? During an OSHA audit, I learned that the audit was the result of a complaint by one of our own employees. I am convinced it was a spiteful act stemming from a poor evaluation. Besides, employees are supposed to notify their supervisors if they think something is wrong. As for OSHA, all we had to do was label some cleaning solutions and update our evacuation plan, but we lost a lot of time and the supervisors were sick with worry for days. Now that we know there was no OSHA violation, can we fire the complainer?

A: No, you cannot fire an employee for making a formal complaint to a federal or state enforcement agency, even if you believe he or she should have gone to company management first.

An employee has a right to complain to OSHA about a potential violation of federal safety or health standards, and the law protects him or her against retaliation for making that complaint. The fact that OSHA required your company to label some cleaning solutions and update your evacuation plan shows that the company may, in fact, have violated an OSHA standard.

But even if OSHA gave you a clean bill of health, you could not fire the complainant as long as the employee had a reasonable and good faith belief that the company had violated an OSHA standard.

Sources: Section 11(c) of the Occupational Safety and Health Act, 29 U.S.C. §660(c).

108. Q: Can I fire an employee for basically broadcasting confidential financial information? One of the employees in our accounting department just sent the senior managers an e-mail accusing the company of fraudulent sales practices because we have different prices for different customers, even of the same product. The owner is furious because our price lists are confidential and there are a lot of perfectly valid reasons for the price differences. He wants to fire the employee. Is his conduct protected whistleblowing?

A: No, this is not protected whistleblowing. You may fire or discipline the employee if you wish.

There is a lot of discussion – and litigation – about whistleblowers these days, and it can be a confusing area of the law. You have probably heard about the Sarbanes-Oxley law, which was enacted by Congress after the scandals involving Enron and other large companies. But keep in mind that Sarbanes-Oxley, which has a whistleblower protection provision, applies only to publicly traded companies. So, it does matter that you are not publicly owned because that means that you do not have to worry about Sarbanes-Oxley.

There are no federal whistleblower protection statutes that would cover the situation you describe. There are no federal laws that protect employees who complain within the company about the company's pricing practices.

But if you have an employment contract with this employee, you should look to see whether there is anything in the contract that is relevant to the issue you raise. For example, is there a provision about confidential information? Did the employee breach this provision by telling senior managers about the company's pricing structure? Are you located in an "employment-at-will" state, which means that you can terminate the employee at your will, so long as you do not violate any laws in doing so?

109. Q: Does whistleblowing have to involve something the company did? We are a private company, but we have a non-retaliation whistleblower policy. An employee was responsible for the arrest of another employee for DWI. A lot of folks here think he was no hero. The employee was never a very good worker and is now the source of a lot of dissension. Is what he did protected whistleblowing under the law?

A: No. There are no federal whistleblower statutes that protect employees who blow the whistle on co-workers' drunk driving.

But you say that your company has a non-retaliation whistleblower policy. What does that policy say? Does it only protect employees who "blow the whistle" about improper company practices? If so, unless his colleague's DWI incident was work-related, your whistleblower may not be protected by the company's non-retaliation policy, and you may be free to terminate him.

Is your company's policy more general? Does it also protect employees who, acting as good citizens, blow the whistle on a colleague (or anyone else) who has run afoul of the law? Even if your employee is protected by your company's non-retaliation policy, you can fire him for what you describe as his chronic poor performance, unless this would merely be an excuse for retaliating against him for blowing the whistle on his colleague.

Leave/Benefits

5

Introduction

Our human resource clients have been telling us for several years that benefits are their companies' number one problem, especially the rising cost of health care and mandated leave. There are a number of federal laws, many of which have state law counterparts, that make leave and benefits issues extremely complicated and difficult to administer.

The most difficult leave law is the Family and Medical Leave Act (FMLA), which requires employers to grant workers up to 12 weeks of job-guaranteed leave for such things as taking care of newborns and illness of close family members. Most states also have leave laws and some of those laws are different than the federal one. How is an employer expected to coordinate those requirements?

And when it comes to coordination, the FMLA, Americans With Disabilities Act and workers' compensation laws are the Bermuda Triangle of leave. With the Iraq war, the Uniformed Services Employment and Reemployment Rights Act has become an issue for many employers.

In addition to questions on those leave issues, this chapter addresses benefits plans, including disability plans, health savings plans and pensions. COBRA and the Health Insurance Portability and Accountability Act both impact health insurance plans.

Unemployment compensation is another type of employee benefit that employers have to deal with, and we have included a couple of your most commonly asked questions about it in this chapter.

When appropriate, forms and checklists are included to give you complete answers to the questions you have asked us.

Questions in This Chapter

Other Types of Leave

Disability Plans

Health Insurance Plans

Health Savings Plans

COBRA

FMLA

110. Q: Can I terminate an employee for excessive absences related to child care? One of my employees had her third child while on my payroll. I'm OK with that; she gets maternity leave, etc. What I am having trouble with is the time missed for "parenting." Very few of these absences qualify for FMLA, and besides, she usually has no leave left. We try to be "family-friendly," but even her co-workers are complaining about having to take up the slack her absences are causing. Is this grounds for termination?

A: Maybe, but think about it carefully first. Sometimes it is hard to be fair because you have to wonder to whom you are being fair.

Let's start with the law. Under the Family and Medical Leave Act (FMLA), eligible employees are entitled to 12 workweeks of unpaid family and medical leave per year for:

- the birth of the employee's son or daughter and care of the infant;
- the placement of a son or daughter with the employee for adoption or foster care;
- the care of the employee's spouse, son, daughter or parent with a serious health condition; or
- the employee's own serious health condition, which makes the employee unable to perform the functions of his or her job.

As you can see, the FMLA is *not* intended to be a childcare statute. FMLA leave is available only when one of the statutory conditions listed above is met. If, as you state, very few of the absences in question qualify as FMLA leave, what you appear to be addressing may have more to do with the administration of your company's other leave programs, such as paid time off, sick leave and vacation. Many companies permit parents to use any available leave to care for a sick child. Those other leave programs are not FMLA and should not be confused with it.

Your question seems to be whether someone with a lot of absences, even absences with a good reason, can be terminated. As far as the FMLA is concerned, after the 12-week (or 60-working-day) leave allotment is exhausted, the employee must return to work or lose reemployment rights.

However, before you take any employment action, you should learn if there are any state laws that provide more leave than the federal law. You also ought to check to see if there have been other similar situations at your company in the past so that any action you take is consistent and non-discriminatory. For example, you do not want to learn later that your company has been lenient and accommodating with men needing additional time off (for any reason) but is being hard-nosed with this woman.

If yours truly is a "family-friendly" business, you can also explore ways to provide more leave to those who need it, such as with leave banks and leave without pay. Remember, good employees are hard to find.

Source: 29 U.S.C.§2612(a)(1).

111. Q: My state has its own family and medical leave law – which rules do I follow, state or federal?

A: The federal FMLA makes it clear that if there is a state law covering the same area, the employee gets the more generous benefit.

Many state leave laws are more "generous" in a variety of ways. For example, smaller employers are covered; "family members" are more broadly defined; more leave is granted; there is no need to exhaust paid leave; and so on, so you must check your state law.

The real complication takes place when the state grants a benefit not covered by the federal law. For example, permitting family leave for someone not covered by the federal law. In that instance, the leave taken under the state law does *not* affect the employee's right to leave under the federal law. In that situation, if the employee has used leave available only under state law, she or he is still entitled to leave under the federal law.

On the other hand, if the leave is covered by both the state law and the FMLA, the 12-weeks of FMLA leave can run concurrently with the state leave. For example, if state law permits 16 weeks of leave for the birth of a child, the employee is entitled to only 16 weeks of leave, not 28.

Source: 29 C.F.R. §825.701(a).

112. Q: Just what is a "serious health condition" under the FMLA? I just had an employee with a head cold ask for FMLA leave.

A: This should be an easy question with an easy answer, but this part of the FMLA has proven to be one of the most difficult to administer.

This is what the regulation says:

A "serious health condition" is defined as an illness, injury, impairment, or physical or mental condition that involves:

- inpatient care (i.e., an overnight stay) in a hospital, hospice or residential medical care facility, including any period of incapacity (defined as an inability to work, attend school or perform other regular daily activities), or any subsequent treatment in connection with such inpatient care; or
- continuing treatment by a health care provider.

A serious health condition involving continuing treatment by a health care provider includes:

- A period of incapacity of more than three consecutive calendar days, and any subsequent treatment or period of incapacity relating to the same condition, that also involves:

  - treatment two or more times by a health care provider, or by a nurse or physician's assistant under direct supervision of a health care provider, or by a provider of health care services (e.g., physical therapist) on referral by a health care provider; or
  - treatment by a health care provider on at least one occasion that results in a regimen of continuing treatment.

- A period of incapacity due to pregnancy, or for prenatal care.
- A period of incapacity or treatment for a "chronic" serious health condition that requires periodic visits for treatment by a health care provider, continues over an extended period, and may cause episodic rather than a continuing period of incapacity (e.g., asthma, diabetes, epilepsy).
- A period of incapacity that is permanent or long-term due to a condition for which treatment may not be effective. The employee or family member need not be receiving active treatment by a health care provider (e.g., Alzheimer's disease, severe stroke, terminal cancer).
- A period of absence to receive multiple treatments for an injury or condition that would result in incapacity of more than three days if not treated (e.g., chemotherapy or radiation for cancer, physical therapy for severe arthritis, or dialysis for kidney disease).

The regulations provide that "treatments" for serious health conditions include examinations to determine if a serious health condition exists, but do not include routine physical, dental or eye examinations.

As a result, the chances are an ordinary head cold does not qualify for FMLA leave. However, if the employee goes to the doctor, is treated and misses at least three days of work, the head cold is no longer "ordinary." If you think you are being victimized by abuse, be sure that you get a medical certification from the health care professional.

Source: 29 C.F.R. §825.114.

113. Q: If an employee goes out on paid sick leave, workers compensation leave or disability leave, can I count that against the 12 weeks of unpaid FMLA leave?

A: Yes, if the underlying illness or injury qualifies as a serious health condition under the FMLA, the absence may be counted against the FMLA leave allotment.

You should make that clear in your policy manual and you should tell the employee, in writing, that the leave is being treated as FMLA leave.

Remember, even though the time off can be counted against the 12-week FMLA allotment, not all states permit you to require the employee to exhaust all paid leave while on FMLA leave. Most states do not permit you to consider time off for a workers' compensation injury as part of any other company leave, such as paid time off or vacation. Always check your state's leave law provisions.

114. Q: If I think the doctor's note is phony or at least not honest, can I get a second opinion before I grant FMLA leave?

A: Yes. If you have a reason to question an employee's original medical certification, you may require the employee to obtain a second certification from a different, independent health care provider that you can choose. However, it is going to be at your expense, including reimbursement to the employee for any reasonable out-of-pocket travel expenses incurred in obtaining the second opinion.

Be sure to get the second opinion before deciding you have been misled and taking any action against the employee. Acting rashly will likely lead to a judicial decision against you. Besides, the employee didn't write a "phony" note, to use your word. If anyone did, it was the doctor.

If there is a conflict between the first and second medical opinions, you can require the employee to obtain a third opinion from another independent health care provider, which will be *binding on both of you*. You must also pay for the third opinion, including any of the employee's out-of-pocket travel expenses.

Pending the ultimate decision on an employee's entitlement to leave, the employee is provisionally entitled to all the benefits of the FMLA, including maintenance of group health benefits. If the certifications ultimately establish that the employee was not entitled to FMLA leave, the leave may be treated as either paid or unpaid non-FMLA leave under your existing leave policies.

Sources: 29 C.F.R. §825.307(a); *Miller v. AT&T Corp.*, 250 F.3d 820 (4th Cir. 2001).

115. Q: Doesn't an employee have to request FMLA leave in advance? I mostly get calls from an employee at home telling me he's sick and he brings a doctor's note either when he comes back or after he sees the doctor a week later. Is that legitimate?

A: An employee is supposed to give as much as 30 days' notice if the reason for the leave is known that far in advance. That's to be expected with voluntary surgery, some newborn deliveries, some adoptions and similar situations.

But what usually happens is what you describe: an employee calls in with an unforeseen illness. This is one of the biggest problems in administering the FMLA.

Remember: to involve the FMLA, the reason for the request for leave must be a "serious health condition"; you can require medical certification (and second and third opinions); and if there is no reasonable excuse for giving you short notice, you can delay the FMLA leave until 30 days after the request. The main question for you, as for most employers, is whether a dew days off is worth all this administrative oversight.

Sources: 29 C.F.R. §§825.302(a) and 825.304(b).

116. Q: When do new employees become eligible for FMLA leave? An employee has been on disability leave since the beginning of the month, but his one-year anniversary with the company comes at the end of next month. The employee has worked 1,250 hours since he was hired. When is he FMLA-eligible?

A: The FMLA requirements state that an employee is eligible for FMLA leave after he or she has worked for an employer for 12 months and for 1,250 hours. In this case, because the employee has already worked the 1,250 hours, he would be eligible for FMLA leave from the date of his one-year anniversary.

The time he is out on disability leave does not count toward his 1,250-hour threshold. In fact, any form of leave, paid or unpaid, does not count toward an employee's hourly requirement.

Source: 29 C.F.R. §825.110.

117. Q: When someone returns from FMLA leave, how "equivalent" to his old job does the new one have to be?

A: It is, of course, best to return the employee to his or her original position. Because it will not always be possible for an employer to restore an employee to the exact position he or she held before taking leave, the definition of "equivalent position" becomes very important.

The FMLA provides that the equivalent position must have equivalent benefits, pay and other terms and conditions of employment.

For a job to be equivalent, it must involve "the same or substantially similar duties and responsibilities, which must entail substantially equivalent skill, effort, responsibility, and authority." Thus, an employee returning from FMLA leave must be restored to a position in which he or she performs essentially the same work for the same compensation and benefits, under equivalent conditions of employment.

The "same" job in a distant location or even in an obviously undesirable place may not be considered "equivalent." A position that is merely "comparable" or "similar" is not enough.

Equivalent benefits include group health insurance, life insurance, disability insurance, sick leave, annual leave, educational benefits and pensions. When an employee returns from FMLA leave, his or her benefits must be resumed in the same manner and at the same levels as provided when the leave began, subject to any changes in benefit levels that may have occurred during the FMLA leave period.

You cannot require an employee to requalify for any benefits enjoyed before FMLA leave began. Thus, if his or her life insurance policy lapses during a period of unpaid FMLA leave, the employee cannot be required to meet any qualifications, such as taking a physical exam, to qualify for life insurance when returning from leave.

With respect to pension and other retirement plans, you must treat a period of FMLA leave as continued service for purposes of vesting and eligibility to participate. If the plan requires an employee to be employed on a specific date to be credited with a year of service, or for vesting, contribution or participation purposes, an employee on unpaid FMLA leave is deemed to have been employed on that date. For other purposes, however, although paid leave is counted as service credit, unpaid leave is not.

Sources: 29 C.F.R. §§825.214(a) and 825.215(a), (d)(1) and (d)(4).

118. Q: Is there a limit on the FMLA's job protection rules? We just lost a big contract and have to reduce our workforce. An employee on FMLA leave is one of those scheduled to be laid off. If I fire him, am I violating the FMLA?

A: No, but be prepared to defend your decision.

Under the FMLA you are permitted to refuse to return someone to work who would otherwise have been laid off or whose position was eliminated. You state that you have used neutral criteria and can support your decision. That is the right way to deal with this difficult issue.

By the way, be sure to check out whether your situation is covered by WARN (the Worker Adjustment and Retraining Notification Act; see Q. 198).

Sources: 29 C.F.R. §825.216(a); *Maxwell v. American Red Cross Blood Services,* 1996 WL 437456 (N.D. Ala. 1996).

119. Q: If an employee uses part or all of her FMLA leave before she needs leave for a pregnancy, does she still have a right to additional FMLA leave?

A: No. Congress may have had pregnancy leave in mind when it passed the FMLA, but only 12 weeks of leave for any and all qualifying events is available.

But that may not be the end to the discussion. Although the federal law provides for 12 weeks of leave under the FMLA, some states, such as California, have separate pregnancy/bonding leaves with separate criteria and separate entitlements. As a result, you should consult your state's law.

Further, there is nothing to prevent you from offering more leave to accommodate your employees' medical events if you do so in a gender-neutral way. And, your pregnant employee may qualify for short-term disability leave, independent of the requirements of the FMLA, depending on her physical condition and your disability leave insurance requirements.

120. Q: Is there a rule about how long before giving birth a pregnant woman can get FMLA leave?

A: No. Moreover, just because a woman is pregnant does not mean she automatically qualifies for FMLA leave.

To qualify, a pregnant woman would need to be incapacitated because of the pregnancy. For example, her doctor would need to order her to be on bed rest for a period of time prior to the birth. Or she could qualify for intermittent FMLA leave for her prenatal doctor's visits, because or morning sickness or the like.

Under the FMLA, no leave is available "to prepare" for the birth. Nonetheless, these are difficult HR situations. One way to avoid being faced with this sort of dilemma is to request that the employee update her medical certification to learn if she may be incapacitated because of the pregnancy before the child is born.

121. Q: Who is supposed to pay for employees' health care coverage when they're on FMLA leave?

A: The FMLA provides that during a period of family or medical leave you (public or private employer) must maintain the employee's coverage under your company's "group health plan ... at the level and under the conditions coverage would have been provided if the employee had continued in employment continuously for the duration of such leave." This means that if the employee contributed to the health care premiums while working, he or she must continue doing so.

But there is more to it. If, as is usually the case, the leave is unpaid, you may request the employee to pay his or her share of the health care premium in any of the following ways:

- payment due at the same time as it would be if made by payroll deduction;
- payment due on the same schedule as payments made under the Consolidated Omnibus Budget Reconciliation Act (COBRA);
- payment prepaid pursuant to a cafeteria plan at the employee's option; or
- another system voluntarily agreed to by employer and employee.

Your existing rules for payment by employees on unpaid leave should be followed, as long as prepayment is not required. Note that whatever method you choose, you must provide the employee with advance written notice of the method to be used.

Your obligation to maintain health coverage is not absolute. It ceases, for example, if an employee's premium payment is more than 30 days late. However, you must provide *written notice* to the employee that payment has not been received 15 days before dropping group health coverage. If you chose to maintain health coverage by paying the employee's share after the 30-day grace period has ended, you may recover the employee's share of any missed premium payments.

If coverage lapses for nonpayment, the employee must still be restored to coverage on his or her return from leave. In this situation, the employee may *not* be required to requalify for coverage, wait for open season, etc. Even if an employee fails to make timely premium payments, the employer's other FMLA obligations, such as reinstatement, continue.

Some employers, aware that meeting insurance premium bills while the employee is on an unpaid leave would create a hardship, fully fund the cost of insurance. However, there are some pitfalls to be aware of. First, the employee might not return to work. You would then be in the position of pursuing a collection action, in certain circumstances. You lose this recovery right in circumstances in which the failure to return to work is due to the continuation, recurrence or onset of a serious health condition, or "other circumstances beyond the employee's control."

Second, even if the employee returns to work, the FMLA regulations do not contain explicit guidelines with respect to the repayment of health care premiums. The Labor Department advises working out a "reasonable" repayment schedule, one not requiring a lump sum repayment.

Sources: 29 C.F.R. §§825.209(a), 825.210(c), 825.212(a) and 825.213; DOL Wage and Hour Division Opinion Letter FMLA-65 (July 13, 1995).

122. Q: Can I let an employee choose when she takes FMLA leave? One employee needs to take medical leave but doesn't want to take it as FMLA leave – she wants to save her FMLA leave for later in the year, when her mother will have surgery.

A: It depends on where you are.

Under the federal law, you *can* let the employee choose when she takes FMLA leave, but that may not be the best management choice, at least in many work settings and circumstances. The FMLA gives you the right to designate FMLA leave (even if it is against the employee's wishes) and you can require the employee to exhaust all paid leave as part of an FMLA leave. Most employers don't want to be seen as giving special benefits to individual employees.

On the other hand, in some states (and the District of Columbia), the employee has the right to choose whether to use available *paid* leave during an FMLA leave. In the situation you describe, the employee in a "choice" jurisdiction may elect to use unpaid FMLA leave for her own medical leave and then use her paid vacation to care for her mother.

Source: 29 C.F.R. §825.208.

123. Q: A guy just asked for FMLA leave to care for his mother, who lives with him. I know his wife is at home and does not work. Do I have to grant him leave?

A: You have to remember that the FMLA creates a statutory right for the eligible employee. The fact that an employee may have someone at home who has time to care for an ill parent or child does not enter at all into an FMLA consideration.

If the employee is eligible to take FMLA leave and asks to care for a family member with a serious health condition, you have no choice: you *must* grant the leave no matter who else may be available to care for the person. In fact, you could be accused of harassing the employee if you respond to a request for FMLA leave by encouraging this employee to have his wife care for his mother.

Intermittent FMLA Leave

124. Q: How do I count intermittent leave time against the 12-week FMLA limit? And can I request a new doctor's note to be sure intermittent leave is still necessary?

A: Let's start with intermittent leave in general, which surveys show to be the biggest problem most employers have in administering the FMLA.

First, the FMLA permits an employee to take leave intermittently or on a reduced leave schedule, but there are two conditions. If the leave is for the birth or placement of a child for adoption or foster care, *you must agree* to the intermittent leave. If the leave is for the "serious health condition" of the employee or the employee's spouse, child or parent, leave may be taken intermittently or on a reduced schedule *only* when medically necessary.

Second, intermittent leave is *part of, not in addition to,* the 12-week FMLA leave allotment. Now, how do you calculate intermittent leave?

Intermittent leave or reduced-schedule leave reduces the total amount of leave by the amount of time actually taken off. For example, if an employee takes four hours of leave for medical treatment, he or she has used four hours of the 12 weeks of leave allowed. Leave taken intermittently and charged to the employee at an hourly rate will not affect the exempt status of an employee who is otherwise exempt from the overtime requirements of the Fair Labor Standards Act.

Intermittent leave may be taken in increments of any size, although you may limit leave increments to the shortest period of time that your payroll system uses to account for absences or use of leave. For many organizations, this means that statutory leave protections can apply to periods as small as six minutes, 10 minutes or 15 minutes.

If an employee normally works a part-time schedule, the amount of leave to which the employee is entitled is determined on a pro-rata basis by comparing the reduced schedule with the employee's normal schedule.

Example: An employee who normally works 30 hours per week, works only 20 hours per week under a reduced-leave schedule. The employee's 10 hours of leave constitutes one-third of a week of FMLA leave for each week she works the reduced schedule.

As for a new medical certification, you may ask for recertification of the employee's medical condition every 30 days from the completion of the original certification, but only in connection with a medically related absence.

Also, you may request recertification sooner than every 30 days if circumstances described by the previous certification have changed significantly, such as the duration or frequency of absences, the severity of the condition or if you have received information that casts doubt on the employee's stated reason for the absence.

It is clear from your question that you are skeptical about the employee's need for leave. One way to prevent FMLA abuse is to start the process on the right footing. The best way to do that is to be sure the employee provides detailed information when he or she requests FMLA leave or provides sufficient information to suggest that time off may qualify as an FMLA absence.

For example, ask what the diagnosis is, the prognosis, whether prescription medication is being taken, the treatment schedule, the name of the doctor, why the employee needs to be absent and what the employee would be doing while absent.

Sources: 29 C.F.R. §§825.203(d), 825.206, 825.208(a), 825.302(c), (d) and (f) and 825.308(a).

125. Q: Do I have to let someone come back to work from FMLA leave on a part-time or reduced-schedule basis? Also, is the reduced schedule considered a kind of intermittent leave?

A: If the employee has FMLA leave left, the decision to return is the employee's. That is, you may not compel the employee to return to a part-time or light-duty job.

However, if the 12 weeks of FMLA leave are exhausted, you are not obliged to return the employee to a different job. Your obligation under the FMLA is to return an employee to the same or equivalent job. But good employees are hard to find and you may want to find a way to assist this one. If so, there are some little-known FMLA rules you should be aware of.

Let's say an employee with a serious health condition has FMLA leave left but chooses to accept a light-duty job to get back on the payroll. The time spent in the light-duty position may *not* be counted against the 12-week allotment of leave, but it can count against the employee's return-to-work restoration rights.

For example, if an employee takes six weeks of FMLA leave for his or her serious health condition and then spends six weeks on light duty, the employee still would have a right to restoration to the original job under the law. On the other hand, if the employee takes six weeks of FMLA leave for a serious health condition and then returns to work for seven weeks of light duty, the entitlement to restoration to the original job expires at the end of the sixth week of light duty.

In the second example, the employee would still be entitled to six more weeks of FMLA leave, but job restoration rights may not be guaranteed. By contrast, if FMLA leave time is still available, and the employee takes further leave for a *different* serious health condition or to care for a family member, the employer should maintain job restoration benefits.

The important thing to remember is that the right to restoration to the same or a position equivalent to the one originally held is available until 12 weeks of FMLA leave *or* light duty have passed within the 12-month period.

The other information needed is the extent of the health condition that led to the FMLA leave. If, for example, the employee qualifies as disabled under the Americans With Disabilities Act (ADA), some things may change.

Although the ADA does not require that you create a part-time or light-duty job as an accommodation, if such openings exist and are offered generally, then regardless of the number of weeks of FMLA leave used, you should offer the same opportunity as an accommodation under the ADA. There is some question as to whether such a position can be required as a permanent accommodation.

As to the second part of your question, light-duty work is not ordinarily considered intermittent leave – if the employee works a full shift, it is not leave of any kind. If the employee still qualifies for FMLA leave for the health care condition, the reduced schedule might be FMLA leave.

Sources: Wage and Hour Opinion Letter FMLA-103, dated March 26, 1999; 29 CFR §825.220(d); *Dalton v. Subaru-Isuzu Automotive,* 141 F.3d 667 (7th Cir. 1998).

126. Q: If an employee asks for intermittent leave, can I ask that his leave meets my business needs?

A: Yes. Employees ordinarily are expected to consult with their employers before scheduling treatment so they can work out a schedule that best suits the needs of both the employer and the employee.

If the employee fails to consult with the employer to make a reasonable attempt to arrange a treatment schedule that will avoid undue disruption of the employer's operations, the employer may initiate those discussions and require the employee to attempt to make such arrangements.

Source: 29 C.F.R. §825.302(e).

127. Q: I have a worker who wants intermittent leave to take care of her emotionally disturbed 20-year-old son whenever he has an "incident." Is something that unpredictable covered by the FMLA?

A: It could be. The first step is to have a health care provider, such as a psychologist, determine whether the son's emotional problems constitute a chronic serious health condition. If so, an eligible employee may take FMLA leave, intermittent or otherwise, to provide care for or provide psychological comfort to an immediate family member with a serious health condition.

Although a family member is defined as a spouse, parent or child *under the age of 18*, the employee may still be eligible to take intermittent FMLA leave to care for her 20-year-old son if he is incapable of self-care because of a disability.

Incapable of self-care means that the individual requires active assistance or supervision to provide daily self-care in three or more of the "activities of daily living," such as bathing, dressing and eating, or "instrumental activities of daily living," such as cooking, cleaning, shopping, taking public transportation, paying bills, etc. "Physical or mental disability" means a physical or mental impairment that substantially limits one or more of the major life activities of an individual.

As you can see, this is a complicated situation. One aspect of it you must try to learn more about is whether the "incidents" you describe are sufficient to support a diagnosis of the son's being "incapable of self-care." In this unfortunate situation, that is the "trigger" to FMLA leave.

Sources: 29 C.F.R. §§825.113(c)(1) and (2), and 825.203(c).

128. Q: Does our policy requiring anyone returning from a sick leave of more than three days to have a doctor's note violate the FMLA?

A: No, but as is so often the case, the FMLA is not the whole story.

The FMLA permits you to require that an employee who takes leave for his or her own serious health condition obtain a medical certification of fitness to return to work. *However,* this requirement is not intended to supersede a valid state or local law or a collective bargaining agreement that governs such employees' return to work. In addition, employers may not require return-to-work certification from employees who take intermittent leave.

The certification must come from the employee's health care provider and must state that the employee is able to return to work. The certification need only be a simple statement that the employee is able to return to work and should have no non-job-related medical information.

You cannot delay the employee's return based on the argument that you need more data. Rather, you need to allow the employee to return to work at the same time that you are seeking more specific information. You should also have a uniformly applied policy or practice that requires all similarly situated employees (i.e., same occupation, same serious health condition) who take leave for their health condition to obtain and present certification from their health care provider.

Remember to treat all employee medical information as confidential, even something as apparently simple as a "fit-for-duty" note.

Source: 29 C.F.R. §§825.310(a)) and (d).

ADA Leave

129. Q: What can I do about an employee who says his health makes it impossible for him to get to work on time? I say this is tardiness, but he says it's intermittent leave. Who's right?

A: This is a complicated question that potentially involves two different laws, the Family and Medical Leave Act (FMLA) and the Americans With Disabilities Act (ADA). The situation has to be evaluated under each law separately.

What is the employee's health problem? Is it a serious health condition under the FMLA that would entitle the employee to take a few hours of leave each day until the equivalent of 12 workweeks of leave in a 12-month period has been exhausted? (See discussion on FMLA, Q. 110-128.) If so, you can require the worker to temporarily transfer to an alternative position with equivalent pay and benefits for the duration of the leave, if there is an alternative job that better suits your business needs. If there is no such position and the employee is qualified for intermittent FMLA leave, such as for medical treatments, you have no option but to give it to him until the equivalent of 12 workweeks is exhausted.

This sounds more like a potential disability under the ADA. The employee has a physical or mental condition that significantly affects a major life activity, such as sleeping, eating or the like, that prevents him from keeping a specific work schedule.

If that is the case, he may be entitled to a modified work schedule as a reasonable accommodation. If coming in late really causes an undue hardship to your business – something more substantial than just inconvenience to you or your other employees – you need to determine if there is another reasonable accommodation that would meet the employee's needs without causing you hardship, such as reassignment. The reassignment can be to a job that pays less, under the ADA.

If no reasonable accommodation exists, your employee probably is not qualified for the job and, therefore, not protected by the ADA.

Sources: 42 U.S.C. § 12111 (9)(B); EEOC Enforcement Guidance: Reasonable Accommodation and Undue Hardship Under the ADA.

130. Q: An employee had a terrible accident and will be out for a while. Do the FMLA, workers' compensation, disability leave and ADA all apply? How do I know which one to follow?

A: It depends on the circumstances of the accident. Once you have the facts about the employee's situation, you have to examine each law separately to determine which, if any, applies.

Let's take the easy one first. If the accident was not work-related, workers' compensation does not apply. If it was, then the employee is covered by your state's workers' comp law.

Your description of a "terrible accident" and the fact that the employee will need to be off work for some time indicates that the employee has a serious health condition and would be entitled to up to 12 weeks of unpaid Family and Medical Leave Act (FMLA) leave if he qualifies. If you have more than 50 employees within a 75-mile radius of his worksite, you are a covered employer. If the injured employee worked for you for a year and at least 1,250 hours during the past 12 months, he is a covered employee and would be entitled to the FMLA leave.

As for the Americans With Disabilities Act (ADA), that is more difficult to tell at this point. Because the accident just happened, there probably is no way to tell whether the employee will end up with a disability. The ADA only applies if someone has a physical or mental impairment that substantially limits a major life activity, such as walking, hearing, seeing, etc.

As for disability leave, that is a company benefit, usually administered by an insurance company or third-party administrator. You are not required to provide this benefit, but a few states have publicly administered disability programs. If your company offers either short-term or long-term disability benefits (public or private), be sure the injured employee makes a timely application for benefits. The administrator will decide if he or she qualifies.

Sources: 29 U.S.C. §§2611 and 2612; 42 U.S.C. §12111; EEOC Guidance: The Family and Medical Leave Act, the Americans With Disabilities Act, and Title VII of the Civil Rights Act of 1964.

131. Q: Is there any flexibility in the ADA regarding accommodations already granted? Because of bad luck and bad timing, we've got more folks on FMLA leave and ADA accommodations than I planned. As a result, we can't let the healthy employees choose their vacation times as in the past, which is causing a huge morale problem. Is this a basis for modifying the ADA accommodations?

A: Possibly, but probably not. Reasonable accommodations under the Americans With Disabilities Act (ADA) are those that do not cause an undue hardship for your business. You would have to determine whether the morale problem is serious enough to really cause an undue hardship.

To do this, you would have to be able to prove that your situation has changed substantially from when the accommodations were first made. Obviously, if you permitted them, the accommodations did not cause an undue hardship at the time.

The law and regulations define an "undue hardship" as one that causes significant difficulty or expense. That means an action that is unduly costly, extensive, substantial or disruptive, or that would fundamentally alter the nature of your business. One factor you can consider in determining whether the accommodations you have granted are causing you an undue hardship is the impact they have on your other employees' ability to perform their job duties.

Even if you can show that the ADA accommodations are causing a real problem for your business, you need to determine whether there are other accommodations that would enable the affected employees to perform the essential functions of their jobs just as well as they can now. You do not have to grant the specific accommodations the employees want, just ones that will enable them to continue working in their jobs without causing your business an undue hardship.

Sources: 29 C.F.R. §1630.2(p)(2); 29 C.F.R. Part 1630 App. §1630.15(d); EEOC Guidance: Reasonable Accommodation and Undue Hardship Under the ADA.

132. Q: Does our policy requiring anyone returning from a sick leave of more than three days to have a doctor's note and a "fitness for duty" clearance violate the ADA?

A: No. The Americans With Disabilities Act (ADA) permits you to require that employees returning from leave for an illness or injury present documentation that they can perform the essential functions of their jobs with or without accommodation.

These "fitness-for-duty" exams or certifications are different from pre-offer medical examinations, which are prohibited by the law. Fitness-for-duty statements following an absence do not have to be required of every employee in the same job category, just of all those in the same circumstances. In other words, as long as you have a policy that is uniformly and consistently enforced, you are not discriminating and, therefore, not violating the law.

Fitness-for-duty requirements also have to be "job related" and a "business necessity." Requiring them to make sure the employee can safely return to the job is sufficient to meet this "job related and business necessity" standard.

What you cannot do is delve too deeply into an employee's health condition. All you need to know is that the employee is fit to safely return to work, not the details of the condition that required the absence. Of course your policy is also designed to make sure that employees who are absent for three or more days are truly ill or injured. Requiring a health care provider to provide a note and clearance should do that, without requiring detailed information about the employee's health or disability.

As with any medical information, fitness-for-duty certifications should be kept confidential.

Source: 29 C.F.R. §1630.14; *Grenier v. Cyanamid Plastics,* 70 F.3d 667 (1st Cir. 1995).

Military Leave

133. Q: Can we put off releasing an employee who just got called to active duty? We're right in the middle of our crunch time.

A: No. Under the Uniformed Services Employment and Reemployment Rights Act, a notification from an employee of the need for leave to perform active uniformed services duty is not a request for permission. While you can request that employees fill out an application for military leave (see Fig. 133-A), you cannot deny the leave.

However, federal regulations do permit you to contact military authorities to discuss concerns over the timing, frequency or duration of an employee's active uniformed service. The Department of Defense requires military authorities to provide assistance to an employer in addressing these issues and the military services must consider and, when military requirements permit, accommodate the legitimate concerns of civilian employers regarding the scheduling of their employees' military service or obligations.

Sources: 32 C.F.R. §§ 104.4(c) and (d), .5(b)(6) and .6(n) and (o).

FIG. 133-A

Application for Leave for Military Service

Name: ______________________________

Job title: ____________________________

Date Leave is to start: __________________

Date Leave is expected to end: ____________

Date of expected return to work: __________

Note: If your period of military service is longer than anticipated, your rights to reemployment will not be affected by dates given on this Request. You are asked to inform your supervisor or Human Resources of changes as soon as you are able.

Regarding Return to work:

Service of 1 to 30 days
If your military service was less than 31 days, you must report not later than the next regularly scheduled work day following completion of service and the expiration of eight hours (i.e., an 8-hour "rest period") after a period allowing for safe transportation home from the place where military service was performed. **NOTE: THIS APPLICATION WILL SERVE AS YOUR REQUEST FOR REEMPLOYMENT; HOWEVER, YOU ARE RESPONSIBLE FOR CONTACTING YOUR SUPERVISOR OR HUMAN RESOURCES TO CONFIRM THE INFORMATION PROVIDED.**

Service of 31 to 180 days
If your military service was more than 30 days but less than 181 days, an application for reemployment must be submitted **no later than 14 days** following completion of military service, or "as soon as possible" if the failure to make timely application is through no fault of the returning employee. Also, for returning employees whose length of service is more than 30 days, an employer may require the employee to provide documentation that the separation from military service was not disqualifying. **NOTE: If the last day of your military service changes, you are responsible for notifying your supervisor or Human Resources as soon as you are able.**

Service of more than 180 days
If your military service was more than 180 days, applications for reemployment must be submitted **not later than 90 days** from completion of military service. **NOTE: If the last day of your military service changes, you are responsible for notifying your supervisor or Human Resources as soon as you are able.**

HFBNFT030

134. Q: Isn't military leave and active duty supposed to be coordinated? We let a guy go on military leave and he's done nothing but hang around town since then. Do I have to consider him on leave or just absent?

A: You have to consider him on leave. There is no limit on the amount of time that can elapse between the date an employee leaves his or her civilian job and the date he or she actually enters the service. The employee does not have to begin military service immediately to retain reemployment rights.

The U.S. Department of Labor's regulations recognize that absence for military service may include a period of time between the date the employee leaves the job and the date the employee actually reports for military training or active duty. Depending on how long he is going to be away, how much notice the military gave him, and the location of the military service, your employee may need time to rest, arrange his affairs and report for duty.

The regulations also recognize that employees may need time off from work prior to reporting for active duty to put their affairs in order. For example, to interview childcare providers, meet with bank officers regarding financial matters, or seek assistance for elderly parents. Because individual situations vary so much, there is no hard and fast rule about what is an appropriate amount of time.

Source: 20 C.F.R. §1002.74.

135. Q: Can I take an employee who is out on military service off the employment rolls?

A: If you are asking whether you can decide to terminate an employee because he or she is on military leave, the answer is "no." The Uniformed Services Employment and Reemployment Rights Act (USERRA) prohibits employers from doing that.

But the question – and answer – is usually a little more complicated. If you are asking whether you can treat the employee the same as other employees who are *not* on military leave and who are terminated during a reduction in force or other layoff, the answer is "not really." The employee on leave has a contingent right to reemployment and related rights regarding credited service.

As a general rule, an employee is entitled to reemployment in the job he or she would have attained with reasonable certainty had it not been for the period of military service. This is known as the "escalator principle," because the employment "escalator" may have gone up or down while the employee was away, and he or she steps back on the escalator at the place he or she would, with reasonable certainty, have been but for the military service. So, if an employee's seniority or job classification would have resulted in the employee being laid off or even terminated during the period of service, he or she may suffer the same fate on return from military duty.

But absent these circumstances, an employee who meets five eligibility requirements must be reinstated after completion of military service. The requirements are:

1. The employee must be absent from a position of civilian employment because of service in the uniformed services – Army, Navy, Marine Corps, Air Force, Coast Guard, reserves of any of those services, Army and Air National Guards, commissioned corps of the Public Health Service and any category of persons designated by the president in time of war or emergency.

2. The employee must notify the employer either orally or in writing as far in advance about impending military service as possible under the circumstances. Thirty days is recommended, when feasible.

3. An employee is generally entitled to a leave of absence for uniformed service for up to five years with each employer. Absence from the job before or after military service does not count against the five-year limit. For example, an employee is entitled to a certain amount of time to travel to the duty station or to report back to work after completing military service and that period does not count against the five-year maximum.

4. The service member must return to work or apply for reemployment at the conclusion of military service. The time limit depends on the length of the active duty. For one to 30 days of active duty, the employee should report back to work by the first regularly scheduled work period after allowing for travel home and an eight-hour rest period. For 31 to 180 days, the request must be submitted no later than 14 days after completion of the active duty. Service of 181 days or more requires application for reemployment no later than 90 days after completion of active duty.

5. Discharge from the uniformed service must have been nothing less than honorable.

Under certain circumstances, an employee can serve in the military for more than five years and still have reemployment rights. For example, some military specialties require a person to serve more than five years because of the amount of time or expense involved in training. In that case, the employee has reemployment rights after the initial period of required service is completed.

USERRA also provides employees with some protections against discharge after they are reemployed. These protections vary, depending on the length of military service. If the employee served for more than 180 days, he or she may not be fired within one year after reemployment, except for cause. With service of 31-180 days, the employee may not be fired within 180 days after reemployment, except for cause. If the employee served for 30 days or less, there is no special protection against discharge, except that you cannot discharge an employee because of military service.

Sources: 38 U.S.C. §4311; 20 C.F.R. §§1002.18, .32, .191, .194 and .247.

136. Q: Do I have to keep health benefits in place for people on military leave? What about other benefits?

A: If the employee was covered under your health plan before he or she left for military training or service, the plan must permit the employee (and dependents, if the plan offers dependent coverage) to elect to continue the coverage for a period that is the shorter of:

- the 24-month period beginning on the date on which the employee's absence begins; or
- the period beginning on the date on which the employee's absence begins, and ending on the date on which the employee fails to return to the job or apply for reemployment.

Note that the 24-month provision reflects amendments made by Congress to USERRA in December 2004. Note, too, that plan administrators may develop reasonable requirements and procedures for the election of continuing coverage.

If the employee leaves work for military service without electing continuing coverage, you may cancel the employee's health insurance unless it was impossible or unreasonable to expect the employee to make an election. If health plan coverage was terminated during military service, coverage must be reinstated at reemployment, if requested by the employee.

The amount the employee must pay for continuing health care coverage varies depending on how long the employee is absent. If the employee performs military service of fewer than 31 days, the employer may not require the employee to pay more than the regular employee share (if any) for coverage. If the employee serves for 31 days or longer, he or she may be required to pay up to 102 percent of the full premium (the employee's share plus the employer's share) for coverage. In either case, the payment obligation begins on the first day of the continuation coverage.

In addition to health care benefits, the employee is entitled to rights and benefits that the employer generally provides to other employees who are on furlough or leave of absence with similar seniority, status and pay. For example, if you offer continued life insurance coverage, holiday pay or bonuses to employees on furlough or other types of leave of absence, you must offer similar benefits to the employee who is on military leave. These do not include rights or benefits that are dependent on seniority. They do, however, include rights and benefits that become effective during the employee's absence.

For pension plan purposes, after reemployment the employee is treated as not having a break in service with the employer for purposes of participation, vesting and accrual of benefits.

Sources: 20 C.F.R. §§1002.149-150, .163-171 and .259.

137. Q: What are the responsibilities of an employee who goes out on military leave?

A: Regulations issued by the U.S. Department of Labor require employees to notify their employers in advance about upcoming military service if they want to be eligible for reemployment with that employer. Notice may be oral or in writing, and the regulations do no dictate any particular format (see Fig. 133-A.)

There is no prescribed time by which an employee must give notice, but the regulations state that an employee should provide notice as far in advance as is reasonable under the circumstances. The Department of Defense has stated that it "strongly recommends that advance notice to civilian employers be provided at least 30 days prior to departure for uniformed service when it is feasible to do so."

An employee is excused from giving advance notice if he or she is prevented from doing so because of military necessity or if notice is otherwise impossible or unreasonable under the circumstances. "Military necessity" generally covers situations in which a mission is classified or could be compromised or otherwise adversely affected by public knowledge. And it may be impossible or unreasonable to give advance notice if the employer is unavailable or if the employee must report for military service in an extremely short period of time.

The service member must return to work or apply for reemployment in a timely manner after the conclusion of military service. Timeliness varies depending on the duration of the military service. (See Application for Reemployment Following Military Leave, Fig. 137-A.)

Sources: 20 C.F.R. §§1002.32(a), 1002.85 and .86; 32 C.F.R. §§104.3 and .6(a)(2)(i)(B).

Fig. 137-A

THOMPSON

Thompson HR Forms
http://forms.thompson.com

APPLICATION FOR REEMPLOYMENT FOLLOWING MILITARY LEAVE

Name: ______________________________

Job title: ____________________________

Date: _______________________________

Date Leave ended : ____________________

Date of expected return to work: __________

Regarding Return to work:

Service of 1 to 30 days
If your military service was less than 31 days, you must report not later than the next regularly scheduled work day following completion of service and the expiration of eight hours (i.e., an 8-hour "rest period") after a period allowing for safe transportation home from the place where military service was performed.

Service of 31 to 180 days
If your military service was more than 30 days but less than 181 days, an application for reemployment must be submitted no later than 14 days following completion of military service, or "as soon as possible" if the failure to make timely application is through no fault of the returning employee. Also, for returning employees whose length of service is more than 30 days, an employer may require the employee to provide documentation that the separation from military service was not disqualifying. **NOTE: This form can serve as your application for reemployment. If the last day of your military service changes, you are responsible for notifying your supervisor or Human Resources.**

Service of more than 180 days
If your military service was more than 180 days, applications for reemployment must be submitted not later than 90 days from completion of military service. **NOTE: This form can serve as your application for reemployment. If the last day of your military service changes, you are responsible for notifying your supervisor or Human Resources.**

HFBNFT031

138. Q: How am I supposed to figure out where a white-collar employee "would have been" if she had not gone on military leave? I can figure that out with our hourly workers, but our white-collar folks aren't on a pay scale. Besides, nothing can replace the experience you get on the job – meeting clients and prospects, learning new product lines, mastering new technology and so on.

A: Frankly, this is very hard and, fortunately, the regulations recognize that.

USERRA and the Department of Labor's regulations require that the returning employee be reemployed in a position that reflects with reasonable certainty the pay, benefits, seniority and other job perquisites that he or she would have attained if not for the period of military service. You must determine the seniority rights, status and rate of pay as though the employee had been continuously employed during the period of military service.

It is typically easier to determine what raises an hourly worker would have received had the worker's employment not been interrupted by military service. But when raises or promotions are discretionary, the regulations recognize that you may have a difficult time reconstructing what position or pay level an employee would occupy but for his or her military service.

A returning service member is entitled to a promotion after reemployment if there is a reasonable certainty that the employee would have been promoted except for the military service. The courts and Labor Department policy recognize that if a promotion depends on an exercise of discretion on the part of the employer, the returning service member may not be entitled to the promotion.

If an opportunity or eligibility for promotion that the employee missed during service is based on a skills test, you should give the employee a reasonable amount of time to adjust to the position and then give a skills test. In determining what is a reasonable amount of time, you may take into account a variety of factors, including the length of time the employee was absent from work, the level of difficulty of the test, the typical time necessary to prepare or study for the test, the duties and responsibilities of the reemployment position and the position into which the employee wants to be promoted, as well as the nature and responsibilities of the service member while serving in the uniformed services.

Sources: 38 U.S.C. §4313; 20 C.F.R. §§1002.191 and .193.

Other Types of Leave

139. Q: Do I set a precedent any time I bend my rules on leave? We have a two-day bereavement leave. An employee's mother just died – in Poland. He has run out of other leave and my heart goes out to him. If I give him extra time off to attend the funeral, have I created a precedent for everyone else?

A: You certainly would be creating a precedent for the next time an employee has a mother die in Poland.

Every time you waive, bend or stretch a company policy, you set a precedent. On the other hand, policies are designed for the usual circumstance; unusual circumstances may require exceptions. There are several things you can do in this instance to prevent future abuse. You could offer just enough leave for the employee to attend the funeral and require that the time be "paid back" out of future vacation or other paid leave. Or you could offer unpaid leave to attend the funeral. By strictly limiting the time to what is absolutely needed to get to Poland and back, your precedent would not stretch very far.

Whatever you do, be careful about discrimination, both now and in the future. All employees in similar circumstances should be treated the same, regardless of gender, race, religion or anything else that could be viewed as an illegal reason to discriminate.

140. Q: Am I supposed to keep paying an employee on jury duty or make up the difference between his pay and his jury fee?

A: Only if your state's laws require you to. Connecticut, Massachusetts and New York currently require employers to pay employees on jury duty for a limited time.

The federal Fair Labor Standards Act does not require payment of wages for time not worked while on jury duty. (An exempt employee must be paid for the week if he or she performs any actual work.) State laws require you to permit your employees to take time off for jury duty. They also generally require you to consider employees to be on leave while serving on jury duty, continue their benefits and return them to their jobs without loss of seniority when their jury duty is finished.

The U.S. Department of Labor reports that 87 percent of employers offer paid jury duty leave. Some employers deduct from employees' wages the amount received from the court for serving on jury duty.

Source: http://www.dol.gov.

Disability Plans

141. Q: Is there a law governing how sick leave, personal leave, vacation leave and disability leave are supposed to work together?

A: Some states and the District of Columbia permit employees who qualify for Family and Medical Leave Act (FMLA) leave to choose whether to use paid sick, vacation and other types of leave while they are on FMLA leave. The federal law permits employers to make that choice. Unless your state law provides otherwise, you would want all paid leave to run concurrently with FMLA leave so the employee cannot "stack" time off. Of course the FMLA only applies if you are a covered employer and your employee is qualified (see Q. 130).

Otherwise, these various types of leave are up to your company policies, collective bargaining agreement if any, and, in the case of long- and short-term disability, your disability insurance plan.

Source: 29 U.S.C. §2612(d).

142. Q: Does our maternity leave program create a precedent for our male employees to take similar leave for a disability? We have a generous maternity leave program – up to four months without a doctor's note. A male IT specialist just had a serious automobile accident and is demanding that we do the same for him. Do I have to?

A: No, although it might be wise to permit him to take up to four months to recover from his injuries to avoid the appearance of reverse gender discrimination and any morale problems that could create.

When it comes to pregnancy, you are dealing with two federal laws: the Family and Medical Leave Act (FMLA) and the Pregnancy Discrimination Act (PDA). Both are implicated in your question. (You also need to examine your state leave laws.)

Let's begin with the FMLA. That law provides for 12 weeks of job-protected leave for the birth of a child for qualified employees of covered employers. Both mothers and fathers are entitled to the 12 weeks of leave, unless they work for the same employer, in which case they must share the 12 weeks between them. There is no requirement for medical certification; the leave is for both recovery from the childbirth and bonding with the child. The first three months of your maternity leave program would count as FMLA leave if you are a covered employer.

There is no equivalent to the "birth-of-a-child without medical certification" leave in the FMLA. Employees with serious health conditions (or injuries) can be required to produce a health care providers' medical certification showing that they qualify for FMLA leave. If they do, if you are a covered employer, and if the employees are otherwise qualified due to hours worked and time on the job, they are entitled to 12 weeks of job-protected FMLA leave. (Of course you need to check your state leave laws to determine whether they provide for more than 12 weeks of job-protected leave for childbirth, sickness or incapacitating injury.)

The PDA prohibits discrimination against women who are pregnant. If an employer permits leave for other temporary health conditions, it must permit women to take the same leave for childbirth and related conditions. The PDA permits employers to establish policies granting more favorable treatment to pregnant female workers than to male employees if the favorable treatment is for the period of actual disability related to pregnancy. However, the PDA does not permit more favorable treatment for "bonding time."

Maternity leave is medical leave provided to female employees in connection with a pregnancy-related disability. Parental leave in the context of a birth is leave to care for the newborn. More favorable treatment of women is permitted for maternity leave, but not for parental leave – new fathers must be permitted to take the same amount of "bonding leave."

Because your maternity leave policy does not require any medical certification of the woman's health condition, it sounds as though it is a combination maternity/parental leave. Moreover, it is four weeks longer than the FMLA's 12-week leave for the birth of a child. A strict interpretation means you would have to provide new fathers with the same four months of leave to avoid discrimination.

But your IT worker is not a new parent. What the PDA requires is that pregnant women be given the same rights as any other employee to temporary disability leave that you provide, and that fathers be given the same parental leave rights as mothers. That leaves your IT worker out.

In fairness, however, isn't an employee's serious injury as important as getting to know a newborn? Because you have voluntarily adopted a more generous leave policy than the law requires for pregnant women, it might be wise to revise your sick leave/disability policy to provide for the same amount of leave when any employee has a serious health condition. However, you should require proof that an employee in that situation qualifies for the leave. Pregnancy is visible; serious health conditions often are not. Therefore, requiring a doctor's certification would not be discriminatory.

Sources: 42 U.S.C. §2000e(k); 29 C.F.R. §825.207(d)(1).

143. Q: Is it against some rule to have a gap between when sick leave ends and disability leave begins? We do this specifically to make sure employees think about going on disability.

A: No. You are not alone in having such a gap. There is no requirement that an employer pay workers who cannot work.

There are workers' compensation benefits for employees injured in the course of their work. Most employers (not all) provide for a specified amount of sick leave. Many (again, not all) provide for short- and/or long-term disability leave through an insurance program. And the federal Family and Medical Leave Act (FMLA) provides covered employees with 12 weeks of job-protected leave for certain specified conditions and situations, including their own serious health condition.

But FMLA leave is *unpaid*. Therefore, while you could not terminate a covered employee during the 12 weeks of FMLA leave (or longer period if your state provides one), you would not have to pay them.

144. Q: How "long-term" is long-term disability supposed to be? We have an employee on long-term disability. He receives no pay and accrues no benefits. How long do I have to consider him an employee?

A: Federal law provides that a covered employee with a serious health condition (someone on long-term disability should certainly qualify) is entitled to 12 weeks of job-protected leave in a 12-month period.

If you have the requisite number of employees (50 within a 75-mile radius of the worksite where this employee is located), and the employee has worked at least 1,250 hours in the past 12 months and has been employed by you for at least one year, this worker is entitled to job-protected leave for 12 weeks (assuming, of course, that he has a serious health condition). After that, unless your state has a leave law that provides for more job-protected leave, you are not required to keep the employee on your employment rolls.

This assumes that because he is on long-term disability, there is no reasonable accommodation that would enable the worker to perform the essential functions of his job. The Americans With Disabilities Act (ADA) does not provide protection for employees who cannot work; it prohibits discrimination in employment against those who, with or without an accommodation, can perform a job's essential functions.

The employee would be entitled to COBRA benefits (see Q. 149-159) for a period of time, generally 18 months (or 29 months if disabled). Your long-term disability insurance plan coverage would determine the amount and length of time for which he is entitled to disability payments from that insurance.

Health Insurance Plans

145. Q: Can I get rid of our health insurance and just give the employees a cash award to let them buy whatever policy they want?

A: Absent a contract (either a collective bargaining contract or an employment contract) to the contrary, yes. But be sure it is what you want to do.

Health insurance is considered to be one of the most valuable, if not *the* most valuable fringe benefit offered. It is also a tax-advantaged benefit. You may find yourself thought of as a less desirable employer. Further, an insured workforce is very often a more productive workforce, because insured employees are more likely to be treated for sickness and injuries and, thus, are more likely to be at work.

Even if you provide a subsidy to buy health insurance, you have no way of guaranteeing the same percentage of your workforce will be insured. Watch out for former employees covered by COBRA. See Q. 154-155 for information on how to deal with COBRA-covered workers.

146. Q: Must I let an employee opt out of our health plan because he can't afford the premiums? Our plan requires employee contributions, and we normally let people opt out only if they are covered by a spouse's plan.

A: No. There are many reasons for you to insist that your employees are covered by health insurance.

For example, an insured workforce is very often a more productive workforce because insured employees are more likely to be treated for sickness and injuries, and, thus, are more likely to be at work.

Nonetheless, rising health care costs are a problem facing many employers. If you have not, you might consider shopping for lower-cost options, such as an HMO, to be added to your health insurance benefit.

Health Savings Plans

147. Q: Please explain these new programs that employees can use to pay some of their own health expenses. Will they really reduce our growing health insurance costs?

A: I think I know what you are asking about, but not all of these programs are employee funded and it is probably too soon to tell whether they will reduce employer health costs. Some studies indicate they may at least slow down the rate of increase.

The idea behind the programs you have heard about is to make employees more responsible for and, thus, more aware of the cost of health care. The common element in all of these programs is a tax-advantaged pre-established account that can be drawn on to pay for medical expenses not covered by insurance. There are three types of accounts that can be used to help fund employee health care expenses – flexible spending accounts, health savings accounts, and health reimbursement arrangements. The latter is *employer* funded. A description of the *employee* funded accounts follows.

Flexible spending accounts (FSA)

Health care flexible spending accounts are *employer-established* benefit plans that reimburse employees for specified medical expenses as they are incurred. Health care premiums, cosmetic surgery and long-term care or coverage are *not* permitted expenses under an FSA.

These accounts are allowed under Section 125 of the Internal Revenue Code and are also referred to as "Cafeteria plans" or "125 plans." The employee contributes funds to the account through a pre-tax salary reduction agreement and is able to withdraw the funds to pay for medical bills as they are incurred.

The salary reduction agreement means that any funds set aside in a flexible spending account escape both income tax and Social Security tax. Employers may contribute to these accounts as well.

There is no statutory limit on the amount of money that can be contributed to health care flexible spending accounts, but because this is a "use it or lose it" account, some companies and most employees place a limit of $2,000 to $3,000 on them.

After the amount of contribution has been designated during the open enrollment period that occurs once each year, the employee is not allowed to change the amount or drop out of the plan during the year, unless he or she experiences a change of family status. Further, the entire amount of the annual contribution is available to be withdrawn on day one, even if the employee is contributing on a monthly basis, which can leave the employer "in the hole." By law, the employee forfeits any unspent funds in the account at the end of the year.

Source: IRS Code §125.

Health Savings Accounts (HSA)

Health savings accounts are a "second-generation" medical savings account without many of the limitations that made those accounts unattractive in the past. However, there are some limiting requirements in HSAs.

An HSA is an individual account for pre-tax funds earmarked to pay for medical expenses not otherwise covered. An HSA can be established by an individual *with or without* employer involvement. The medical expense can be for oneself, a spouse or dependent.

However, an HSA account is available only to people who are covered by a high-deductible health plan and *no other plan*, including Medicare. The HSA cannot provide benefits until the annual deductible is paid. In 2007, the minimum deductible for such a plan is $1,100 for an individual and $2,200 for a family. Also, the HSA must be funded through a trust in the United States established exclusively for qualified medical expenses.

There are also contribution limits. In 2007, the contribution limits are $2,850 for individuals and $5,650 for families. One of the benefits of such an arrangement is that the HSA funds are "owned" by the beneficiary, are portable and can "roll-over" from year to year.

But there are complications, including avoidance of ERISA requirements, that mean that any business or individual establishing an HSA should seek out sophisticated assistance in designing and administering it.

Source: Treas. Reg. §54.4980G-1 *et seq.*

148. Q: Is there a plan I can set up that would reimburse my employees for medical expenses and let me keep my tax break for health insurance?

A: Yes. They're called health reimbursement arrangements (HRA), also known as "health reimbursement accounts." They are a type of health insurance plan.

Health reimbursement accounts consist of funds set aside *by employers* to reimburse employees for qualified medical expenses, just as an insurance plan reimburses covered individuals for the cost of services incurred. HRAs may not be part of a cafeteria plan.

The guidance provided by the Treasury Department makes it clear that health reimbursement accounts are not a new type of account designated within the Internal Revenue Code. Rather, employers qualify for preferential tax treatment of funds placed in a health reimbursement account in the same way that they qualify for tax advantages by funding an insurance plan. (Employers can deduct the cost of an insurance plan – and now a health reimbursement account – as a business expense under Internal Revenue Code §162.)

Health reimbursement arrangements are open to employees of companies of all sizes. A health reimbursement account provides "first-dollar" medical coverage and payment of insurance premiums until funds are exhausted.

Under a health reimbursement account, the employer provides funds, not the employee. All unused funds are *rolled over* at the end of the year. Former employees, including retirees, can have continued access to unused reimbursement amounts. Health reimbursement accounts may remain with the originating employer or the program can permit the fund to follow an employee to new employment or retirement. HRAs can be offered along with health insurance and FSAs. Thus, HRAs can be stand-alone offerings or part of an integrated health care program.

Source: Rev. Ruling 2002-41; Notice 2002-45.

COBRA

149. Q: Do I have to provide COBRA coverage?

A: Only if you have enough employees to be covered and if you offer those employees health insurance.

Basically, COBRA applies to employers that offer their employees health care coverage and that employed 20 or more employees on 50 percent of the business days during the preceding calendar year. All full- and part-time employees are considered in determining whether an employer had fewer than 20 employees. However, each part-time employee counts as a fraction of a full-time employee.

Sources: 29 U.S.C. §1161; 26 C.F.R §54.4980B-2.

150. Q: What do I have to tell my employees about COBRA and when do I have to tell them?

A: COBRA requires you to provide a number of notifications to your employees based on the following timeframes:

1. When COBRA becomes effective for a plan, all covered employees (including retirees) and their spouses should be notified of their rights. Send the U.S. Department of Labor (DOL) general notice (see Fig. 150-A for a copy) to all covered employees and spouses, if any.

2. After COBRA is effective for any plan, employees and their spouses, if any, should be notified of their rights when they become covered under the plan. Notices should be provided within a 90-day period after group health coverage begins. This notice should be included in the summary plan description (SPD) that is given to each employee and spouse. Until the explanation is included in the SPD, provide individuals with the DOL general notice.

3. You must notify the plan administrator of an employee's termination or reduction in hours of employment, death or entitlement to Medicare within 30 days of the qualifying event.

4. The plan administrator must notify employees, spouses and dependent children, if any, that they would lose coverage because of a qualifying event and subsequently have rights to elect coverage. This notice must be sent within 14 days of the notification described above. Any notice to an employee's spouse is considered notice to any beneficiaries living with the spouse. If an individual had single coverage in effect immediately before a qualifying event, his or her spouse or dependent children may not elect COBRA coverage.

COBRA requires that each qualified beneficiary must be offered a separate opportunity to make an independent COBRA election. This obligation can be fulfilled by sending separate notices addressed to each affected qualified beneficiary.

However, a single mailing addressed to all qualified beneficiaries living at the same address will meet this obligation as long as it is clear from the COBRA notices in that mailing that each qualified beneficiary has a separate right to elect COBRA coverage.

Sources: 29 U.S.C. §1166; 29 C.F.R. §§2590.606-2 and -4.

Fig. 150-A

MODEL COBRA CONTINUATION COVERAGE ELECTION NOTICE
(For use by single-employer group health plans)

[*Enter date of notice*]

Dear: [*Identify the qualified beneficiary(ies), by name or status*]

This notice contains important information about your right to continue your health care coverage in the [*enter name of group health plan*] (the Plan). Please read the information contained in this notice very carefully.

To elect COBRA continuation coverage, follow the instructions on the next page to complete the enclosed Election Form and submit it to us.

If you do not elect COBRA continuation coverage, your coverage under the Plan will end on [*enter date*] due to [*check appropriate box*]:

☐ End of employment
☐ Death of employee
☐ Entitlement to Medicare
☐ Reduction in hours of employment
☐ Divorce or legal separation
☐ Loss of dependent child status

Each person ("qualified beneficiary") in the category(ies) checked below is entitled to elect COBRA continuation coverage, which will continue group health care coverage under the Plan for up to ___ months [*enter* 18 *or* 36, *as appropriate and check appropriate box or boxes; names may be added*]:

☐ Employee or former employee
☐ Spouse or former spouse
☐ Dependent child(ren) covered under the Plan on the day before the event that caused the loss of coverage
☐ Child who is losing coverage under the Plan because he or she is no longer a dependent under the Plan

If elected, COBRA continuation coverage will begin on [*enter date*] and can last until [*enter date*]. [*Add, if appropriate:* You may elect any of the following options for COBRA continuation coverage: [*list available coverage options*].

COBRA continuation coverage will cost: [*enter amount each qualified beneficiary will be required to pay for each option per month of coverage and any other permitted coverage periods.*] You do not have to send any payment with the Election Form. Important additional information about payment for COBRA continuation coverage is included in the pages following the Election Form.

If you have any questions about this notice or your rights to COBRA continuation coverage, you should contact [*enter name of party responsible for COBRA administration for the Plan, with telephone number and address*].

continued on next page

Fig. 150-A (cont.)

COBRA CONTINUATION COVERAGE ELECTION FORM

INSTRUCTIONS: To elect COBRA continuation coverage, complete this Election Form and return it to us. Under federal law, you must have 60 days after the date of this notice to decide whether you want to elect COBRA continuation coverage under the Plan.

Send completed Election Form to: [*Enter Name and Address*]

This Election Form must be completed and returned by mail [*or describe other means of submission and due date*]. If mailed, it must be post-marked no later than [*enter date*].

If you do not submit a completed Election Form by the due date shown above, you will lose your right to elect COBRA continuation coverage. If you reject COBRA continuation coverage before the due date, you may change your mind as long as you furnish a completed Election Form before the due date. However, if you change your mind after first rejecting COBRA continuation coverage, your COBRA continuation coverage will begin on the date you furnish the completed Election Form.

Read the important information about your rights included in the pages after the Election Form.

I (We) elect COBRA continuation coverage in the [*enter name of plan*] (the Plan) as indicated below:

Name Date of Birth Relationship to Employee SSN (or other identifier)

a. ______________________________

[*Add if appropriate:* Coverage option elected: ______________]

b. ______________________________

[*Add if appropriate:* Coverage option elected: ______________]

c. ______________________________

[*Add if appropriate:* Coverage option elected: ______________]

______________________ ______________________
Signature Date

______________________ ______________________
Print Name Relationship to individual(s) listed above

____
____
______________________ ______________________
Print Address Telephone number

continued on next page

Fig. 150-A (cont.)

IMPORTANT INFORMATION
ABOUT YOUR COBRA CONTINUATION COVERAGE RIGHTS

What is continuation coverage?

Federal law requires that most group health plans (including this Plan) give employees and their families the opportunity to continue their health care coverage when there is a "qualifying event" that would result in a loss of coverage under an employer's plan. Depending on the type of qualifying event, "qualified beneficiaries" can include the employee (or retired employee) covered under the group health plan, the covered employee's spouse, and the dependent children of the covered employee.

Continuation coverage is the same coverage that the Plan gives to other participants or beneficiaries under the Plan who are not receiving continuation coverage. Each qualified beneficiary who elects continuation coverage will have the same rights under the Plan as other participants or beneficiaries covered under the Plan, including [*add if applicable:* open enrollment and] special enrollment rights.

How long will continuation coverage last?

In the case of a loss of coverage due to end of employment or reduction in hours of employment, coverage generally may be continued only for up to a total of 18 months. In the case of losses of coverage due to an employee's death, divorce or legal separation, the employee's becoming entitled to Medicare benefits or a dependent child ceasing to be a dependent under the terms of the plan, coverage may be continued for up to a total of 36 months. When the qualifying event is the end of employment or reduction of the employee's hours of employment, and the employee became entitled to Medicare benefits less than 18 months before the qualifying event, COBRA continuation coverage for qualified beneficiaries other than the employee lasts until 36 months after the date of Medicare entitlement. This notice shows the maximum period of continuation coverage available to the qualified beneficiaries.

Continuation coverage will be terminated before the end of the maximum period if:

- any required premium is not paid in full on time,
- a qualified beneficiary becomes covered, after electing continuation coverage, under another group health plan that does not impose any pre-existing condition exclusion for a pre-existing condition of the qualified beneficiary,
- a qualified beneficiary becomes entitled to Medicare benefits (under Part A, Part B, or both) after electing continuation coverage, or
- the employer ceases to provide any group health plan for its employees.

Continuation coverage may also be terminated for any reason the Plan would terminate coverage of a participant or beneficiary not receiving continuation coverage (such as fraud).

[*If the maximum period shown on page 1 of this notice is less than 36 months, add the following three paragraphs:*]

continued on next page

FIG. 150-A (CONT.)

How can you extend the length of COBRA continuation coverage?

If you elect continuation coverage, an extension of the maximum period of coverage may be available if a qualified beneficiary is disabled or a second qualifying event occurs. You must notify [*enter name of party responsible for COBRA administration*] of a disability or a second qualifying event in order to extend the period of continuation coverage. Failure to provide notice of a disability or second qualifying event may affect the right to extend the period of continuation coverage.

Disability

An 11-month extension of coverage may be available if any of the qualified beneficiaries is determined by the Social Security Administration (SSA) to be disabled. The disability has to have started at some time before the 60th day of COBRA continuation coverage and must last at least until the end of the 18-month period of continuation coverage. [*Describe Plan provisions for requiring notice of disability determination, including time frames and procedures.*] Each qualified beneficiary who has elected continuation coverage will be entitled to the 11-month disability extension if one of them qualifies. If the qualified beneficiary is determined by SSA to no longer be disabled, you must notify the Plan of that fact within 30 days after SSA's determination.

Second Qualifying Event

An 18-month extension of coverage will be available to spouses and dependent children who elect continuation coverage if a second qualifying event occurs during the first 18 months of continuation coverage. The maximum amount of continuation coverage available when a second qualifying event occurs is 36 months. Such second qualifying events may include the death of a covered employee, divorce or separation from the covered employee, the covered employee's becoming entitled to Medicare benefits (under Part A, Part B, or both), or a dependent child's ceasing to be eligible for coverage as a dependent under the Plan. These events can be a second qualifying event only if they would have caused the qualified beneficiary to lose coverage under the Plan if the first qualifying event had not occurred. You must notify the Plan within 60 days after a second qualifying event occurs if you want to extend your continuation coverage.

How can you elect COBRA continuation coverage?

To elect continuation coverage, you must complete the Election Form and furnish it according to the directions on the form. Each qualified beneficiary has a separate right to elect continuation coverage. For example, the employee's spouse may elect continuation coverage even if the employee does not. Continuation coverage may be elected for only one, several, or for all dependent children who are qualified beneficiaries. A parent may elect to continue coverage on behalf of any dependent children. The employee or the employee's spouse can elect continuation coverage on behalf of all of the qualified beneficiaries.

continued on next page

Fig. 150-A (cont.)

In considering whether to elect continuation coverage, you should take into account that a failure to continue your group health coverage will affect your future rights under federal law. First, you can lose the right to avoid having pre-existing condition exclusions applied to you by other group health plans if you have more than a 63-day gap in health coverage, and election of continuation coverage may help you not have such a gap. Second, you will lose the guaranteed right to purchase individual health insurance policies that do not impose such pre-existing condition exclusions if you do not get continuation coverage for the maximum time available to you. Finally, you should take into account that you have special enrollment rights under federal law. You have the right to request special enrollment in another group health plan for which you are otherwise eligible (such as a plan sponsored by your spouse's employer) within 30 days after your group health coverage ends because of the qualifying event listed above. You will also have the same special enrollment right at the end of continuation coverage if you get continuation coverage for the maximum time available to you.

How much does COBRA continuation coverage cost?

Generally, each qualified beneficiary may be required to pay the entire cost of continuation coverage. The amount a qualified beneficiary may be required to pay may not exceed 102 percent (or, in the case of an extension of continuation coverage due to a disability, 150 percent) of the cost to the group health plan (including both employer and employee contributions) for coverage of a similarly situated plan participant or beneficiary who is not receiving continuation coverage. The required payment for each continuation coverage period for each option is described in this notice.

[*If employees might be eligible for trade adjustment assistance, the following information may be added*: The Trade Act of 2002 created a new tax credit for certain individuals who become eligible for trade adjustment assistance and for certain retired employees who are receiving pension payments from the Pension Benefit Guaranty Corporation (PBGC) (eligible individuals). Under the new tax provisions, eligible individuals can either take a tax credit or get advance payment of 65% of premiums paid for qualified health insurance, including continuation coverage. If you have questions about these new tax provisions, you may call the Health Coverage Tax Credit Customer Contact Center toll-free at 1-866-628-4282. TTD/TTY callers may call toll-free at 1-866-626-4282. More information about the Trade Act is also available at www.doleta.gov/tradeact/2002act_index.asp.

When and how must payment for COBRA continuation coverage be made?

First payment for continuation coverage

If you elect continuation coverage, you do not have to send any payment with the Election Form. However, you must make your first payment for continuation coverage not later than 45 days after the date of your election. (This is the date the Election Notice is post-marked, if mailed.) If you do not make your first payment for continuation coverage in full not later than 45 days after the date of your election, you will lose all continuation coverage rights under the Plan. You are responsible for making sure that the amount of your first payment is correct. You may contact

continued on next page

Fig. 150-A (cont.)

[*enter appropriate contact information, e.g., the Plan Administrator or other party responsible for COBRA administration under the Plan*] to confirm the correct amount of your first payment.

Periodic payments for continuation coverage

After you make your first payment for continuation coverage, you will be required to make periodic payments for each subsequent coverage period. The amount due for each coverage period for each qualified beneficiary is shown in this notice. The periodic payments can be made on a monthly basis. Under the Plan, each of these periodic payments for continuation coverage is due on the [*enter due day for each monthly payment*] for that coverage period. [*If Plan offers other payment schedules, enter with appropriate dates:* You may instead make payments for continuation coverage for the following coverage periods, due on the following dates:]. If you make a periodic payment on or before the first day of the coverage period to which it applies, your coverage under the Plan will continue for that coverage period without any break. The Plan [*select one:* will *or* will not] send periodic notices of payments due for these coverage periods.

Grace periods for periodic payments

Although periodic payments are due on the dates shown above, you will be given a grace period of 30 days after the first day of the coverage period [*or enter longer period permitted by Plan*] to make each periodic payment. Your continuation coverage will be provided for each coverage period as long as payment for that coverage period is made before the end of the grace period for that payment. [*If Plan suspends coverage during grace period for nonpayment, enter and modify as necessary:* However, if you pay a periodic payment later than the first day of the coverage period to which it applies, but before the end of the grace period for the coverage period, your coverage under the Plan will be suspended as of the first day of the coverage period and then retroactively reinstated (going back to the first day of the coverage period) when the periodic payment is received. This means that any claim you submit for benefits while your coverage is suspended may be denied and may have to be resubmitted once your coverage is reinstated.]

If you fail to make a periodic payment before the end of the grace period for that coverage period, you will lose all rights to continuation coverage under the Plan.

Your first payment and all periodic payments for continuation coverage should be sent to:

[*enter appropriate payment address*]

For more information

This notice does not fully describe continuation coverage or other rights under the Plan. More information about continuation coverage and your rights under the Plan is available in your summary plan description or from the Plan Administrator.

If you have any questions concerning the information in this notice, your rights to coverage, or if you want a copy of your summary plan description, you should contact [*enter name of party responsible for COBRA administration for the Plan, with telephone number and address*].

continued on next page

Fig. 150-A (cont.)

For more information about your rights under ERISA, including COBRA, the Health Insurance Portability and Accountability Act (HIPAA), and other laws affecting group health plans, contact the U.S. Department of Labor's Employee Benefits Security Administration (EBSA) in your area or visit the EBSA website at www.dol.gov/ebsa. (Addresses and phone numbers of Regional and District EBSA Offices are available through EBSA's website.)

Keep Your Plan Informed of Address Changes

In order to protect your and your family's rights, you should keep the Plan Administrator informed of any changes in your address and the addresses of family members. You should also keep a copy, for your records, of any notices you send to the Plan Administrator.

151. Q: What is a COBRA "qualifying event"?

A: A "qualifying event" is defined as any of the following events that cause a loss of health insurance coverage:

For covered employees:

- termination of employment (other than for gross misconduct) or reduction in hours of employment.

For spouses or dependent children:

- the covered employee's termination of employment (other than for gross misconduct) or reduction in hours of employment;
- the covered employee's death;
- a divorce or legal separation of a spouse from a covered employee;
- a covered employee's entitlement to Medicare; or
- a child's loss of dependent status.

For retirees, their spouses and dependent children:

- the start of a bankruptcy proceeding.

The occurrence of one of these events does not in itself create any COBRA rights. For COBRA to apply, the event must cause a qualified beneficiary to lose coverage. For example, if retirement does not cause an employee or the employee's spouse or dependent children to lose coverage before the end of the maximum period of coverage under COBRA, that retirement is not a qualifying event. (Sample notices of some qualifying events begin with Fig. 151-A.)

Source: 26 C.F.R. §54.4980B-4.

FIG. 151-A

Employer Notice to Plan Administrator of a Qualifying Event for COBRA Coverage

[If the qualifying event is the employer's bankruptcy filing or the covered employee's termination (other than by reason of gross misconduct) or reduction in hours of employment, death, or Medicare entitlement, the employer must notify the plan administrator of the event within 30 days. This assumes that the employer and the plan administrator are separate entities.]

Date of Notice: ___________

FROM: EMPLOYER **TO:** PLAN ADMINISTRATOR

Address: ______________________

____

Plan Name/Group #:_______________

Name: Last, First, Middle **Social Security Number**

Home Address **Street** **City** **State** **Zip**

Date of Birth: __/__/__ **Marital Status:** **Single** **Married**

No. of Dependent Children: _____ **Date of Hire:** __/__/__

On____(date)_____, the above qualified beneficiary incurred the following "qualifying event" that caused the qualified beneficiary to lose group health coverage under the Plan for purposes of COBRA continuation coverage:

Termination of employment

Reduction in hours of employment due to (reason:_____________________)

Death of employee

Employee's Medicare entitlement

Start of bankruptcy proceeding

Divorce or legal separation from employee

Cessation of dependent child status

Policy Number:_____________________________________

Type of Coverage: _________ _________ _________ Other__________

Level of Coverage: Single____ Family______ Other______

Dependent on plan, if any:

Name ____ Relationship:______________

Coverage under the plan will terminate on __________. Please send the aforementioned person (and his or her spouse and dependent child(ren), if any) the appropriate election notices and forms for COBRA continuation coverage within 14 days of the receipt of this notice, as required under COBRA.

Signature:_________________________________Title:________________

FIG. 151-B

Employee/Qualified Beneficiary Notice to Plan Administrator of a Multiple Qualifying Event for COBRA Coverage

Date of Notice: ____________

FROM: ______________________ **TO:** PLAN ADMINISTRATOR

Address: ______________________

____

Plan Name/Group #: ____________

Qualified Beneficiary Information

Name: Last, First, Middle **Social Security Number**

Home Address **Street** **City** **State** **Zip**

Date of Birth: __/__/__

No. of Dependent Children: _____

Marital Status: ❒ **Single** ❒ **Married**

Date of Hire: __/__/__

COBRA Qualifying Event Information

On______(date)________, the above-referenced qualified beneficiary incurred the following second or multiple "qualifying event" which would entitle the qualified beneficiary to extend COBRA continuation coverage under the Plan for a total of up to 36 months of COBRA continuation coverage measured from the date of the first qualifying event (the original termination or reduction in hours of employment):

❒ Termination of employment
❒ Reduction in hours of employment due to (reason:________________)
❒ Death of employee
❒ Employee's Medicare entitlement
❒ Divorce from employee
❒ Legal separation from employee
❒ Cessation of dependent child status

NOTE: These events can be a second qualifying event only if they would have caused the qualified beneficiary to lose coverage under the Plan if the first qualifying event had not occurred. You must notify the Plan within 60 days after a second qualifying event occurs if you want to extend your continuation coverage. If you do not provide this notice within 60 days after the second qualifying event occurs, you will not be entitled to any extension of COBRA continuation coverage.

Signature:________________Name (please print):________________Date:________

Fig. 151-C

Employee/Qualified Beneficiary Notice to Plan Administrator of a Qualifying Event for COBRA Coverage

Date of Notice:____________

FROM: ______________________________ **TO:** PLAN ADMINISTRATOR

Address: ________________________

____

Plan Name/Group #:____________

Qualified Beneficiary Information

Name: Last, First, Middle **Social Security Number**

____

Home Address **Street** **City** **State** **Zip**

____

Date of Birth: ___/___/___ **Marital Status:** ❒ **Single** ❒ **Married**

No. of Dependent Children: _____ **Date of Hire:** ___/___/___

COBRA Qualifying Event Information

On_______(date)_________, the above-referenced qualified beneficiary incurred the following "qualifying event" which caused the qualified beneficiary to lose group health coverage under the Plan for purposes of COBRA continuation coverage:

❒ Divorce from employee
❒ Legal separation from employee
❒ Cessation of dependent child status

NOTE: You must notify the Plan within 60 days after a qualifying event occurs if you want to elect COBRA continuation coverage. If you do not provide this notice within 60 days after the qualifying event occurs, you will not be entitled to any COBRA continuation coverage.

Coverage under the plan [*Choose ONE:* will terminate/has terminated] on ____________. Please send the appropriate COBRA election notices and forms for COBRA continuation coverage within 14 days of the receipt of this notice, as required under COBRA.

Signature:__________________Name (please print):________________Date:__________

152. Q: What is a COBRA election?

A: Although a covered employer must provide COBRA coverage, in large part because the employee has to pay for the coverage (102 percent of the premium) the employee (now called a "qualified beneficiary") has the option of electing to be covered under COBRA.

The general rule is that the qualified beneficiary always has 60 days from the loss of coverage date to elect COBRA coverage. However, if the plan administrator provides a qualifying event notice after the loss of coverage date, the qualified beneficiary has 60 days from the notice date to elect COBRA coverage.

For example, let's say coverage ends immediately on termination of employment and the employee terminates employment on March 1. The employer has until March 31 to notify the plan administrator. From this date, the plan administrator has 14 days to notify the former employee of his or her rights. The ex-employee then has 60 days from the date of the plan administrator's notice to elect COBRA coverage. (See Fig. 152-A for a chart showing COBRA notice timeframes.)

Sources: 29 U.S.C. §1165; 26 C.F.R. §54.4980B-6.

FIG. 152-A

COBRA Notification Timeframes

(Note: Multi-employer plans may extend the 14- and 30-day notice periods.)

Scenario 1: Qualifying Event and Loss of Coverage on Same Day, All COBRA Periods Measured From That Date

Qualifying Events: Covered Employee's Termination/Reduction in Hours/Death

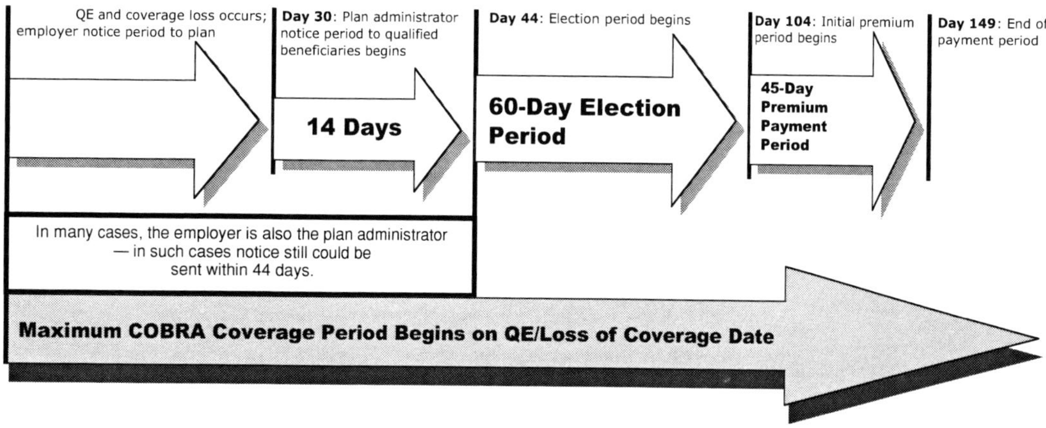

Qualifying Events: Divorce or Legal Separation/Cessation of Dependent Status

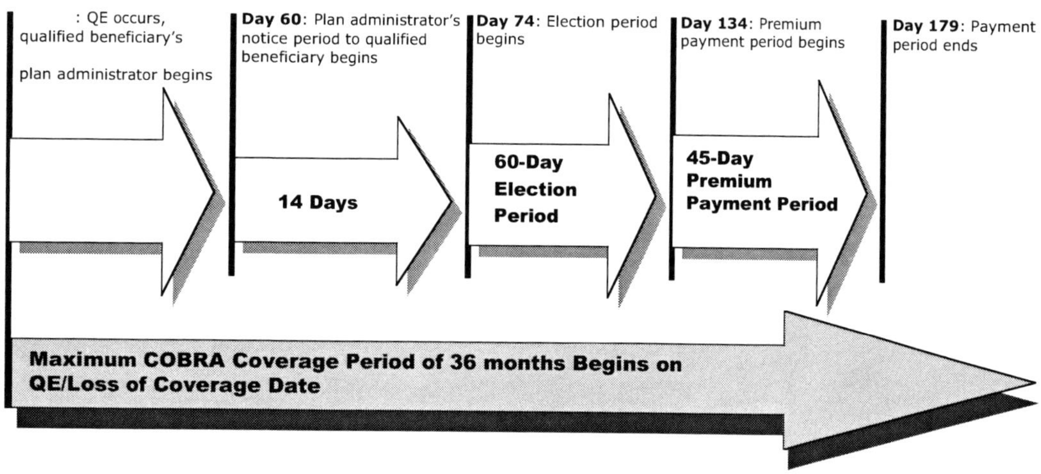

continued on next page

FIG. 152-A (CONT.)

Scenario 2: Loss of Coverage Occurs 30 Days After Qualifying Event, Coverage Period Measured From Qualifying Event Date

Qualifying Events: Covered Employee's Termination/Reduction in Hours/Death

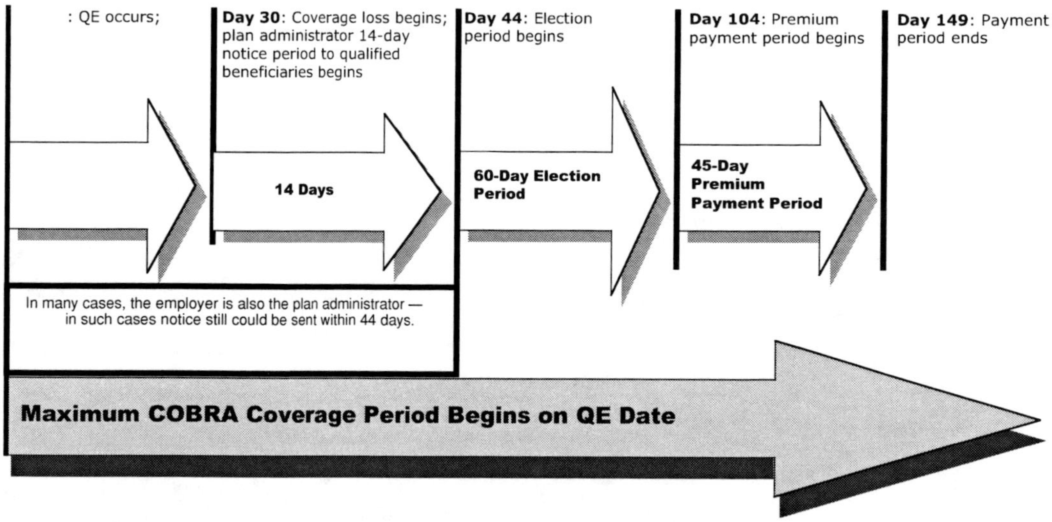

Scenario 3: Loss of Coverage Occurs 30 Days After Qualifying Event, All Notice and Coverage Periods Measured From the Coverage Loss Date

Qualifying Events: Termination/Reduction in Hours/Death

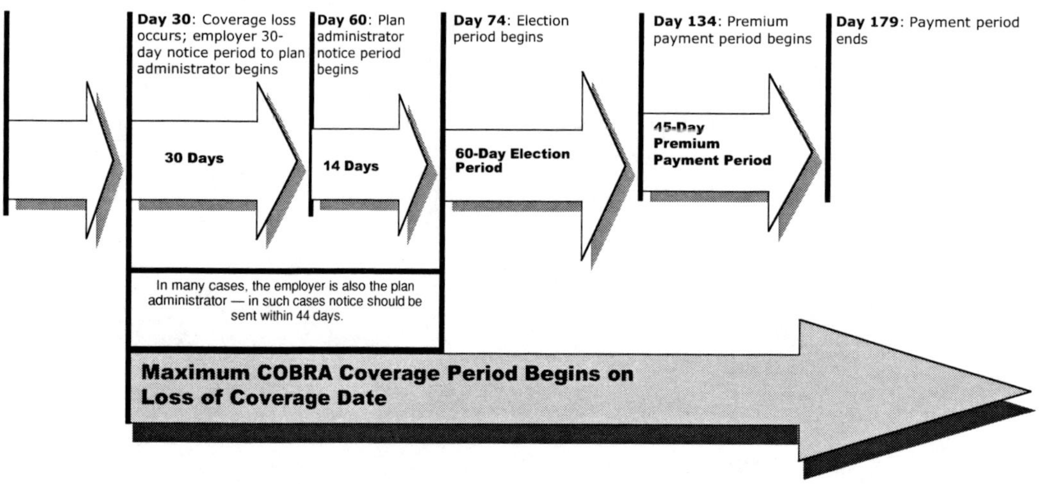

153. Q: Do we have to offer COBRA coverage to employees' domestic partners who have enrolled in our health plan?

A: Generally domestic partners and same-gender spouses cannot qualify as "spouses" under federal law. Therefore, you are not required to provide COBRA coverage to them. However, you could choose to draft your plan to provide COBRA-like rights to those individuals.

Sources: 29 U.S.C. §1167; 26 C.F.R. §54.4980B-3.

154. Q: If I eliminate all of my health care options and provide only an HMO, can I limit coverage for qualified beneficiaries who are receiving COBRA coverage under the old plan? If I cancel all of my health care plans, can I cancel the people on COBRA too?

A: Yes, but be careful. If the HMO is offered by a new company, many potential insurers only want to cover active employees.

Unfortunately, because you and the insurer are not yet under a contract, you may find it difficult to require potential insurers to cover qualified beneficiaries. Because you have the ultimate responsibility to provide coverage, make sure you can do so for qualified beneficiaries covered under the current plan.

If you terminate all health care coverage, you may terminate coverage for qualified beneficiaries who are covered by your existing plan. However, if active employees are either covered under another group health plan or are permitted to switch coverage to other plans you offer, qualified beneficiaries who were covered under the terminated plan must be allowed those same rights.

Sources: 29 U.S.C. §1162; 26 C.F.R. §§54.4980B-5 and B-7.

155. Q: Is there a way to get our retirees off COBRA and onto Medicare? We are looking for ways to reduce our exposure to higher health care premiums.

A: There are rules and they are a little complicated. One big issue is when someone is eligible for Medicare and entitled to Medicare. Another issue is if the entitlement occurs after the date of the COBRA election.

Under COBRA, a *qualified* beneficiary is ineligible for COBRA coverage only when he or she becomes entitled to Medicare – not just eligible for Medicare – after the date of the COBRA election.

"Entitled" essentially means that a qualified beneficiary is covered under Medicare. Persons who are covered under Medicare will have applied for coverage – either directly or indirectly by reaching age 65 and applying for Social Security income benefits – and may be paying premiums for that coverage.

Someone who has turned 65 and is eligible for Medicare will not necessarily be entitled to it. This means that the retiree has the option of retaining COBRA coverage or enrolling in Medicare.

Sources: 29 U.S.C. §1162; 26 C.F.R. §54.4980B-7.

156. Q: Are we required to send COBRA election notices to employees when they retire? We automatically offer all these people a retiree plan.

A: Generally, if coverage under the retiree plan is not identical to COBRA coverage, an employee must be given the opportunity to elect COBRA at the same time the retiree plan is offered. If the retiree plan is identical to COBRA coverage, the employer has two basic choices.

It could:

1. Provide an election notice within the required time period after the termination of employment begins. In that case, the retiree plan and COBRA coverage would run concurrently.
2. Provide an election notice after coverage under the retiree plan ends. In this instance coverage under COBRA and your retiree plan would run consecutively.

Sources: 29 U.S.C. §1162; 26 C.F.R. §§54.4980B-4 and B-5.

157. Q: Must we provide COBRA coverage to an employee while she is out on family and medical leave?

A: The Family and Medical Leave Act (FMLA) and IRS final COBRA regulations provide that family and medical leave is not a qualifying event. You are required to permit the employee to continue whatever group health insurance you offer at the same premiums she would pay if not on leave. (See Q. 121 for the FMLA's requirements.)

However, if the employee does not or cannot return to work when the protected leave period ends, the COBRA coverage period begins on that date, even if the affected individual is not covered under the plan at that time.

Source: 26 C.F.R. §54.4980B-10.

158. Q: How can I check to see if an employee on COBRA has enrolled in another employer's plan? If this is true, I want to get him off our plan.

A: This is one of the biggest problems under COBRA. No sure way exists of checking for subsequent coverage.

Some employers periodically send a letter to qualified beneficiaries requesting such information. Others provide qualified beneficiaries with a series of 18 or 36 identical coupons attesting to their lack of other group coverage. The beneficiaries are then required to provide a signed coupon each month along with their premium payments.

A check for other coverage may also be made when a claim is filed and coordination-of-benefits information is gathered.

Sources: 29 U.S.C. §1162; 26 C.F.R. §54.4980B-7.

159. Q: What types of notice must an employee or other qualified beneficiary provide to a plan administrator under COBRA?

A: A qualified beneficiary must provide notice to the plan administrator when any of the following events occurs:

1. divorce or legal separation from the covered employee;
2. the cessation of dependent child status under the plan;
3. a Social Security Administration determination of an individual's disability within the first 60 days of COBRA coverage; or
4. a Social Security Administration determination of cessation of disability.

Sources: 29 U.S.C. §1166; 29 C.F.R. §2590.606-3.

HIPAA

160. Q: What is the Health Insurance Portability and Accountability Act (HIPAA)?

A: HIPAA amended the Employee Retirement Income Security Act (ERISA) to provide new rights and protections for participants and beneficiaries in group health plans.

There are two parts to HIPAA. One is designed to assist employees in maintaining health insurance coverage if they change jobs (portability). The other is designed to ensure that an employee's personal health information is protected (accountability). For the employer, it is important to know what you must do in each situation.

> **Sources:** 29 U.S.C. §1181 et seq.; 42 U.S.C. §§1320a-7a, and d et seq. Pub. L. 104-191.

161. Q: How do the portability provisions work?

A: If you have a health plan and an employee in the plan leaves, you must provide him or her (or covered dependents) with a "certificate of coverage," stating how long the individual has been continuously covered by the plan (see model form Fig. 161-A).

The period of coverage is called "creditable coverage" in HIPAA. You must provide the certificate. You should have procedures to provide the certificate automatically to employees who lose coverage under the plan or otherwise become entitled to elect COBRA continuation coverage, and again when COBRA continuation coverage ceases.

A certificate may also be requested (and must be provided free of charge) for 24 months after the date coverage ends. When you are the employer hiring a new employee you should ask about the certificate and the employee should be able to obtain one if coverage ended no more than 24 months previously. HIPAA also requires that no employee or dependent can be denied health insurance because of his or her health status.

> **Sources:** 29 U.S.C. §1181(e); 29 C.F.R. §2590.701-5.

Fig. 161-A

Certificate of Group Health Plan Coverage

Note: Separate certificates should be furnished if information is not identical for the participant and each dependent.

1. Date of this certificate: ____________________
2. Name of group health plan: ____________________
3. Name of participant: ____________________
4. Identification number of participant: ____________________
5. Name of individuals to whom this certificate applies: ____________________
6. Name, address, and telephone number of plan administrator or issuer responsible for providing this certificate:

   ____

   ____

   ____
7. For further information, call: ____________________
8. If the individual(s) identified in line 5 has (have) at least 18 months of creditable coverage (disregarding periods of coverage before a 63-day break), check here _____ and skip lines 9 and 10.
9. Date waiting period or affiliation period (if any) began: ____________________
10. Date coverage began: ____________________
11. Date coverage ended (or if coverage is continuing as of the date of this certificate, enter "continuing"): __________.

continued on next page

Fig. 161-A (cont.)

Statement of HIPAA Portability Rights

[*Editor's Note: The shaded text represents proposed language.*]

IMPORTANT — KEEP THIS CERTIFICATE. This certificate is evidence of your coverage under this plan. Under a federal law known as HIPAA, you may need evidence of your coverage to reduce a pre-existing condition exclusion period under another plan, to help you get special enrollment in another plan, or to get certain types of individual health coverage even if you have health problems.

Pre-existing condition exclusions. Some group health plans restrict coverage for medical conditions present before an individual's enrollment. These restrictions are known as "pre-existing condition exclusions." A pre-existing condition exclusion can apply only to conditions for which medical advice, diagnosis, care or treatment was recommended or received within the six months before your "enrollment date." Your enrollment date is your first day of coverage under the plan, or, if there is a waiting period, the first day of your waiting period (typically, your first day of work). In addition, a pre-existing condition exclusion cannot last for more than 12 months after your enrollment date (18 months if you are a late enrollee). Finally, a pre-existing condition exclusion cannot apply to pregnancy and cannot apply to a child who is enrolled in health coverage within 30 days after birth, adoption or placement for adoption.

If a plan imposes a pre-existing condition exclusion, the length of the exclusion must be reduced by the amount of your prior creditable coverage. Most health coverage is creditable coverage, including group health plan coverage, COBRA continuation coverage, coverage under an individual health policy, Medicare, Medicaid, State Children's Health Insurance Program (SCHIP), and coverage through high-risk pools and the Peace Corps. Not all forms of creditable coverage are required to provide certificates like this one. If you do not receive a certificate for past coverage, talk to your new plan administrator.

You can add up any creditable coverage you have, including the coverage shown on this certificate. However, if at any time you went for 63 days or more without any coverage (called a break in coverage) a plan may not have to count the coverage you had before the break.

➡ Therefore, once your coverage ends, you should try to obtain alternative coverage as soon as possible to avoid a 63-day break. You may use this certificate as evidence of your creditable coverage to reduce the length of any pre-existing condition exclusion if you enroll in another plan.

Right to get special enrollment in another plan. Under HIPAA, if you lose your group health plan coverage, you may be able to get into another group health plan for which you are eligible (such as a spouse's plan), even if the plan generally does not accept late enrollees, if you request enrollment within 30 days. (Additional special enrollment rights are triggered by marriage, birth, adoption and placement for adoption.)

➡ Therefore, once your coverage ends, if you are eligible for coverage in another plan (such as a spouse's plan), you should request special enrollment as soon as possible.

continued on next page

FIG. 161-A (CONT.)

Prohibition against discrimination based on a health factor. Under HIPAA, a group health plan may not keep you (or your dependents) out of the plan based on anything related to your health. Also, a group health plan may not charge you (or your dependents) more for coverage, based on health, than the amount charged a similarly situated individual.

Right to individual health coverage. Under HIPAA, if you are an "eligible individual," you have a right to buy certain individual health policies (or in some states, to buy coverage through a high-risk pool) without a pre-existing condition exclusion. To be an eligible individual, you must meet the following requirements:

- you have had coverage for at least 18 months without a break in coverage of 63 days or more;
- your most recent coverage was under a group health plan (which can be shown by this certificate);
- your group coverage was not terminated because of fraud or nonpayment of premiums;
- you are not eligible for COBRA continuation coverage or you have exhausted your COBRA benefits (or continuation coverage under a similar state provision); and
- you are not eligible for another group health plan, Medicare or Medicaid, and do not have any other health insurance coverage.

The right to buy individual coverage is the same whether you are laid off, fired or quit your job.

➡ Therefore, if you are interested in obtaining individual coverage and you meet the other criteria to be an eligible individual, you should apply for this coverage as soon as possible to avoid losing your eligible individual status due to a 63-day break.

Special information for people on FMLA leave. If you are taking leave under the Family and Medical Leave Act (FMLA) and you drop health coverage during your leave, any days without health coverage while on FMLA leave will not count towards a 63-day break in coverage. In addition, if you do not return from leave, the 30-day period to request special enrollment in another plan will not start before your FMLA leave ends.

➡ Therefore, when you apply for other health coverage, you should tell your plan administrator or health insurer about any prior FMLA leave.

State flexibility. This certificate describes minimum HIPAA protections under federal law. States may require insurers and HMOs to provide additional protections to individuals in that state.

For more information. If you have questions about your HIPAA rights, you may contact your state insurance department or the U.S. Department of Labor, Employee Benefits Security Administration (EBSA) toll-free at 1-866-444-3272 (for free HIPAA publications ask for publications concerning changes in health care laws). You may also contact the CMS publication hotline at 1-800-633-4227 (ask for "Protecting Your Health Insurance Coverage"). These publications and other useful information are also available on the Internet at: http://www.dol.gov/ebsa, the DOL's interactive Web pages — Health Elaws, or http://www.cms.hhs.gov/hipaageninfo.

162. Q: What is the certificate for and why does the length of creditable coverage matter?

A: This is where the portability comes in. A health plan may exclude pre-existing conditions for up to 12-months (and up to 18 months for late enrollees). However, if a departing (or arriving) employee gets reemployed within 63 days of losing coverage, the period of creditable coverage counts against the pre-existing conditions exclusion period. So, if the employee has 12 months or more of creditable coverage, the exclusion period has been satisfied.

Up to 18 months of creditable coverage is counted against the exclusion period, so any creditable coverage is important to list on the certificate. However, you should not list more than 18 months of continuous coverage.

Sources: 29 C.F.R. §§2590.701-3 and -4(b).

163. Q: Are we allowed to have a waiting period before an employee can enroll? If so, how does that factor in with the creditable coverage and break-in-service rules?

A: If your plan has a waiting period prior to enrollment, days in a waiting period during which the employee has no other coverage are not creditable coverage under the plan, but these days are not taken into account when counting whether a 63-day-break in coverage has occurred. This length of the break period may be different under state law. If the state law time period is more generous than the federal 63 days, you should use the state law provision.

Sources: 29 C.F.R. §§2590.701-4(b)(2)(i) and (iv).

164. Q: If a new employee is currently on COBRA through her former employer's plan, does that count as creditable coverage?

A: Yes. Under HIPAA any period of time that you are receiving COBRA continuation coverage is counted as previous health coverage, as long as the coverage occurred without a break of 63 days or more.

For example, if you were covered continuously for five months by a previous health plan and then received seven months of COBRA continuation coverage, you would be entitled to receive credit for 12 months of coverage by your new group health plan.

Sources: DOL Employee Benefits Security Administration, Health Benefits Coverage Under Federal Law, p. 11; see http://www.dol.gov/ebsa/compliance_assistance.html.

165. Q: What is a pre-existing condition?

A: It has a special definition under HIPAA. The only pre-existing conditions that may be excluded under a pre-existing condition exclusion for HIPAA purposes are those for which medical advise, diagnosis, care or treatment was recommended or received within the six-month period before your enrollment date. (Your enrollment date is your first day of coverage, or if there is a waiting period to get into the plan, the first day of the waiting period.)

If you had a medical condition in the past, but have *not* received any medical advice, diagnosis, care or treatment within the six months prior to your enrollment date in the plan, the old condition is not a pre-existing condition to which an exclusion can be applied. Moreover, under HIPAA, pre-existing condition exclusions cannot be applied to pregnancy, regardless of whether the woman had previous health coverage.

In addition, a pre-existing condition exclusion cannot be applied to a newborn, an adopted child under age 18, or a child under age 18 placed for adoption as long as the child became covered under health coverage within 30 days of the birth, adoption or placement for adoption and provided that the child does not incur a subsequent 63-day break in coverage.

Finally, genetic information may not be treated as a pre-existing condition in the absence of a diagnosis. If your coverage is through an insurance company or offered through an HMO, state law may provide additional protections.

Sources: 29 C.F.R. §§2590.701-3(a) and (b).

HIPAA Security/Accountability

166. Q: What does HIPAA require me to do to protect our employees' medical information?

A: Let's start with a technicality. HIPAA regulates the conduct of health plans and plan sponsors – who are usually the employer – but not the employer itself. This is the source of a lot of the confusing language in HIPAA and a lot of confusion about the law. If you are the plan sponsor, when you read materials about HIPAA if you find instructions for plans and plan sponsors, just recognize they are almost always talking about you.

Your question about protecting employees' privacy is a critical one, because much of HIPAA is concerned with keeping health information confidential. The first thing you must do is have written privacy procedures, including a description of staff that has access to protected information, how it will be used and when it may be disclosed.

In our sample notice, you will see a reference to the *authorized* use of personal health information. You must get the employee's permission to disclose personal health information when it is for a purpose not expressly permitted in the law.

You do *not* need authorization to disclose health information for purposes of treatment, to pay for health care services or to complete official government reports such as public health reports and police reports. You are also permitted to disclose health information to family or pre-identified others who may be assisting the employee in taking care of health care bills. Other disclosures require a signed authorization.

See the sample Notice of Privacy Practices for Protected Health Information, Fig. 166-A, and the sample Authorization Form, Fig. 166-B.

Sources: 29 U.S.C. §1181 et seq.; 43 C.F.R. §164.302 et seq.; 45 C.F.R. §164.500 *et seq.*

FIG. 166-A

Notice of Privacy Practices for Protected Health Information

HIPAA's privacy rules require covered entities to provide individuals with a "notice of information practices." Special rules also require group health plans to give notices to plan participants and, in certain cases, allocate that responsibility to health insurance issuers. Generally, the notice must describe: (1) the uses and disclosures of protected health information (PHI) that a covered entity may make; (2) an individual's rights; and (3) a covered entity's responsibilities.

The sample notice below is drafted for a self-insured group health plan that is not subject to state medical privacy laws. Group health plans that are subject to state law may have more stringent requirements that also must be described in the notice.

* * * *

NOTICE OF PRIVACY PRACTICES

[Note: The following header is required and must be prominently displayed. 45 CFR §164.520(b)(1)(i).]

THIS NOTICE DESCRIBES HOW MEDICAL INFORMATION ABOUT YOU MAY BE USED AND DISCLOSED AND HOW YOU CAN GET ACCESS TO THIS INFORMATION. PLEASE REVIEW IT CAREFULLY.

Effective Date of Notice: [The effective date must be the same as or later than the date of publication.]

The [Name of Group Health Plan] (the "Plan") is required by law to take reasonable steps to ensure the privacy of your personally identifiable health information and to inform you about:

- the Plan's uses and disclosures of Protected Health Information (PHI);
- your privacy rights with respect to your PHI;
- the Plan's duties with respect to your PHI;
- your right to file a complaint with the Plan and to the Secretary of the U.S. Department of Health and Human Services; and
- the person or office to contact for further information about the Plan's privacy practices.

The term "Protected Health Information" (PHI) includes all individually identifiable health information transmitted or maintained by the Plan, regardless of form (oral, written, electronic).

Section 1. Notice of PHI Uses and Disclosures

Required PHI Uses and Disclosures

Upon your request, the Plan is required to give you access to certain PHI in order to inspect and copy it.

Use and disclosure of your PHI may be required by the Secretary of the Department of Health and Human Services to investigate or determine the Plan's compliance with the privacy regulations.

Uses and disclosures to carry out treatment, payment and health care operations

The Plan and its business associates will use PHI without your consent, authorization or opportunity to agree or object to carry out treatment, payment and health care operations. The Plan also will disclose PHI to the Plan Sponsor [Name of Plan Sponsor] for purposes related to treatment, payment and health care operations. The Plan Sponsor has amended its plan documents to protect your PHI as required by federal law.

Treatment is the provision, coordination or management of health care and related services. It also includes but is not limited to consultations and referrals between one or more of your providers.

For example, the Plan may disclose to a treating orthodontist the name of your treating dentist so that the orthodontist may ask for your dental X-rays from the treating dentist.

Payment includes but is not limited to actions to make coverage determinations and payment (including billing, claims management, subrogation, plan reimbursement, reviews for medical necessity and appropriateness of care and utilization review and preauthorizations).

For example, the Plan may tell a doctor whether you are eligible for coverage or what percentage of the bill will be paid by the Plan.

Health care operations include but are not limited to quality assessment and improvement, reviewing competence or qualifications of health care professionals, underwriting, premium rating and other insurance activities relating to creating or renewing insurance contracts. It also includes disease management, case management, conducting or arranging for medical review, legal services and auditing functions including fraud and abuse compliance programs, business planning and development, business management and general administrative activities.

For example, the Plan may use information about your claims to refer you to a disease management program, project future benefit costs or audit the accuracy of its claims processing functions.

HIDE-AD57

continued on next page

FIG. 166-A (CONT.)

Uses and disclosures that require your written authorization

Your written authorization generally will be obtained before the Plan will use or disclose psychotherapy notes about you from your psychotherapist. Psychotherapy notes are separately filed notes about your conversations with your mental health professional during a counseling session. They do not include summary information about your mental health treatment. The Plan may use and disclose such notes when needed by the Plan to defend against litigation filed by you.

Uses and disclosures that require that you be given an opportunity to agree or disagree prior to the use or release

Disclosure of your PHI to family members, other relatives and your close personal friends is allowed if:

- the information is directly relevant to the family or friend's involvement with your care or payment for that care; and
- you have either agreed to the disclosure or have been given an opportunity to object and have not objected.

Uses and disclosures for which consent, authorization or opportunity to object is not required

Use and disclosure of your PHI is allowed without your consent, authorization or request under the following circumstances:

(1) When required by law.

(2) When permitted for purposes of public health activities, including when necessary to report product defects, to permit product recalls and to conduct post-marketing surveillance. PHI may also be used or disclosed if you have been exposed to a communicable disease or are at risk of spreading a disease or condition, if authorized by law.

(3) When authorized by law to report information about abuse, neglect or domestic violence to public authorities if there exists a reasonable belief that you may be a victim of abuse, neglect or domestic violence. In such case, the Plan will promptly inform you that such a disclosure has been or will be made unless that notice would cause a risk of serious harm. For the purpose of reporting child abuse or neglect, it is not necessary to inform the minor that such a disclosure has been or will be made. Disclosure may generally be made to the minor's parents or other representatives although there may be circumstances under federal or state law when the parents or other representatives may not be given access to the minor's PHI.

(4) The Plan may disclose your PHI to a public health oversight agency for oversight activities authorized by law. This includes uses or disclosures in civil, administrative or criminal investigations; inspections; licensure or disciplinary actions (for example, to investigate complaints against providers); and other activities necessary for appropriate oversight of government benefit programs (for example, to investigate Medicare or Medicaid fraud).

(5) The Plan may disclose your PHI when required for judicial or administrative proceedings. For example, your PHI may be disclosed in response to a subpoena or discovery request provided certain conditions are met. One of those conditions is that satisfactory assurances must be given to the Plan that the requesting party has made a good faith attempt to provide written notice to you, and the notice provided sufficient information about the proceeding to permit you to raise an objection and no objections were raised or were resolved in favor of disclosure by the court or tribunal.

(6) When required for law enforcement purposes (for example, to report certain types of wounds).

(7) For law enforcement purposes, including for the purpose of identifying or locating a suspect, fugitive, material witness or missing person. Also, when disclosing information about an individual who is or is suspected to be a victim of a crime but only if the individual agrees to the disclosure or the covered entity is unable to obtain the individual's agreement because of emergency circumstances. Furthermore, the law enforcement official must represent that the information is not intended to be used against the individual, the immediate law enforcement activity would be materially and adversely affected by waiting to obtain the individual's agreement and disclosure is in the best interest of the individual as determined by the exercise of the Plan's best judgment.

(8) When required to be given to a coroner or medical examiner for the purpose of identifying a deceased person, determining a cause of death or other duties as authorized by law. Also, disclosure is permitted to funeral directors, consistent with applicable law, as necessary to carry out their duties with respect to the decedent.

(9) The Plan may use or disclose PHI for research, subject to conditions.

(10) When consistent with applicable law and standards of ethical conduct if the Plan, in good faith, believes the use or disclosure is necessary to prevent or lessen a serious and imminent threat to the health or safety of a person or the public and the disclosure is to a person reasonably able to prevent or lessen the threat, including the target of the threat.

(11) When authorized by and to the extent necessary to comply with workers' compensation or other similar programs established by law.

Except as otherwise indicated in this notice, uses and disclosures will be made only with your written authorization subject to your right to revoke such authorization.

continued on next page

FIG. 166-A (CONT.)

Section 2. Rights of Individuals

Right to Request Restrictions on PHI Uses and Disclosures

You may request the Plan to restrict uses and disclosures of your PHI to carry out treatment, payment or health care operations, or to restrict uses and disclosures to family members, relatives, friends or other persons identified by you who are involved in your care or payment for your care. However, the Plan is not required to agree to your request.

The Plan will accommodate reasonable requests to receive communications of PHI by alternative means or at alternative locations.

You or your personal representative will be required to complete a form to request restrictions on uses and disclosures of your PHI.

Such requests should be made to the following officer: [insert name or title of person or office responsible for managing requests, telephone number and address].

Right to Inspect and Copy PHI

You have a right to inspect and obtain a copy of your PHI contained in a "designated record set," for as long as the Plan maintains the PHI.

"Protected Health Information" (PHI) includes all individually identifiable health information transmitted or maintained by the Plan, regardless of form.

"Designated Record Set" includes the medical records and billing records about individuals maintained by or for a covered health care provider; enrollment, payment, billing, claims adjudication and case or medical management record systems maintained by or for a health plan; or other information used in whole or in part by or for the covered entity to make decisions about individuals. Information used for quality control or peer review analyses and not used to make decisions about individuals is not in the designated record set.

The requested information will be provided within 30 days if the information is maintained on site or within 60 days if the information is maintained offsite. A single 30-day extension is allowed if the Plan is unable to comply with the deadline.

You or your personal representative will be required to complete a form to request access to the PHI in your designated record set. Requests for access to PHI should be made to the following officer: [insert name or title of person or office responsible for managing requests, telephone number and address].

If access is denied, you or your personal representative will be provided with a written denial setting forth the basis for the denial, a description of how you may exercise those review rights and a description of how you may complain to the Secretary of the U.S. Department of Health and Human Services.

Right to Amend PHI

You have the right to request the Plan to amend your PHI or a record about you in a designated record set for as long as the PHI is maintained in the designated record set.

The Plan has 60 days after the request is made to act on the request. A single 30-day extension is allowed if the Plan is unable to comply with the deadline. If the request is denied in whole or part, the Plan must provide you with a written denial that explains the basis for the denial. You or your personal representative may then submit a written statement disagreeing with the denial and have that statement included with any future disclosures of your PHI.

Requests for amendment of PHI in a designated record set should be made to the following officer: [insert name or title of person or office responsible for managing requests].

You or your personal representative will be required to complete a form to request amendment of the PHI in your designated record set.

[The covered entity may require individuals to make requests for amendment in writing and to provide a reason to support a requested amendment, provided that it informs individuals in advance of such requirements.]

The Right to Receive an Accounting of PHI Disclosures

At your request, the Plan will also provide you with an accounting of disclosures by the Plan of your PHI during the six years prior to the date of your request. However, such accounting need not include PHI disclosures made: (1) to carry out treatment, payment or health care operations; (2) to individuals about their own PHI; (3) prior to the compliance date; or (4) based on your written authorization.

If the accounting cannot be provided within 60 days, an additional 30 days is allowed if the individual is given a written statement of the reasons for the delay and the date by which the accounting will be provided.

If you request more than one accounting within a 12-month period, the Plan will charge a reasonable, cost-based fee for each subsequent accounting.

The Right to Receive a Paper Copy of This Notice Upon Request

To obtain a paper copy of this Notice contact the following officer: [insert name or title of person or office responsible for managing requests].

A Note About Personal Representatives

You may exercise your rights through a personal representative. Your personal representative will be required to produce evidence of his/her authority to act on your behalf before that person will be given access to your PHI or allowed to take any action for

continued on next page

FIG. 166-A (CONT.)

you. Proof of such authority may take one of the following forms:

- a power of attorney for health care purposes, notarized by a notary public;
- a court order of appointment of the person as the conservator or guardian of the individual; or
- an individual who is the parent of a minor child.

The Plan retains discretion to deny access to your PHI to a personal representative to provide protection to those vulnerable people who depend on others to exercise their rights under these rules and who may be subject to abuse or neglect. This also applies to personal representatives of minors.

Section 3. The Plan's Duties

The Plan is required by law to maintain the privacy of PHI and to provide individuals (participants and beneficiaries) with notice of its legal duties and privacy practices.

This notice is effective beginning [Date] and the Plan is required to comply with the terms of this notice. However, the Plan reserves the right to change its privacy practices and to apply the changes to any PHI received or maintained by the Plan prior to that date. If a privacy practice is changed, a revised version of this notice will be provided [to all past and present participants and beneficiaries] for whom the Plan still maintains PHI. [The plan must describe how the notice will be provided.]

Any revised version of this notice will be distributed within 60 days of the effective date of any material change to the uses or disclosures, the individual's rights, the duties of the Plan or other privacy practices stated in this notice.

Minimum Necessary Standard

When using or disclosing PHI or when requesting PHI from another covered entity, the Plan will make reasonable efforts not to use, disclose or request more than the minimum amount of PHI necessary to accomplish the intended purpose of the use, disclosure or request, taking into consideration practical and technological limitations.

However, the minimum necessary standard will not apply in the following situations:

- disclosures to or requests by a health care provider for treatment;
- uses or disclosures made to the individual;
- disclosures made to the Secretary of the U.S. Department of Health and Human Services;
- uses or disclosures that are required by law; and
- uses or disclosures that are required for the Plan's compliance with legal regulations.

This notice does not apply to information that has been de-identified. De-identified information is information that does not identify an individual and with respect to which there is no reasonable basis to believe that the information can be used to identify an individual is not individually identifiable health information.

In addition, the Plan may use or disclose "summary health information" to the plan sponsor for obtaining premium bids or modifying, amending or terminating the group health plan, which summarizes the claims history, claims expenses or type of claims experienced by individuals for whom a plan sponsor has provided health benefits under a group health plan; and from which identifying information has been deleted in accordance with HIPAA.

Section 4. Your Right to File a Complaint With the Plan or the HHS Secretary

If you believe that your privacy rights have been violated, you may complain to the Plan in care of the following officer: [insert name or title of person or office responsible for managing complaints and street address, telephone number and e-mail address].

You may file a complaint with the Secretary of the U.S. Department of Health and Human Services, Hubert H. Humphrey Building, 200 Independence Avenue S.W., Washington, D.C. 20201.

The Plan will not retaliate against you for filing a complaint.

Section 5. Whom to Contact at the Plan for More Information

If you have any questions regarding this notice or the subjects addressed in it, you may contact the following officer: [insert name or title of person or office responsible for handling inquiries and street address, telephone number and e-mail address.]

Conclusion

PHI use and disclosure by the Plan is regulated by a federal law known as HIPAA (the Health Insurance Portabilty and Accountability Act). You may find these rules at 45 *Code of Federal Regulations* Parts 160 and 164. This notice attempts to summarize the regulations. The regulations will supersede any discrepancy between the information in this notice and the regulations.

Fig. 166-B

Sample Employer Authorization Form

Under HIPAA's privacy rules, an authorization allows the use and disclosure of protected health information (PHI) both by the covered entity requesting the authorization and a third party. It must be written in specific terms to allow PHI use and disclosure for purposes *other than* those of treatment, payment and health care operations (TPO), although HHS guidance has reduced the degree of specificity originally thought to be required.

The sample authorization below is drafted for an employer that is not subject to state medical privacy laws. Employers that are subject to state law may have more stringent requirements.

The elements in this authorization are core elements, but the authorization may need additional information to comply with HIPAA.

AUTHORIZATION FOR RELEASE OF HEALTH INFORMATION

I _______________ [Employee Name] hereby authorize the use or disclosure of my health information as described in this authorization.

(1) *Specific person/organization (or class of persons) authorized to provide the information*:

____

(2) *Specific person/organization (or class of persons) authorized to receive and use the information*:

____

(3) *Specific and meaningful description of the information:*

> [For example, medical examination report and conclusions related to a fitness-for-work exam, or results of drug testing for employment-related purposes.]

____

(4) *Purpose of the request:*

(*Please state the purpose of the request below. If you do not wish to state a purpose, please state, "At the request of the individual."*)

____

(5) *Right to revoke:* I understand that I have the right to revoke this authorization at any time by notifying [Employer or Plan Sponsor] in writing at [list address where revocation must be delivered]. I understand that the revocation is only effective after it is received and logged by [Employer or Plan Sponsor]. I understand that any use or disclosure made prior to the revocation under this authorization will not be affected by a revocation.

(6) I understand that after this information is disclosed, federal law might not protect it and the recipient might redisclose it.

(7) I understand that my initial and continued employment and position are subject to my agreement to this authorization, and any additional authorization [Employer] requests.

> [Employers must review their employment handbooks and any applicable collective bargaining or state-law restrictions to ensure that the authorization does not conflict with other employee rights or requirements (imposed either voluntarily or by law).]

(8) I understand that I am entitled to receive a copy of this authorization.

HIDE-AD85

continued on next page

FIG. 166-B (CONT.)

Sample Employer Authorization Form, *continued*

(9) I understand that this authorization will expire when my employment with [Employer] terminates.

> [The authorization must include a terminal date based on a specific date or event. Here, the event used is the termination of employment. If an employer or plan sponsor desires to extend the time for post-employment use of authorizations, it must modify item 8 accordingly.]

Signature of Employee ______________________________ Date________________

Personal Representatives section

If a Personal Representative executes this form, that Representative warrants that he or she has authority to sign this form on the basis of: ____

Pensions

167. Q: Do I have to have a pension plan?

A: No. You do not have to provide a pension plan, although there are some tax advantages to both employees and employers who do so. If you choose to provide a pension, however, you must comply with the applicable laws and regulations.

> **Source:** IRS Web site: www.irs.gov/retirement/sponsor/article/0,,id=136475,00.html.

168. Q: What is a Roth 401(k) or Roth 403(b)? Are they new?

A: No, these are not new types of plans, but there are some new amendments to the tax law that have made some important changes.

The main thing about a Roth plan is that the contributions are made post-tax so that when the money (including any investment or interest gain) is withdrawn after age 59 ½, it is *tax-free*. With a traditional 401(k) plan, contributions are made on a pre-tax basis but the money (plus any gain) is taxed when withdrawn.

Beginning in 2006, elective contributions come in two types: traditional, pre-tax elective contributions (elective contributions are also referred to as elective deferrals), and designated Roth contributions.

> **Sources:** This feature is permitted under a code section added by the Economic Growth and Tax Relief Reconciliation Act of 2001 (EGTRRA), effective for years beginning on or after Jan. 1, 2006; IRS Code §§401(k) and 402A; Treas. Reg. §§1.401(k)-1 and 1.402A-1.

169. Q: Are there any limits on how much may be contributed to a designated Roth account?

A: Yes. The combined amount contributed to all designated Roth accounts and traditional, pre-tax accounts in any one year for any individual is limited by the 402(g) limit – $15,500 in 2007 plus an additional $5,000 in catch-up contributions if age 50 or older.

> **Sources:** IRS Code §402(g); Treas. Reg. §1.402(g)-1.

170. Q: Do the same income restrictions that apply to Roth IRAs apply to designated Roth contributions?

A: No, there are no limits on income in determining if designated Roth contributions can be made. Of course, you have to have salary from which to make any 401(k) or 403(b) deferrals.

> **Sources:** IRS online resource guide for IRAs: www.irs.gov/retirement/article/0,,id=137307,00.html; IRS Code §402A; proposed Treas. Reg. §1.402-1.

Summary Plan Descriptions

171. Q: What is a Summary Plan Description?

A: Every employee pension or benefit plan must be explained in plain language to the employees/participants. This is done in a Summary Plan Description, also called an SPD. The SPD is a very important document. Although it is only a summary and less explicit than the terms of the plan it is describing, many courts have ruled that the explanation of benefits in it may be relied on by participants, even if the actual complete plan document is different. This is especially true if the explanation in the SPD is more favorable to a participant than the plan itself. As a result, considerable care should be taken to make sure that the SPD accurately states the terms of the plan.

Sources: 29 U.S.C. §1022; 29 C.F.R. §2520.102-3; *Burstein v. Retirement Account Plan for Employees of Allegheny Health Education and Research Foundation,* 334 F.3d 365 (3rd Cir. 2003); *Burke v. Kodak Retirement Income Plan,* 336 F.3d 103 (2nd Cir. 2003); *Palmisano v. Allina Health Systems, Inc.,* 190 F.3d 881, 887-88 (8th Cir. 1999); *Maxa v. John Alden Life Ins. Co.,* 972 F.2d 980, 984 (8th Cir. 1992), *cert. denied,* 506 U.S. 1080 (U.S. Sup. Ct. 1993).

172. Q: What should I do if there are differences between our SPD's explanations of our benefits and the descriptions of those same benefits in the plan itself? Our SPD is written by our insurer.

A: First, there should not be any differences between the benefits descriptions in the plan and those in the SPD. You should have those clarified immediately. Second, it doesn't matter who wrote the SPD, the plan sponsor (the employer, in most cases) will be responsible. You may be able to sue the insurer, but who wants to get involved in lengthy and expensive lawsuits? Have the SPD corrected and give corrected copies to all plan participants.

Source: *Hansen v. Continental Co.,* 940 F.2d 971 (5th Cir. 1991).

173. Q: Can we automatically enroll new employees in our 401(k) plan? We are concerned that too many of them, especially the lower-paid ones, are choosing not to sign up.

A: In general, yes, but you are a little ahead of the curve. Although you may begin automatic enrollment now, it is still a bit complicated, with a number of steps that will not be required in 2008, when the new law takes full effect. It might be wisest to take 2007 to get yourself fully prepared to begin auto enrollment in 2008. Even then, there are a number of rules and regulations.

Perhaps the most important consideration is that to enroll employees automatically, the employer *must make a contribution* to employee accounts. There are some rather complicated rules for determining the contribution, and the best way for each employer to do that will depend on the make-up of each workforce, but the bottom line is that an employer contribution has to be made. Here are some of the other main rules:

- The new automatic enrollment rule generally applies only to new employees. However, current employees that have not made an affirmative election to participate (or not participate) may be covered.
- Participants must be 100 percent vested in employer matching or non-elective contributions after completing two years of service.
- Notice must be given to employees (as you do under current law).

The above rules also apply to 403(b) plans.

Source: Pension Protection Act of 2006, §§901-904, including amendments to IRS Code §§401(a), 401(k) and 411(a); 29 U.S.C. §1144.

Workers' Compensation

174. Q: Can I count workers' compensation leave, disability leave or paid sick leave against the 12 weeks of unpaid FMLA leave?

A: In general, and under federal law, yes, if the reason the employee is on leave qualifies as a "serious health condition" under the Family and Medical Leave Act (FMLA) and is thus covered by that law.

Under federal law, you can require that the employee exhaust all paid leave during FMLA leave. However, a number of states and the District of Columbia permit the employee to decide whether time on FMLA leave will be paid. In those jurisdictions, an employee may decide to save paid vacation for something like a planned future trip, and take unpaid FMLA leave. You must check the leave law in your state to find out what its provisions are.

The situation is a little different for workers' compensation leave. If an employee is receiving pay from a workers' compensation fund, you may not require the employee to substitute any paid vacation or other leave that is covered by the workers' compensation fund.

But to return to the original question, just because someone is being paid during an FMLA leave, whether by you, an insurer or a state program, does not mean the time does not count against the 12-week FMLA leave allotment.

175. Q: Are small employers exempt from having to pay workers' compensation premiums? Can I self-insure this expense? I run a small bookkeeping business with just eight employees.

A: Although 11 states exempt very small employers, five employees is the highest exemption allowed.

For the most part, workers' compensation is an "omnibus" law that is designed to cover employees, including part-time and temporary employees. Workers' compensation laws are designed to ensure that employees who are injured or disabled on the job are provided with fixed monetary awards, without litigation. It is a kind of "no-fault" insurance.

These laws also provide benefits for dependents of those workers who are killed because of work-related accidents or illnesses. Some laws also protect employers and fellow workers by limiting the amount an injured employee can recover from an employer and by eliminating the liability of co-workers for most accidents.

Although there are federal statutes, most workers' compensation programs are created and administered by state law, which means that there is considerable variety in how these programs are administered. Many states require that employers provide insurance to cover workplace injuries and deaths, but some states permit some entities, often nonprofits, to self-insure.

Please note, not every employee qualifies for workers' compensation benefits in every state. For example, some states have more detailed definitions of the term "employee," which include officers of a corporation, sole proprietors or partners, and independent contractors under certain conditions. Other persons may be excluded from the definition of employee for workers' compensation purposes, such as:

- real estate sales agents;
- band, orchestral, musical and theatrical performers and disc jockeys;
- owner-operators of motor vehicles who transport property under a written agreement;
- persons whose employment is "casual";
- volunteers; and
- taxicab, limousine or other passenger-for-hire drivers.

You must check your state's workers' compensation law.

176. Q: If I let an employee on workers' comp come back in a light-duty job, do I have to let everyone have that option?

A: This is a difficult question because it implicates other laws. The short answer is "no," because the federal Americans With Disabilities Act (ADA) does not require that you create a new position as an accommodation, and most light-duty jobs are unrelated to the original job of the disabled worker seeking an accommodation.

Therefore, light-duty jobs may be limited to workers' compensation situations. However, be careful. If such positions are offered more broadly, a precedent for wider use may very well have been established.

You should also be aware of a possible complication under the federal Family and Medical Leave Act (FMLA). It is the Department of Labor's position that if an employee qualifies for FMLA leave, the employee *may not be forced* to return to work in a light-duty position before the employee's FMLA leave entitlement has expired.

Forcing the employee to return to such a position would violate his or her right to be restored to the *same or an equivalent* position. Thus, if an employee is injured on the job, and the injury also qualifies as an FMLA "serious health condition," the employee will qualify for both workers' compensation benefits and FMLA leave. This would allow the employee to receive workers' compensation benefits for replacement of lost wages, and have his or her health benefits maintained under the FMLA.

If, as part of the workers' compensation process, the employee is offered a medically approved light-duty position, the employee may decline the position and instead choose to exercise his or her FMLA rights. (The employee may lose workers' compensation payments in that case.)

If the employee accepts the light-duty position in lieu of FMLA leave or returns to work on or before the 12 weeks of FMLA leave are up, he or she retains the right to the original or an equivalent position.

> **Sources:** EEOC's Technical Assistance Manual on Title I of the ADA, 9.4; Wage Hour Opinion Letter FMLA-55 (March 10, 1995).

177. Q: Do I have to hire an employee back from a workers' compensation leave? If so, must I put him in the same or an equivalent job?

A: This is a difficult question because it implicates other laws. Workers' compensation is a program designed to support workers who are injured on the job. Because the program is administered by the states, there is tremendous variety in how these programs are handled.

In some states, an employer does not have to reemploy an employee returning from a workers' compensation leave. In those states where reemployment is required, the employee does not have to be returned to the same or an equivalent job.

However, workers' compensation laws long pre-date the enactment of the Americans With Disabilities Act (ADA) and the Family and Medical Leave Act (FMLA). Those federal laws are "superior" to the state laws whenever the benefits mandated by Congress are greater than those provided by state law. So, how does it work in the situation you asked about?

If the employee on workers' compensation leave also qualifies for and is considered as being on FMLA leave, she or he has the rights conferred by the FMLA. That means if the employee can return to work within the 12-week leave allotment of the FMLA, you must return that worker to the same or an equivalent job.

If the employee on workers' compensation leave also qualifies for leave as an accommodation under the ADA, when that employee is able to return to work, you may have to provide a reasonable accommodation to permit him or her to perform the essential functions of the job, and you *must* return him or her to the *same* job, unless the employee agrees to another position as an accommodation for his or her disability.

Although there is no statutory time limit on the length of an ADA leave, many courts have imposed the requirement of "reasonableness." Leaves cannot be indefinite and, for most courts, there must be a reasonable expectation that the leave will improve the health of the worker so that he or she can return to work.

Unemployment Compensation

178. Q: Are small employers exempt from having to pay unemployment compensation premiums? Can I self-insure this expense? We only have 12 employees.

A: In general, small employers are not exempt, but you may be nonetheless.

Some employment is not covered by the state-federal funding partnership that is the core of unemployment compensation, because the federal government will not subsidize the cost of unemployment insurance for these workers. As a result, the following employment is *generally* not covered:

1. self-employment;
2. certain agricultural labor and domestic service;
3. service for relatives;
4. service of patients in hospitals;
5. certain student interns;
6. certain alien farmworkers;
7. certain seasonal camp workers; and
8. railroad workers (who have their own unemployment program).

If your employees are in these categories, you may be exempted. Please note, states are free to provide coverage greater than that offered by the federal government and some do.

As for self-insurance, that doesn't make a lot of sense (even if it were possible) because it would deprive you of the governmental subsidy.

179. Q: Can I just ignore an unemployment insurance claim I believe to be vindictive? An employee we fired is filing for UI. He was insubordinate and unreliable, but he is claiming in his papers that he was discriminated against. I don't have the time or resources to fight about UI, but I am concerned that if I don't fight him on this now, he'll use a decision in his favor as evidence in a discrimination suit against me later. What should I do?

A: I wouldn't be too concerned. A number of years ago, there were a handful of cases that accepted the findings (sometimes uncontested) of unemployment insurance (UI) hearings in subsequent discrimination cases. Since then, the courts have recognized that an employer has such a different incentive to defend and the tribunal has such different standards of evidence and proof, that the findings of a UI hearing are given no weight, even when they are admitted into evidence. This is based on the general principle that the "same" issue with the same stakes must be decided in one case to affect a second case.

In any event, if you believe that the reason for the termination is one that precludes the award of UI, this might be an instance when you should find the time and resources to contest formally. It may deter the employee from pursuing his claim and/or you may prevail on the merits.

Sources: *Bonder-Tongue Laboratories, Inc. v. University of Illinois,* 402 U.S. 313 (U.S. Sup. Ct. 1971); *Victory Highway Village, inc. v. Weaver,* 634 F.2d 1099 (8th Cir. 1980); *Yak v. Bank Brussels Lambert, BBL,* 252 F.3d 127 (2d Cir. 2001).

Termination

6

Introduction

We began at the beginning of the employment relationship. Termination by any means – retirement, reduction-in-force, change of jobs or firing – is the end. The end can be full of traps for the unwary and is probably the point from which the most lawsuits arise. Employees who are fired are usually unhappy. They want someone to blame, they want recourse and they probably want money.

The way you handle a termination can mean the difference between a lawsuit and a peaceful parting of the ways. You need to know whether your state follows the employment-at-will doctrine or requires "cause" for discharge. What about releases? How can you avoid a retaliation claim? Are there different requirements for older workers? And what about reductions-in-force?

How do you decide about a severance package? Is there some kind of notice that has to be given if you have a plant shutdown? And after an employee has left, what documents do you need to keep on file?

The answers to these questions and others are in this final chapter. The list of questions is on the back of this page.

Questions in This Chapter

Litigation

180. Q: What can I do to reduce the chances of getting sued by a terminated employee?

A: As long as you understand that there really are no guarantees, there are things to consider and steps to take that can help reduce the likelihood of a lawsuit. Many are included in the Checklist for Terminations, Fig. 180-A.

Proper and thorough documentation of performance is probably the most important thing you can do to protect your company. Having policies that are followed and applied consistently also is important. Releases, too, can help (see Q. 191-194). Unless the termination is for violent behavior, it is prudent to think through the situation before terminating a worker. Termination is, after all, capital punishment for an employee. You always want to make sure the process if fair and necessary.

FIG. 180-A

THOMPSON

Thompson HR Forms
http://forms.thompson.com

CHECKLIST FOR TERMINATION & CONDUCTING TERMINATIONS AND LAYOFFS

JUST CAUSE FOR DISCHARGE:

THE SEVEN TESTS

1. *Notice:* Did the employer forewarn the employee of the possible consequences of his conduct?

- **a. Knowledge of the misconduct: What actions could lead to discipline?; and**
- **b. Knowledge of the penalty for such misconduct, especially if the penalty is discharge.**

2. *Reasonable of the Order:* Was the employer's rule reasonably related to the orderly, efficient and safe operation of the business and reasonably related to performance that the employer might properly expect of the employee?

3. *Investigation:* Did the employer, before administering discipline, make an effort to discover whether the employee did, in fact, violate a rule?

4. *Fair Investigation:* Was the employee's investigation conducted fairly and objectively?

5. *Proof:* Did the investigation yield substantial evidence or proof that the employee was guilty as charged?

6. *Equal Treatment:* Has the employer applied its rules and penalties evenhandedly and without discrimination, to all employees?

7. *Penalty:* Was the degree of discipline imposed by the employer reasonably related to:

- **a. the seriousness of the employee's proven offense; and**
- **b. the employee's record of service with the employer?**

continued on next page

Fig. 180-A (cont.)

A. TERMINATION CONFERENCE

1. The employee's supervisor, together with a representative of the human resources department or a senior manager, should communicate the termination decision to the employee. There should always be two (2) company representatives at the termination meeting.

2. Tell the employee the true reason for the termination decision and, where appropriate, provide a few specific examples of the problems (whether they be performance or economic related, or otherwise) leading up to the company's decision. However, do not debate the merits of the decision; make it clear to the employee that the decision is final. Try to keep the meeting brief and to the point.

3. If the termination is to be immediate, at the conclusion of the termination meeting, ask the employee to return all company property, including building passes, card keys, hard keys, office equipment, credit cards, documents, etc.

4. Do not make any false statements to the employee(s) regarding termination or recall rights.

5. Inform the employee of rights respecting unemployment benefits and, in RIF situations, consider having someone from the local office of Employment Security present to start collecting applications.

6. Inform the employee of rights, if any, to continued company benefits or severance pay.

7. Specifically inform the employee of COBRA rights to continued health insurance.

8. In RIF situations, consider having employment counselors present to help employees find new jobs.

9. Consider having the final paycheck ready for distribution when notice of termination or layoff is given or, on the last day of work. At the latest, pursuant to the NY and NJ labor laws, a terminated employee should be paid in full by the next regular pay date after separation, in order to comply with state wage payment laws.

10. Within five days of the discharge, the New York Labor Law requires that the employer advise the employee in writing of the date of the termination and the last date in which his medical insurance coverage is effective.

continued on next page

FIG. 180-A (CONT.)

B. CONDUCT AN "EXIT INTERVIEW"

Under some circumstances, where the employee has advance notice of the termination decision, it will be a good idea to conduct an exit interview the last day the employee is on the job. Such an interview helps to close off loose ends. It gives the employer a chance to collect company property, issue a final paycheck, review COBRA information and, importantly, to listen to any concerns that the employee may raise. This is particularly important for three reasons:

1. It allows the employer to modify and improve the discipline and discharge process based on employee concerns. This may alleviate future litigation.

2. It may afford the employer the opportunity to determine if this employee intends to sue.

3. It may let the employer know if the employee has prospects for future employment (an important damages issue if a lawsuit is forthcoming).

C. INTERNAL COMMUNICATIONS ABOUT THE TERMINATION OR LAYOFFS

1. In individual termination scenarios, active employees should be advised that the former employee has departed in the ordinary course. No information as to the reasons for the discharge should be provided to anyone other than those with a need to know (*e.g.*, the employee's supervisor, human resources director or senior management).

2. In RIF cases, once the termination decisions are made, active employees should be advised that as a result of financial or other applicable reasons, the company is undergoing a RIF resulting in the layoffs of the departing employees. Where appropriate, active employees should be advised that no further layoffs are anticipated at this time.

D. REFERENCES

Handling inquiries about former employees has become increasingly difficult. Many defamation suits have been brought by employees who received negative references. A United States Supreme Court case, *Robinson v. Shell Oil*, has made references even more difficult to handle. In *Robinson*, the court ruled that a *former* employee can bring suit under Title VII for retaliation. This now means that if an employee receives what is perceived to be a negative reference letter, the employee may be able to sue the employer under Title VII (assuming the employee is protected by Title VII) even though the employee no longer works for the employer.

continued on next page

FIG. 180-A (CONT.)

As a result, employers should choose from one of the following options when it comes to references:

1. Do not give employment references for any employee.

2. Only give out an employee's name, dates employed, and jobs held (the so called "name, rank and serial number").

3. Prepare a reference letter at the exit interview that the employee approves, and use that letter in response to all subsequent inquiries.

4. Obtain a release from the employee respecting any references provided to prospective employers.

E. CONCLUSION

The termination of employment is a difficult area that often spurs litigation. However, if the termination decision is arrived at thoughtfully and conducted properly, an employer can dramatically decrease its risk of being held liable for employment discrimination or other types of wrongful termination. Once again, the key elements to remember are:

- ➢ Proceed with Caution
- ➢ Thoroughly Investigate
- ➢ Review all Pertinent Contracts and Policies
- ➢ Act Consistently
- ➢ Think Through Every Decision
- ➢ Consult with Counsel
- ➢ Document, Document, Document

Employment-at-Will

181. Q: Can you explain "wrongful discharge" and "employment-at-will"?

A: In the strictest sense, "employment-at-will" means the employment relationship can be terminated by either the employer or employee at any time for any reason. The only limits for the employer are those that exist in the constitution, statutes or an employment contract. For example, most anti-discrimination statutes include an anti-retaliation provision, prohibiting employers from firing a worker for filing a discrimination complaint.

The employment-at-will and wrongful discharge concepts are controlled primarily by state law. With some exceptions, states generally are divided between those that recognize employment-at-will, and those that recognize causes of action for wrongful discharge. There are numerous variations among the states in applying the two doctrines and there are some states that fall in the middle, not strictly in one camp or the other.

New York is a fairly strict employment-at-will state. A private New York employer could terminate a worker for wearing brown shoes simply because of a dislike for brown shoes.

The states that have departed from the employment-at-will concept generally use one of three rationales, or some combination of them. These are: violations of public policy; breach of an express or implied contract; or breach of the covenant of good faith and fair dealing.

Public policy is the community conscience about what is right and fair. For example, firing an employee who refused to participate in an illegal act would be against public policy.

Every employment relationship is a contractual one, although often the contract is an unwritten agreement. Sometimes a personnel manual forms the basis for the contract. The employee has a right to enforce the employment contract the same as he or she does any other contract in the states that adhere to this doctrine.

The "covenant of good faith and fair dealing" means that all parties are expected to treat each other fairly and act in good faith. If it is obvious that the employer was unfair or acted with bad intent when it hired or discharged a worker, the states that recognize this concept permit the employee to sue to enforce the implied agreement that the employer would be fair.

In states that recognize a cause of action for wrongful discharge, employers must have a cause, or good reason, for terminating employees and be able to prove that reason if the termination is challenged in court.

182. Q: Is it possible to be an at-will employer and also have a graduated discipline policy? I've been told that our graduated discipline policy undermines our at-will status, and that the two can't co-exist.

A: Probably not. The extent to which your "graduated" or "progressive" discipline policy undermines your at-will status depends in large part on whether all appropriate disclaimers have been included in your discipline policy, employee handbook, procedures manual or other summary of employment policies.

These disclaimers must be displayed prominently within the policy or handbook, and should include statements clearly emphasizing that the discipline policy does not create an employment contract or in any other way affect an employee's employment-at-will status. (See section on "For Cause," Q. 185-189, for specifics.)

With appropriate disclaimers, at-will status and a discipline policy certainly can co-exist. However, the employer should bear in mind that any failure to comply with established policies and procedures concerning discipline will be the kiss of death in any form of employment litigation.

183. Q: Can an employee I recently fired have a valid "wrongful termination" claim? We are an at-will employer, which is stated in our employment handbook and standard offer and termination letters. Nonetheless, an ex-employee just sued us for wrongful termination.

A: Anyone can file a lawsuit. Is it valid? Probably not, but we need more facts.

"Wrongful termination" is a recognized cause of action in only a few states. But there are exceptions to the right to terminate an employee-at-will. Both federal and state law require that adverse employment actions, including virtually all forms of discipline, be applied in a nondiscriminatory fashion, without regard to race, sex, age, national origin or other protected status. Some states enforce laws prohibiting termination from employment for particular reasons, such as jury service or filing a workers' compensation or wage claim.

In addition, some states have created the following exceptions to the employment-at-will doctrine, limiting the employer's right to terminate employees based on:

- Public policy exceptions, prohibiting termination for whistleblowing, for example.
- Implied contract exceptions for failure to follow promises documented in an employee policy or handbook or for implied promises made verbally during an interview that require just cause to terminate.
- Implied covenants of good faith and fair dealing such as terminating long-term employees just before they're due to receive some anticipated financial benefit. ERISA prohibits a termination to prevent someone from qualifying for a pension or similar benefit.

From what you said, it doesn't sound as though you terminated your employee for any of those reasons and you started out on the right track by including an employment-at-will statement in the appropriate documents. Nevertheless, while employment-at-will statements and appropriate disclaimers in an employee handbook can provide a helpful defense to wrongful termination claims, an employer can do virtually everything right and still be sued. Unfortunately, it can get very expensive to prove that you had the right to terminate someone.

Accordingly, there is always some value in at least considering a severance agreement that provides the affected employee with some monetary compensation and the opportunity to resign, in exchange for a comprehensive release of claims and a commitment to confidentiality.

184. Q: Does an employee have a right to know why he's being terminated? We are an at-will employer.

A: There is no specific legal requirement that the employee be told exactly why he or she is being terminated from employment.

However, the far better practice, to minimize potential liability, is to follow the two fundamental principles of due process by according the employee:

- notice of what he or she has done to warrant termination; and
- an opportunity to provide an explanation and/or defense, if he or she so chooses.

The best way to accomplish these goals is to conduct an exit interview. The interview not only accords the employer a chance to collect company property, issue a final paycheck and review COBRA information, it provides an opportunity to listen to any concerns the employee may raise. Specifically, the exit interview:

- allows the employer to modify and improve the discipline and discharge process based on employee concerns, which may limit future litigation;
- affords the employer the opportunity to determine if the employee intends to sue, and if so, to offer a severance agreement option; and
- may provide helpful information about the employee's prospects for future employment, an important issue affecting damages if a lawsuit is filed.

It is important to keep in mind that some wrongful termination claims arise from the specific manner in which the termination was conducted. Accordingly, the departing employee should always be treated with dignity and respect, regardless of the terminating offense.

For Cause

185. Q: Who gets to decide what constitutes "good cause" – the employer or the employee? Our employee handbook says we will only fire for good cause, and I've just had an argument with an employee I am about to terminate about whether the term applies to him.

A: "Good cause" is a synonym for "just cause," and refers to the basis for an adverse employment action. It is determined by examining the reasonableness of the proposed termination in light of the surrounding facts and circumstances according to whatever guidelines the employer has established for discipline and discharge. Here those guidelines would be in your employee handbook and your past practices.

An employment-at-will employee can be terminated for any reason or no reason, as long as the firing does not violate a state or federal law. A good or just cause requirement restricts your right to terminate at-will employees. Most states (the exceptions are California, Colorado and Montana) are employment-at-will states, so restrictions on termination would be for illegal discrimination, violation of a whistleblower provision, or similar public policy issues.

Employee handbooks are deemed in some circumstances to constitute binding employment contracts that negate at-will employment. Commitments to fire only for good cause have been enforced in many instances, to the employers' detriment. The basic concept is that although an employer need not establish personnel policies or practices, once established, they must be followed.

Appropriate disclaimers can sometimes preserve the employer's right to invoke any or none of its specified termination procedures. Accordingly, the following disclaimers should be prominently displayed in your employee handbook because they will determine whether a "good" or "just cause" standard will be enforced:

- This handbook does not create a contract, express or implied.
- This handbook is not all inclusive, and provides guidelines only, to which exceptions may be made within the employer's discretion.
- This handbook does not alter the at-will relationship between employer and employee.
- This handbook does not guarantee employment for any definite period of time.
- This handbook can be changed by the employer unilaterally, at any time, with or without notice, as business needs change.

Having said all that, many employers have concluded that, if given the chance, they would not promise to terminate employees only for good cause. The good cause promise creates factual disputes as to whether a particular offense constitutes good cause for termination, which can lead to expensive and time-consuming litigation.

Whether a particular employee is entitled to protection from termination absent a showing of good cause depends on several factors:

- In a non-union setting or when a management employee is involved, the terms of the employee handbook generally will determine whether the particular individual is entitled to good cause protections. For example, many handbooks establish a probationary period for new employees to assess their competence in the actual work environment. Because probation is designed to accord the employer maximum flexibility in determining whether a new hire is the right "fit" for the position, the employer has virtually absolute discretion to terminate during the probationary period, for any reason or no reason at all except unlawful discrimination.

- Layoffs for lack of work or based on other adverse financial circumstances affecting the employer's business will provide good cause for terminations. The issue would be the selection of particular individuals for termination. The terms of the employer's policies or applicable collective bargaining agreement would govern that.

- If your business is covered by a collective bargaining agreement, the employees generally cannot be terminated absent just cause. Such an employee, with assistance from the union representative, usually is entitled to challenge a termination in arbitration. The arbitrator will assess whether there was just cause for the termination, or whether a less severe form of discipline should have been imposed based on the provisions contained in the collective bargaining agreement and the employer's past practice.

When a good or just cause standard applies, the employer must ensure prior to approving the proposed termination that the two basic principles of due process have been satisfied:

- Employees deserve the opportunity to understand what their employer expects of them with respect to job performance and workplace conduct, and how he or she has failed to meet these expectations. The employee must have been adequately forewarned that the particular behavior or level of performance would result in discipline or termination.

- Employees deserve an opportunity to explain misconduct, and/or to change their behavior or performance through corrective action.

To accomplish these goals, discipline generally should be progressive. A failure to improve triggers increasingly severe consequences (from verbal counseling to final warning), culminating in termination from employment. Of course, there are certain types of misconduct that are so severe they warrant immediate termination (e.g., theft or insubordination).

In addition, there must be documentation that management conducted a thorough, impartial, pre-termination investigation that applicable policies and procedures have been applied in a consistent, non-discriminatory manner, and that termination is warranted given the seriousness of the offense.

186. Q: What benefits, if any, do we have to give a worker who is fired for good cause?

A: The benefits provided to an employee terminated for good or just cause (such as severance pay or accrued but unused vacation pay) are governed by the terms of the applicable collective bargaining agreement, if any, the employee handbook and your benefits policies.

In addition, most employees and their covered dependents – depending on the employer's size and other factors – generally are entitled under COBRA to continue their health insurance coverage at group rates, absent a clear showing that they were terminated for gross misconduct.

Employees terminated for cause and/or misconduct normally are not entitled to unemployment compensation.

187. Q: How much can I say about a terminated employee's departure without getting into legal trouble? I fired a very well-liked employee for theft. When I am asked about why she left, I've been saying, "we don't talk about personnel decisions." I won't lie about it, but the silence about her departure has started a distracting rumor mill.

A: It is best not to elaborate to co-workers without a need to know on the circumstances surrounding your employee's termination, given the potential for defamation and invasion of privacy claims.

Stating that an employee was terminated for theft is defamatory on its face, meaning that all an employee needs to do to establish liability is to show that the words were publicized. It is true that communications made in good faith by an employer concerning job performance or other job-related matters are subject to a qualified privilege and generally are not grounds for a defamation action. But the privilege is not absolute and can be lost when statements are made with actual malice or inflammatory language or to individuals without a legitimate business interest in receiving the information. The real question is "why do you even want to get into that?"

Of course, dealing with the rumor mill remains extremely frustrating. About the best that can be done is to circulate a short, carefully worded memo or e-mail stating simply that the employee has left your company to pursue other opportunities, and that management is not free to discuss the circumstances surrounding her departure. The statement should emphasize that out of respect for the employee's privacy, such information must remain confidential. One option is to ask the departing employee how she would like her departure to be announced, and to honor her preference, if possible.

188. Q: Can I get sued because I don't have a written policy on termination? We don't have an employee handbook, so we don't have any written policies. An employee keeps mouthing off at his supervisor and I want to fire him "for cause" to make sure he doesn't get unemployment insurance.

A: No law requires that an employer establish personnel policies or practices. Of course anybody can sue anyone for anything. The key is not whether you can be sued, but whether you can win.

The determination as to whether an employee was terminated "for cause" or "misconduct," and thus disqualified from receiving unemployment benefits, is a factual one, not dependent on whether you enforce a "for cause" policy. When there are no written policies, the state unemployment agency will look to past practices in dealing with other workers who committed the same or similar offenses.

"Mouthing off" to a supervisor sounds like a synonym for insubordination, a generally accepted ground for denying unemployment. The key to success will be contemporaneous documentation of the incidents on which the termination is based, any prior incidents of misconduct, and how similar incidents were treated in the past.

189. Q: As part of our graduated discipline policy, do I have to list everything that can result in immediate termination?

A: Obviously, it is impossible to anticipate every single type of misconduct that warrants immediate termination. The best approach is to implement a Discipline and Discharge Policy, stating that "some examples of grounds for immediate termination include (list), although immediate termination may occur for other reasons." Also, listing broad categories of misconduct warranting immediate termination accords the employer more flexibility.

Bear in mind, however, that regardless of how serious the misconduct may appear, there is simply no reason to terminate on the spot. Temporarily suspending the employee pending an investigation into the incident is the far better practice, and will result in a documented record to support the termination should it be subject to legal challenge. A temporary suspension provides all parties the opportunity to cool down, and the employer time to conduct an investigation that should include the following steps:

- Examine any physical evidence, such as drugs, alcohol or stolen property.
- Interview all witnesses and document their statements in writing.
- Review prior discipline imposed on other employees who committed similar offenses.

- If the employee is in a protected group (minority, female, disabled, etc.), determine whether he or she has received the same treatment and consideration as his or her similarly situated non-protected co-workers.
- Review the employee's past work record and performance.
- Get the employee's side of the story, and document his or her explanation in writing.
- Have HR and legal representatives review the proposed termination whenever possible.

Retaliation

190. Q: Do I still have to be extra careful when terminating minorities or women when I'm certain there was no discrimination involved?

A: You are right to be concerned. Employers accused of discrimination have successfully defended themselves against that charge but ended up losing the lawsuit because they retaliated against the employee who complained.

Retaliation is covered in Chapter 5 of this book. Briefly, it is taking an adverse employment action against a worker who participated in "protected activity," such as filing a discrimination complaint. If an employee was involved in such activity and you took adverse action against him or her shortly thereafter, a retaliation claim is sure to follow.

Regardless of whether the employee participated in protected activity, you should always have sufficient documentation to prove a legitimate business reason for taking adverse employment action against a worker. This is especially true when a termination is involved. Employees who lose their jobs and livelihoods are understandably upset and often want restitution of some kind. A lawsuit may provide the perfect avenue for that.

Releases

191. Q: Can I ask an employee to waive his FMLA rights when I fire him? We are in the process of terminating an employee because of poor performance. He claims that we're firing him because he took FMLA leave. This isn't true, but rather than have him go to court against us, we want to give him some extra payment in his severance package and ask him to sign a release so he can't sue us under the FMLA. Is that okay?

A: Maybe, but it depends on which court you ask.

The U.S. Department of Labor (DOL), which interprets and enforces the federal Family and Medical Leave Act (FMLA), has a regulation that provides that "employees cannot waive, nor may employers induce employees to waive, their rights under FMLA."

According to DOL, the regulation only prohibits the prospective waiver of rights by a current employee. It does not prohibit an employer from obtaining a release of the right to bring suit to remedy past violations. This means that you can*not* ask a current employee or a new hire to waive the right to take FMLA leave, even if you give the worker a bonus or other inducement to sign such a waiver. But you *can* get a terminated employee to sign a release of the right to sue your company for FMLA violations that may have occurred before the employee left.

Federal courts do not all agree with the Labor Department. The U.S. Court of Appeals for the 4th Circuit, which handles cases from Maryland, Virginia, West Virginia, North Carolina and South Carolina, held that a waiver of the right to sue, even by a departing employee, was not enforceable. But the court later rescinded that decision at the urging of DOL, and has not yet issued a new opinion. A federal court in Pennsylvania agreed with the 4th Circuit's first decision.

The 5th U.S. Circuit Court of Appeals, which covers cases from Louisiana, Mississippi and Texas, and a lower federal court in Georgia, have held that the Department of Labor's regulation prohibits only the prospective waiver of FMLA rights, not the retrospective settlement of FMLA claims. Those courts decided that a departing employee's agreement not to sue the employer for FMLA violations is valid and must be given full effect.

There are not yet enough appeals court decisions to completely settle the issue. DOL's interpretation of its own regulation should be persuasive to other courts, but there is at least one decision that neither current nor former employees can waive FMLA rights with a release.

Sources: 29 C.F.R. § 825.220(d); *Taylor v. Progress Energy, Inc.*, 415 F.3d 364 (4th Cir. 2005), *rehearing granted and judgment vacated,* June 14, 2006); *Faris v. Williams WPC-I, Inc.*, 332 F.3d 316 (5th Cir. 2003); *McRae v. Master Craft Engineering, Inc.*, 2005 WL 3874359 (Nov. 3, 2005).

192. Q: Can I ask an employee to waive his right to sue us when I fire him? We are in the process of terminating an employee because of poor performance. He claims we owe him some overtime pay. We disagree, but we're willing to give him what he says we owe him if he'll sign a release agreeing not to sue us.

A: No. The U.S. Supreme Court has held that the Fair Labor Standards Act prohibits such waivers or releases.

The only time an employee can effectively waive the right to sue his employer for overtime compensation is if the waiver is part of a settlement approved by the Department of Labor as part of an audit by that agency, or by a court as part of a settlement of a lawsuit.

Sources: 29 U.S.C. §216(c); *Brooklyn Savings Bank v. O'Neil,* 324 U.S. 697 (1945).

193. Q: Is a settlement with the U.S. Department of Labor limited to the federal government, or does it offer additional protection? We just went through a wage and hour audit by the DOL, and they are asking us to settle the matter with a back pay settlement. If I sign this, are we protected from wage and hour suits from employees or our state labor department?

A: If the Department of Labor's Wage and Hour Division has conducted an audit and has determined that your company owes employees back wages for unpaid overtime, the agency will give you a Form WH-56, which will tell you how much money you owe each employee.

After your company's representative has signed that form, the Wage-Hour investigator will give you Form WH-58. This form is entitled "Receipt for Payment of Lost or Denied Wages, Employment Benefits, or Other Compensation." You must fill out a Form WH-58 for each employee to whom the company is offering back wages, and present the form to the employee at the time a back-wage check is tendered. There is a place on the form for the employee to sign and date it.

The Form WH-58 provides the following notice to employees:

> Your acceptance of back wages due under the Fair Labor Standards Act means that you have given up any right you may have to bring suit for back wages under Section 16(b) of that Act. Section 16(b) provides that an employee may bring suit on his/her own behalf for unpaid minimum wages and/or overtime compensation and an equal amount as liquidated damages, plus attorneys' fees and court costs. The statute of limitations for Fair Labor Standards Act suits requires that a suit for unpaid minimum wages and/or overtime compensation must be filed within 2 years of a violation of the Act, except that a suit for a willful violation must be filed within 3 years of the violation. Do not sign the receipt unless you actually have received payment of all back wages due.

If the employee accepts the payment and signs the Form WH-58, the employee will be deemed to have waived his right to bring suit against your company.

194. Q: I gave our employees the Department of Labor release to settle an overtime dispute, and one of them refused to sign it. What am I supposed to do now?

A: Nothing, yet. Wait to see if the employee cashes the back wages check. If the employee endorses and cashes the check, he or she will be considered to have waived the right to bring suit without having signed the DOL form.

Note that the language on Form WH-58 states that the employee's "acceptance of back wages due" means that he or she has given up the right to bring suit. Courts have held that the employee's signature on the back-wage check constitutes the employee's acceptance of those back wages.

If the employee does not cash the check and chooses to sue, you have the defense of attempting to correct your error by offering the back wages that were due according to the DOL audit.

OWBPA

195. Q: How much do I have to put in a termination release for an older employee? I am terminating a 63-year-old employee and giving him a severance package in addition to his early retirement benefits. I am over 50 and so are the rest of his supervisors. In the release I am going to offer him, do I have to put in all that language about getting 21 days to think it over, getting a lawyer, waiting a week to change your mind, etc.?

A: Yes, if you want the release to be upheld.

In response to a U.S. Supreme Court ruling that permitted discrimination on the basis of age in an employee retirement package (*Public Employees Retirement System v. Betts*, 492 U.S. 158 (U.S. Sup. Ct. 1989)), Congress amended the Age Discrimination in Employment Act (ADEA) in 1990 with the Older Workers Benefit Protection Act (OWBPA).

The ADEA generally covers employees over the age of 40 from discrimination in all aspects of employment. Although the U.S. Supreme Court has held that citizens cannot sue states in federal court for money damages to enforce the ADEA, the law is still very much applicable to private employers such as yourself.

The OWBPA made provisions concerning age for pension plans, early retirement and deductions from severance pay. It also included specific provisions for waivers of the right to file suit under the ADEA. Such waivers are commonly used by employers in general releases when an employee takes early retirement or is terminated.

To be enforceable, a waiver of ADEA rights has to be part of an agreement between you and your employee that is written in clear, understandable language. The waiver must refer specifically to the ADEA and must clearly state that it applies only to rights that arose prior to the release being signed. Any discrimination that occurs after the release is signed cannot be waived in that release.

You must give your employee something of value in return for the release. In this case, the severance package would suffice. And yes, your employee must be given 21 days to consider the release before signing it and seven days after that to revoke his signature. The release must specifically advise your employee to consult a lawyer before he signs.

Simply put, your waiver must include the following:

- be in writing;
- be in plain, understandable language that specifically refers to the ADEA;
- state that it does not cover future rights;
- be in exchange for something of value in addition to what the employee would otherwise be entitled to;

- provide 21 days for prior thought (45 days if the waiver is in connection with a general termination or offer of early retirement);
- provide seven days for revocation after signing; and
- advise the employee to discuss the matter with a lawyer before signing.

Fig. 195-A is a sample waiver.

The point of all this is to ensure that your employee knew what he was giving up and was not coerced into doing so at the time he signed the release. If the validity of the release is challenged, the burden is on you to show that it was given knowingly and voluntarily.

Source: 29 U.S.C. §626(f).

Fig. 195-A

SETTLEMENT AGREEMENT AND GENERAL RELEASE

[For use for employees over 40 years of age.]

Please note that this is written for a female employee; change the gender accordingly

THIS SETTLEMENT AGREEMENT and GENERAL RELEASE (the "Release") is made and entered into effective for all purposes and all respects as of (date)__, 20__, by and between [The Company] ("EMPLOYER") and [Name] ("EMPLOYEE"), together, "the parties."

WHEREAS, EMPLOYEE's employment with EMPLOYER has ended, effective (date), ____, 20__;

WHEREAS, the parties seek to resolve all claims or causes of action which could be asserted by or against any of the parties, and even though the parties deny the basis of any and all such claims or causes of action if any such existed, the parties desire that this employment relationship end with a Settlement and Release;

WHEREAS, EMPLOYER has agreed to pay certain consideration to EMPLOYEE in return for this Release;

WHEREAS, EMPLOYEE has made commitments and promises of acknowledged value to EMPLOYER; and

WHEREAS, each party to this Release has made the decision and determination that it or she has sufficient information necessary to enter into and execute this Release;

NOW, THEREFORE, for and in consideration of the agreements, covenants, releases, and obligations contained herein and other valuable considerations, the receipt and sufficiency of which are hereby acknowledged, the parties hereto, intending legally to be bound, hereby agree as follows:

continued on next page

Fig. 195-A (cont.)

1. Upon execution of this Release by both parties and the fulfillment of all its terms, EMPLOYER agrees to pay to EMPLOYEE (i) ------ Thousand ----Hundred dollars ($--,---.00), less statutory deductions, to be paid in a lump sum (the "severance payment"); [the following are optional examples, to be included only if these benefits are part of the severance agreement]: (ii) twenty-one (21) days of unused accrued vacation, amounting to -----Thousand ----Hundred dollars ($----.00), to be paid in a lump sum, and (iii) the cost of health insurance under COBRA for three (3) months, to be paid monthly, if such coverage is elected by EMPLOYEE (together, the "Settlement Amount"), as and in full and complete satisfaction and settlement of any and all claims or causes of action which EMPLOYEE could assert arising directly or indirectly out of, or in any way connected with, based upon, or related to her employment by EMPLOYER or to the termination of that employment, pursuant to or arising under or out of any statute, common law, regulation, and/or ruling, whether federal or municipal. The Employee agrees and acknowledges that she is entitled to no other severance payments or severance benefits and that no payments described here will be made unless and until the provisions of Paragraph 13 below have been complied with. Nothing herein can or is intended to affect EMPLOYEE's pension rights or the amount (if any) of any pension payments to which she is entitled.

2. This Release is made by the parties to avoid the threat of future litigation and shall never at any time for any purpose be considered as an admission of liability, fault, or responsibility on the part of any party or representative thereof.

3. EMPLOYEE hereby absolutely, unconditionally, and forever releases, acquits, and discharges EMPLOYER and EMPLOYER's representatives, officers, directors, employees, and agents, from any and all actions, causes of action, suits, debts, costs, expenses, damages, losses, claims, liabilities, and demands of any character, nature or kind, whether known or

continued on next page

Fig. 195-A (cont.)

unknown, matured or contingent, liquidated or unliquidated, in law, equity, or otherwise, which any party ever had, now has or can, shall or may have arising from or relating to EMPLOYEE's employment by EMPLOYER and/or the cessation of that employment. This release expressly extends to all claims based on the present and future effects of past acts of EMPLOYER. The general release in this paragraph is intended specifically to include, but is not limited to, all claims or causes of action which any party could, might or may assert arising under any federal, state, or local statute or ordinance providing any remedy, including, but not limited to, claims or causes of action arising under Title VII of the Civil Rights Act of 1964, as amended, the Age Discrimination in Employment Act, as amended, and the Older Workers Benefit and Protection Act (identify all other statutes that may apply here).

4. The agreements, covenants, representations, and warranties of the parties set forth in this Release shall survive the date of the Release and the performance by the parties of any and all obligations under it. All such agreements and covenants shall be binding and enforceable against the parties bound thereby in accordance with their terms.

5. Notwithstanding anything contained in this Release to the contrary, nothing herein, expressed or implied, is intended to confer on any person or entity other than the parties hereto or their respective officers, directors, representatives, employees, agents, successors, heirs, executors, estates, and personal and legal representatives, any rights, remedies, obligations, or liabilities under, or by reason of, this Release.

6. This Release constitutes the final written expression of all of the agreements between the parties with respect to the subject matter hereof and is a complete and exclusive statement of those terms. The only consideration for the EMPLOYEE's execution of this Release is as set out above, and the EMPLOYEE agrees that no representations, promises or

continued on next page

Fig. 195-A (cont.)

agreements of any kind, other than the express terms of this Release, have been made to or with her by any person or entity whatsoever to cause her to sign this Release.

7. It is understood and agreed that the payments and any other consideration referred to above shall not be deemed to be an admission of liability by EMPLOYER.

8. EMPLOYEE promises never to file or participate in a lawsuit, arbitration or other legal proceeding asserting any claims that are released pursuant to this Agreement, except to enforce rights created by this Release, as stated in Paragraph 4, *above*. [*Optional:* If the EMPLOYEE breaches her promise and files or participates in a legal proceeding based on any such released claims, EMPLOYER's obligation to make the payments and benefits referred to in Paragraph 1 above shall terminate immediately, and the EMPLOYEE will (i) repay to EMPLOYER any money paid to her pursuant to this Release; (ii) pay for all costs incurred by EMPLOYER, including reasonable attorneys' fees, in defending against her claim; and (iii) pay all other damages awarded by a court of competent jurisdiction.]

9. The parties promise that the contents of this Release are and shall remain confidential. The parties may reveal the contents of this Release only to its officers and executives, members of her immediate family, her or its tax counselor, and to her or its attorney.

10. EMPLOYEE promises that she will not disparage, debase, or demean EMPLOYER and EMPLOYER's representatives, officers, directors, employees, and agents. EMPLOYER promises it will not disparage, debase, or demean EMPLOYEE. EMPLOYER promises to provide EMPLOYEE with a neutral reference.

11. EMPLOYEE promises and agrees that she will not seek employment from EMPLOYER in the future. EMPLOYER promises it will not contest EMPLOYEE's claim for

continued on next page

Fig. 195-A (cont.)

unemployment benefits provided such claim is submitted no sooner than twelve (12) weeks after the execution of this Release.

12. The persons who have executed this Release represent and warrant that they understand all the terms of this Release, that they are duly authorized and permitted to enter into this Release on behalf of the respective party for whom they are signing, and that they enter into this Release voluntarily.

13. EMPLOYEE acknowledges that:

(i) she has been advised to consult an attorney prior to signing this Release;

(ii) she has twenty-one (21) days after the date this Release is given to her to sign and deliver the signed copy of the Release to EMPLOYER (although she may choose to sign and deliver the Release sooner);

(iii) she has a period of seven (7) days after a signed copy of this Release is delivered to EMPLOYER to cancel and revoke it;

(iv) she has read and fully understands all of the provisions of this Release and she is knowingly and voluntarily agreeing to its terms;

(v) should she rescind her acceptance of this Release as provided in sub-paragraph (iii), above, EMPLOYER has no obligation to pay to her any part of the Settlement Amount described herein.

IN WITNESS WHEREOF, EMPLOYER and EMPLOYEE have executed this Release as of the date above stated.

continued on next page

FIG. 195-A (CONT.)

I, [Employee's Name], understand that I have twenty-one (21) days to consider the offer made to me in this Release. My signature below affirms that I have knowingly and voluntarily elected to shorten that period.

WITNESS:	The Company's Name
______________________________	______________________________
	By:___________________________
	Title:_________________________
WITNESS:	
______________________________	______________________________
	Employee's Name

Reduction-in-Force

196. Q: How can I protect the company from lawsuits following a reduction-in-force?

A: Probably the most important thing to do is make the process as neutral as possible. That is, make the decision on who to let go based on documented performance and business needs.

If you have some jobs your company can do without, eliminating those jobs regardless of who holds them is a neutral way to reduce your workforce. If you have a seniority policy or union contract, follow the requirements to the letter. "Last hired, first fired" is a neutral way to make decisions.

Usually things are not so simple and employers want to "cherry pick" the employees to discharge based on performance. That is when your documentation of performance is critical. There should never be any surprises among your workers about the quality of their work. If performance evaluations have been done properly with adequate communication between supervisors and employees, not only will you have good documentation of performance, but your workers will know whether their performance has been poor or excellent.

You can protect your company to a large extent with severance packages and releases in which the employees give up their right to sue you for past conduct. (See Q. 191-194 for information about releases.)

If some of the employees you discharge are over the age of 40, you need to follow the requirements of the Older Workers Benefit Protection Act (OWBPA) (see Q. 195). The time for deciding whether to sign a release in conjunction with a general termination program under the OWBPA is 45 days, not the usual 21 days. You are required to give employees the job titles and ages of those selected for discharge as well as the ages in the same job classifications or unit of those not selected.

If possible, it is a good idea to bring in someone from the outside to make the selection of employees to be discharged in connection with a reduction-in-force. If those individuals have no knowledge about workers' ages, gender or other protected class, there is less chance of bias creeping into the process. The selection criteria will then be based on documented performance and business necessity.

Severance

197. Q: Do I have to give severance pay to a terminated employee?

A: As a matter of law, no. But you may have company policies or employment contracts that require a different response. Obviously, you must conform to your company policies or to the terms of any contracts.

There is a great deal of confusion about this question because severance pay has become quite common in the American workplace. However, no federal law requires that you give severance pay to any employee. The widespread use of severance pay may be a function of the increase in employment-related litigation. Many employers offer severance pay but link it to the signing of a release of claims from terminated (as opposed to resigning or retiring) employees. Doing so is perfectly legitimate.

You should recognize that if severance pay becomes a common occurrence at your business, you have very likely established it as an expectation or a practice. In that case, you should not be surprised that your terminated employees expect severance pay. One way to avoid this is to have a written policy stating that the granting of severance pay is in the sole discretion of the company and then to live up to the policy by adjusting both the award and the amount of the severance pay to reflect the particular circumstances of the employee. A long-term employee whose job has been eliminated should be treated differently from others who do not match that profile.

Many employers with general severance policies also have a "two weeks pay in lieu of notice" practice, in which a terminated employee is asked to leave promptly and not given any notice. In any case, even that kind of severance payment is only made if a release of claims is signed.

WARN Act

198. Q: Do I have give employees advance notice that we're planning mass layoffs or even a plant closure?

A: Probably, depending on how large your business is and how many employees get laid off. If your company has 100 or more full-time workers (not counting employees who have less than six months on the job and employees who work fewer than 20 hours per week), or if your company employs 100 or more workers who work at least a combined 4,000 hours per week, you must provide notice. The federal Worker Adjustment and Retraining Notification Act (WARN) requires you to provide *written* notice to affected employees at least 60 calendar days in advance of a plant closing or mass layoff.

A *plant closing* that will trigger WARN Act requirements occurs if you are permanently or temporarily shutting down a single site of employment and the shutdown results in an employment loss for 50 or more employees during any 30-day period.

If a *mass layoff* will last more than six months, the layoff will trigger WARN Act coverage if at least one-third of the employees at a single site have an employment loss during any 30-day period and at least 50 employees are affected; or at least 500 employees at a single site during any 30-day period have an employment loss.

For purposes of both plant closings and mass layoffs, an employment loss is defined as a:

- termination, other than a discharge for cause, voluntary departure or retirement;
- layoff exceeding six months; or
- reduction in hours of work of individual employees of more than 50 percent during each month of any six-month period.

An employment loss does not include a situation in which a worker is reassigned or transferred to employer-sponsored programs such as retraining or job search activities, the reassignment does not constitute an involuntary termination or a constructive discharge, and the employee continues to be paid.

If your planned closing or layoff triggers WARN Act requirements, the affected employees to whom you must provide notice include the following:

- hourly and salaried workers;
- employees who will be terminated, laid off for more than six months, or who will have their hours reduced 50 percent or more in any six-month period as a result of the closing or lay-off;
- workers who are on temporary lay-off, including those on maternity leave, Family and Medical Leave Act leave or workers' comp leave, but who have a reasonable expectation of recall; and
- part-time employees, even if they were not required to be counted for purposes of determining whether WARN Act rights were triggered.

The required notice must be given to employees, either individually or through their employee representative, if there is one; the State Rapid Response Dislocated Worker Unit (a unit designated by the governor of each state); and the local chief elected official.

The notice given to the State Rapid Response Dislocated Worker Unit and the local chief elected official must include at least the following information:

- the name and address where the mass layoff or plant closing is to occur;
- the name and telephone number of a company official to contact for further information;
- the expected date of separation; and
- the number of affected employees.

The notice given to each affected union must contain at least the following information:

- the name and address where the mass layoff or plant closing is to occur, along with the name and telephone number of a company contact person who can provide additional information;
- a statement about whether the planned action is expected to be permanent or temporary and, if the entire plant is to be closed, a statement to that effect;
- the expected date of the first separation and the anticipated schedule for making separations; and
- the job titles of positions to be affected and the number of affected employees in each job classification.

To help you plan for a mass layoff, see Fig. 198-A, "Avoiding Liability in Mass Layoffs and Downsizing."

Sources: 29 U.S.C. §2101, *et seq.*; 20 C.F.R. Part 639.

FIG. 198-A

Avoiding Liability in Mass Layoffs and Downsizing

TABLE OF CONTENTS

continued on next page

Fig. 198-A (cont.)

Avoiding Liability in Mass Layoffs and Downsizing

I. BEFORE YOU EVEN PLAN

A. Decide why a layoff or reduction in force ("RIF") is necessary. Typical reasons include expected economic savings, increased worker efficiency, and prior business downturns.

B. Document objective data supporting the need for a layoff or RIF.

II. PLANNING: POSSIBLE LAWS THAT COULD BE IMPLICATED

A. The Worker Adjustment and Retraining Notification Act ("WARN") and similar state plant closing laws[1] may apply.

1. WARN applies to employers with 100 or more full-time employees, or 100 or more full and part-time employees who work over 4000 hours of non-overtime work per week.[2]

2. WARN requires covered employers to give 60 days advance notice of plant closings affecting at least 50 full-time workers (except for the instances discussed below).

   - A *plant closing* is a temporary or permanent shutdown of a single site of employment,[3] if the shutdown results in an employment loss during any thirty day period of 50 or more employees.

     - An *employment loss* includes: (1) a termination other than a discharge for cause or a voluntary departure or retirement, (2) a layoff exceeding six months, and (3) reductions of more than 50% of an employee's working hours.

3. WARN also requires covered employers to give 60 days notice of mass layoffs that will last more than six months. A *mass layoff* occurs when:

   a. at least one-third (1/3) of the employees at a single site during any thirty day period have an employment loss, **and** the number of employees affected is at least 50; **or**

   b. at least 500 employees at a single site during any thirty (30) day period have an employment loss.

[1] A number of states and some local jurisdictions have similar laws. Please check with you employment counsel regarding what the locality of the worksite in question requires.

[2] This 100 employee threshold test includes all employees regardless of whether they are located at separate sites of employment.

[3] A "single site of employment" can include a single location or a group of contiguous locations. It can also include separate locations in the same geographic area if the locations share the same staff and equipment and are used for the same purpose. Contiguous buildings, however, that are owned by the same employer, but which have separate management, separate workforces, employ different workers and produce different products are not a single site.

continued on next page

Fig. 198-A (cont.)

4. WARN also provides for a 90-day aggregation threshold test ("rolling WARN"), whereby WARN applies if the 50-employee termination test, or either of the mass layoff tests are cumulatively met, during any rolling 90-day period, unless an employer can show that the employment losses were the result of separate causes. When counting employees for the purpose of the 90-day test, do not count losses within the 90-day period that would have triggered the WARN notice obligation in and of themselves in the 30-day test.

5. The required WARN notice must be given to:
   a. the employees, either individually or through their employee representative if they have one;
   b. the state dislocated worker units;
   c. the chief elected official of the unit of local government within which the closing or layoff is to occur.

6. Content of the required notice:
   a. name and address of employment site where closing or layoff will occur;
   b. description of the action, *i.e.* whether closing or layoff, permanent or temporary;
   c. expected date(s) of the terminations or layoffs (if the notice is going to an individual employee, it must state the date of that employee's termination);
   d. the job titles of the positions affected, the number of employees in each job classification, and the names of the employees affected (for notice that is provided to non-union employees, this item need not be included);
   e. a statement as to whether any bumping rights apply, *e.g.* the right of a senior employee under a collective bargaining agreement to "bump" a junior employee from his job rather than being terminated or laid off;
   f. identification of each union representing affected employees and the name and address of the chief elected union officers of each union (this item need only be included in notice provided to state and local government officials);
   g. the name and address of a company official to contact for further information.

7. **WARN provides for several exceptions to the 60-day notice rule**:
   a. If the employer in good faith is actively seeking capital which, if successful, would obviate the need for a closing or layoff, the 60-day period is not required. The employer must still provide notice, however, as soon as is practicable.

continued on next page

Fig. 198-A (cont.)

b. If the reason for closing or layoff is caused by business circumstances that were not reasonably foreseeable (loss of a major customer or contract), the 60-day requirement may not be required, although notice is still required as soon as is practicable.

c. If the closing or layoff is due to any type of natural disaster, the 60-day requirement may not be required, but notice must still be given as soon as is practicable.

d. Closings or layoffs affecting employees who were forewarned at the time of their hire that they were only being hired temporarily, are exempt from the notification requirements.

e. Closings or layoffs that constitute strikes or lockouts that were not designed to evade WARN are also exempt from notification requirements.

B. If workers over the age of forty will be affected, the Age Discrimination in Employment Act ("ADEA") will be implicated.

1. The ADEA generally prohibits an employer from discriminating against an employee because of his or her age.

2. As part of a layoff or RIF, an employer will often want to consider implementing a Voluntary Early Retirement Program ("VERP"). The ADEA, however, specifically prohibits an employer from forcing an employee to accept an early retirement plan. The courts have held that VERPs are only lawful if they are truly voluntary and in accord with the principles of the ADEA.

   Whether retirement is considered voluntary or forced depends on the following factors:

   a. The employee must have sufficient time to consider the options offered under the retirement plan.

   b. Full and accurate information about the plan must have been given to the employees.

   c. Coercion is not allowed, but attractive incentives may be permissible. Possibilities include:

      (1) bonus payments;

      (2) performance of certain extra services;

      (3) extra pension benefits.

3. For any releases that are obtained from employees over forty years old, the Older Workers Benefits Protection Act ("OWBPA") prescribes very specific requirements. These requirements will be outlined in detail in the section on releases (Section VI(D)(2)).

continued on next page

FIG. 198-A (CONT.)

C. The Employee Retirement Security Income Act ("ERISA") may be implicated.

1. ERISA, among other things, prohibits interference with the vesting of an employee's pension. It is a violation of §510 of ERISA to terminate an employee **in order to** avoid the vesting of his or her rights under a pension or welfare benefit plan.

2. If, as a matter of a fairly consistent past practice, severance payments have been given to departing employees, ERISA may also be implicated. Some courts have held that the practice of making severance payments may, in some circumstances, rise to the level of a benefit plan. Once a severance practice is deemed a benefit plan, then any employee who is terminated may have a claim for the severance payments "due" to him under that plan. This means that if, as a past practice, severance payments have been made pursuant to a published policy or routinely made in any event, an employer should consider making those payments a part of the RIF. Factors that are considered in determining whether an ERISA plan exists include:

   a. whether there are intended benefits;

   b. whether there is an intended class of beneficiaries;

   c. whether there is a source of funding; and

   d. whether there are procedures in place for recovery of the intended benefits.

3. A RIF may also raise an ERISA issue of a partial plan termination. If a significant number of employees are terminated, an ERISA plan termination may be held to have occurred. If that occurs, employers/plan administrators may be required to vest the interests of the terminated employees, as of the date of the plan termination, even if the employees have not yet qualified for vesting.

D. If union employees will be affected, the National Labor Relations Act ("NLRA") may, under certain conditions, require the employer to bargain about a plant closure or, more generally, about the effects, that is, the terms and conditions of the RIF. The collective bargaining agreement ("CBA") must also be reviewed. The following clauses are typical of the types of clauses in a CBA that may affect a RIF.

1. *Management Rights:* Does the employer have complete discretion through a clear and unmistakable waiver to implement layoffs?

2. *Layoff:* Are there limits on when an employer can conduct a layoff, and/or are there notice requirements?

3. *Seniority:* Is there a restriction on the selection of employees?

4. *Recall:* Is there a specified order for recall of employees when the company starts hiring again?

5. *Bumping:* Are there requirements that certain junior employees be "bumped" from their jobs in order to make room for more senior employees who would otherwise be laid off?

continued on next page

Fig. 198-A (cont.)

6. *Work-sharing:* Is there a provision that requires that there be a broad scale reduction in hours in lieu of a layoff?

7. *Benefits and Severance:* What are the requirements for the continuation of benefits and/or severance after the RIF?

E. If the employer employs over 20 employees, the Consolidated Omnibus Budget Reconciliation Act of 1985 ("COBRA") applies.

1. COBRA is applicable to employers with over twenty (20) employees. This numerical threshold includes full and part-time employees.

2. COBRA provides that a covered employer must allow a terminated employee to continue his or her health insurance for up to eighteen (18) months after the date of termination, or up to twenty-nine (29) months if the employee or his or her qualified beneficiary is or becomes disabled during the first eighteen (18) months of COBRA benefits.

3. Under COBRA, an employer may charge employees an administrative fee in addition to the applicable premium for the period of the extended health insurance.[4]

4. Covered employers must tell each employee and his/her spouse, by first-class mail, of their right to continuation of their existing health insurance coverage from the benefit plan

5. The employee must have at least sixty (60) days from the date of notice of the termination of his health benefits or from the date of termination, whichever is later, in which to elect to continue his/her continuing coverage.

6. If the employer does not administer the plan itself, it must notify the plan administrator of the termination or layoff.

F. Consideration should be given to the state Wage Payment and Collection Law.

- State wage payment laws generally require that an employee must be paid all earned wages including accrued but unused vacation and benefits not later than the employee's next regular payday after his separation from employment. Employer set-offs are generally not allowed.

G. *Practical Tips.* Consideration should be given to the following in advance of creating the RIF plan:

1. whether the employer will offer an early retirement incentive;

2. whether the employer will attempt to get signed releases from employees;

fee is adjusted occasionally; please check with your insurer to determine the applicable fee. The applicable premium is generally the cost to the benefit plan the applicable time period for similarly situated employees.

continued on next page

FIG. 198-A (CONT.)

3. what benefits in terms of severance will be offered;
4. whether the employer wishes to retain valued employees until the closing or layoff occurs

III. CREATING A LAYOFF/RIF PLAN AND WHAT IT SHOULD CONTAIN

A. *A statement of the facially valid business justification for the layoff or RIF.* This statement should be a written recitation of the reasons for the action. Any objective data documenting the justifications for the layoff or RIF should also be included. If possible, include data evaluating possible alternatives to a layoff or RIF, and ultimately supporting the actions taken.

B. *A selection policy including objective criteria for deciding which jobs will be eliminated.* The criteria chosen to be part of the selection policy should be relevant to the expected needs of the company after the layoff or RIF.

1. Consider the following possible criteria:
   a. Past practice, if any.
   b. Seniority.
   c. Attendance records.
   d. Safety records.
   e. *Performance records.* This factor should be made as specific as possible to the job performed. The more objective the standards the better. Subjective evaluation criteria are always risky in the case of a later challenge to termination, but the following procedures will help to support an employer's decision:
      (1) any task-oriented objective evaluations;
      (2) written guidelines for evaluators;
      (3) review of evaluations to guard against arbitrary grading.
   f. Productivity.
   g. Compensation levels.
2. When deciding on the criteria to be used, remember that any later deviation from the selection policy will look bad in any later challenges by subject employees.

C. *Identification of the selection procedure and who the actual decision-makers will be.* All of the procedures in the plan must be followed.

D. If any jobs will be eliminated entirely, document the objective reasons why the job functions are now obsolete or would better be consolidated with other positions. If possible, do not mention any specific

continued on next page

Fig. 198-A (cont.)

names of these job-holders when discussing the job elimination decisions.

E. Include a statement of whether layoffs will be permanent or temporary.

IV. SELECTING EMPLOYEES FOR LAYOFF

A. For union employees, follow any provisions in the collective bargaining agreement.

B. Transfers, reassignments, and demotions should be considered where appropriate.

C. Consider whether certain job functions are obsolete and can be eliminated completely.

D. When less than an entire unit of same-job employees is terminated, individually evaluate all employees in the unit based on the selection criteria before deciding which employees to keep and which to terminate.

E. Follow the selection criteria contained in the Plan. Apply them consistently.

F. If formal performance evaluations are regularly used, consider making lists ranking the relative performance of employees being considered for termination or layoff.

G. Be aware of any potential breach of contract claims by reviewing any individual employee contracts, and verifying with management employees that no promises extending tenure have been made to any individual employees.

H. Be aware of any potential retaliation claims that could be brought by any employee who is terminated or laid off for exercising a legal claim against the company.

I. Be aware of any potential whistleblower claims that could be exercised by any employee who is terminated for opposing or reporting possible legal violations by the company.

J. Be aware of possible discrimination claims. Equal employment opportunity ("EEO") laws prohibit employment decisions based on certain protected characteristics. EEO laws also prohibit otherwise valid employment decisions that disparately impact on protected groups. Protected characteristics include, but are not limited to the following:

1. Sex (Title VII, state and local laws)
2. Race (Title VII, state and local laws)
3. Color (Title VII, state and local laws)
4. National origin (Title VII, state and local laws)
5. Religion (Title VII, state and local laws)
6. Age (ADEA)

continued on next page

Fig. 198-A (cont.)

7. Marital or Familial status (some state and local laws)
8. Handicap (Americans with Disabilities Act, Rehabilitation Act, state and local laws)
9. Political activity (some state and local laws)
10. Veteran status (Uniform Services Employment and Reemployment Rights Act, Veterans Reemployment Act)
11. Sexual orientation (an increasing number of state and local laws)

K. Be very careful about terminating any employees on temporary leave for medical reasons or leave to care for a family member. Failure to return these employees to their former jobs may be a violation of the Family and Medical Leave Act.

V. REVIEWING EMPLOYEE SELECTIONS

A. Perform statistical analyses on selected employees to determine impact on EEO protected groups.

B. Set up a committee to review selection decisions and confirm that they were made based on the selection criteria in the Plan and not for unlawful reasons.

VI. END-STAGE PLANNING

A. Plan a time for employees to remove personal belongings from the office, and consider having extra security present at the time of removal.

B. Adopt a policy for employees returning to the company's premises after the date of termination or layoff. Notify the affected employees of this policy.

C. Assign all public relations to a specific individual or individuals.

D. Execute all releases, if any, that have been negotiated.

1. In order to be enforceable, releases should include the following:
    a. clear and plain language describing the terms of the release, so that they are easily understandable by the employee;
    b. an express identification of all claims waived in the release by named statutory reference or by class or type of claim;
    c. a statement by the employee that the waiver was knowing and voluntary and understood by the employee;

continued on next page

Fig. 198-A (cont.)

d. a statement that the employee was encouraged to consult with counsel;

e. consideration should be given in exchange for the employee's release of all claims;

f. any possible actual negotiation of terms and time for individual consideration of the release by the employee will also be helpful if the validity of the release is ever challenged.

2. If the worker is over 40 years old, the provisions in the Older Workers Benefits Protection Act ("OWBPA") apply. The following additional requirements are then necessary for a release:

a. The release must specifically release claims arising under the ADEA.

b. The release cannot cover claims or rights that arise after the release is signed.

c. The release must state, in writing, that the employee was advised to consult with an attorney before signing.

d. The employee must be given twenty-one (21) days to consider the agreement before signing (or 45 days if the termination is part of group plan offered to a group or class of employees).

e. There must be a seven (7) day period following the signing of the agreement during which the agreement is revocable by the employee.

f. For group terminations or early retirement options, each member of the group must be informed in writing, at the beginning of the forty-five (45) day period, how many people are subject to the termination or program, the criteria for being made part of the program, and any applicable time limits for the program. The ages and job titles of all eligible employees and the ages of all ineligible employees must also be made public.

g. To comply with current EEOC regulations, the release should contain a provision specifying that any forfeiture of monies, if a charged based upon a released claim is filed, shall be inapplicable in matters involving the ADEA.

E. If WARN applies, give the employees the required notice. Even if WARN or any state closing laws do not apply, consider giving some advance notice, as it may lessen the shock to affected employees.

VII. CONDUCTING THE TERMINATIONS OR LAYOFFS

A. Consider having extra security present when conducting terminations or layoffs.

B. Inform the affected employees of their rights for unemployment benefits, and consider having someone from the local office of Employment Security present to start collecting applications.

C. Inform the employees of their rights, if any, to continued company benefits or severance pay.

continued on next page

Fig. 198-A (cont.)

D. Specifically inform employees of their COBRA rights to continued health insurance.

E. Consider having employment counselors present to help employees find new jobs.

F. Consider having final paychecks ready for distribution when notice of the terminations or layoffs is given, or, on the last day of work. At the latest, all employees should be paid in full by the next regular pay date after separation, in order to comply with state wage payment laws.

VIII. AFTER THE TERMINATIONS OR LAYOFFS

A. Do not make any derogatory comments about any of the affected employees to potential employers or anyone else.

B. Adopt guidelines for any references to be given out, and select a particular employee or group of employees to handle all reference requests.

C. Do not make any false statements to affected employees regarding their termination or recall rights.

PLEASE NOTE: This document is for general information only and does not include a full legal analysis of the matters presented. It should not be construed or relied upon as legal advice or legal opinion on any specific facts or circumstances.

Documentation

199. Q: Am I supposed to keep records of absences, including FMLA leaves, out of an employee's personnel file?

A: Records of absenteeism that do not contain any confidential medical information may be kept in the employee's personnel file.

Similarly, documentation of FMLA leave confirming solely the dates of leave and amount taken may be kept in the employee's personnel file. Moreover, records of the use of FMLA leave for a reason other than a health condition may be retained in his or her personnel file. For example, if the employee takes FMLA leave for the adoption of a child, information concerning that leave may appropriately be kept in the employee's personnel file.

Any records containing medical information for the employee or his or her dependents or family members must be kept confidential and separate from other personnel files.

200. Q: Should we keep some record of oral warnings? With supervisor turnover, I've noticed that we are losing track of when some employees are supposed to move to the next level of discipline.

A: It is essential that some record be kept of oral warnings. Otherwise, it is the employee's word against the employer's that a oral warning took place and when it occurred. And, as you pointed out, it is difficult to keep track from a supervisory standpoint of when the appropriate next level of discipline is due.

The record can be a memo to the file or notes on a daily calendar. Electronic notes in an e-mail format will suffice. No particular format is required. Keeping it simple is the best approach.

201. Q: Is there any law about how long I must keep discipline records in a personnel file?

A: Under Title VII of the 1964 Civil Rights Act and the Americans With Disabilities Act, employers with at least 15 employees must retain applications and other personnel records relating to hires, rehires, tests used in employment, promotion, transfers, demotions, selection for training, layoff, recall, terminations or discharge for one year from the date the record was made or the personnel action taken. The Age Discrimination in Employment Act requires that such records be retained for at least three years.

Federal contractors are required to maintain records concerning all employment transactions for their current affirmative action plan year and the prior year – in short, two years. The Family and Medical Leave Act requires the retention of certain records with respect to payroll and demographic information as well as information related to the individual employee's leave for a period of three years. Such information may include disciplinary records if any issue of abuse of leave or excessive absenteeism is presented.

Accordingly, it is recommended that employee disciplinary records be retained for at least three years. Be advised, however, that any records relevant to an employment discrimination charge or employment-related lawsuit must be kept until the final disposition of the charge or suit, which, given our system, might well exceed three years.

Summaries of Main Employment Laws

Title VII of the Civil Rights Act of 1964

Title VII prohibits employment discrimination based on race, color, religion, gender, and national origin. The law applies to employers with 15 or more employees, including state and local governments. It also applies to employment agencies and labor organizations, as well as to federal government employers. Because the law is so broad, each of its main divisions is described separately.

Race/Color Discrimination

It is unlawful to discriminate against any employee or applicant for employment because of his or her race or color in regard to hiring, termination, promotion, compensation, job training or any other term, condition or privilege of employment. Title VII also prohibits employment decisions based on stereotypes and assumptions about abilities, traits or the performance of individuals of certain racial groups. Title VII prohibits both intentional discrimination and neutral job policies that disproportionately exclude minorities and that are not job related.

Equal employment opportunity cannot be denied because of marriage to or association with an individual of a different race, membership in or association with ethnic-based organizations or groups, or attendance or participation in schools or places of worship generally associated with certain minority groups.

Title VII violations include:

- *Race-Related Characteristics and Conditions* – Discrimination on the basis of an immutable characteristic associated with race, such as skin color, hair texture, or certain facial features violates Title VII, even though not all members of the race share the same characteristic. Title VII also prohibits discrimination on the basis of a condition that predominantly affects one race unless the practice is job related and consistent with business necessity. For example, since sickle cell anemia predominantly occurs in African-Americans, a policy that excludes individuals with sickle cell anemia must be job related and consistent with business necessity. Similarly, a "no-beard" employment policy may discriminate against African-American men who have a predisposition to pseudofolliculitis barbae (severe shaving bumps) unless the policy is job related and consistent with business necessity.

- *Harassment* – Harassment on the basis of race and/or color violates Title VII. Ethnic slurs, racial "jokes," offensive or derogatory comments, or other verbal or physical conduct based on an individual's race/color constitutes unlawful harassment if the conduct creates an intimidating, hostile, or offensive working environment or interferes with the individual's work performance.

- *Segregation and Classification of Employees* – Title VII is violated when employees who belong to a protected group are segregated by physically isolating them from other employees or from customer contact. In addition, employers may not assign employees according to race or color. For example, Title VII prohibits assigning primarily African-Americans to predominantly African-American establishments or geographic areas. It is also illegal to exclude members of one group from particular positions or to group or categorize employees or jobs so that certain jobs are generally held by members of a certain protected group. Coding applications/resumes to designate an applicant's race, by either an employer or employment agency, constitutes evidence of discrimination where people of a certain race or color are excluded from employment or from certain positions.

- *Pre-Employment Inquiries* – Requesting pre-employment information that discloses or tends to disclose an applicant's race strongly suggests that race will be used unlawfully as a basis for hiring. Therefore, if members of minority groups are excluded from employment, the request for such pre-employment information can be construed to be evidence of discrimination.

  If an employer legitimately needs information about its employees' or applicants' race for affirmative action purposes and/or to track applicant flow, it may obtain racial information and simultaneously guard against discriminatory selection by using "tear-off sheets" for the identification of an applicant's race. After the applicant completes the application and the tear-off portion, the employer separates the tear-off sheet from the application and does not use it in the selection process.

It is also unlawful to retaliate against an individual for opposing employment practices that discriminate based on race or color, or for filing a discrimination charge, testifying, or participating in any way in an investigation, proceeding, or litigation under Title VII.

Religious Discrimination

Title VII prohibits employers from discriminating against individuals because of their religion in hiring, firing, and other terms and conditions of employment. Title VII covers employers with 15 or more employees, including state and local governments. It also applies to employment agencies and to labor organizations, as well as to the federal government. Under Title VII:

- Employers may not treat employees or applicants less or more favorably because of their religious beliefs or practices. For example, an employer may not refuse to hire individuals of a certain religion, may not impose stricter promotion requirements for persons of a certain religion, and may not impose more or different work requirements on an employee because of that employee's religious beliefs or practices.

- Employees cannot be forced to participate – or not participate – in a religious activity as a condition of employment.

- Employers must reasonably accommodate employees' sincerely held religious beliefs or practices unless doing so would impose an undue hardship on the employer. A reasonable religious accommodation is any adjustment to the work environment that will allow the employee to practice his religion. Flexible scheduling, voluntary substitutions or swaps, job reassignments and lateral transfers and modifying workplace practices, policies and/or procedures are examples of how an employer might accommodate an employee's religious beliefs.

- An employer is not required to accommodate an employee's religious beliefs and practices if doing so would impose an undue hardship on the employers' legitimate business interests. An employer can show undue hardship if accommodating an employee's religious practices requires more than ordinary administrative costs, diminishes efficiency in other jobs, infringes on other employees' job rights or benefits, impairs workplace safety, causes co-workers to carry the accommodated employee's share of potentially hazardous or burdensome work, or if the proposed accommodation conflicts with another law or regulation. This is a less burdensome standard than that used under the Americans With Disabilities Act.

- Employers must permit employees to engage in religious expression if employees are permitted to engage in other personal expression at work, unless the religious expression would impose an undue hardship on the employer. Therefore, an employer may not place more restrictions on religious expression than on other forms of expression that have a comparable effect on workplace efficiency.

- Employers must take steps to prevent religious harassment of their employees. An employer can reduce the chance that employees will engage unlawful religious harassment by implementing an anti-harassment policy and having an effective procedure for reporting, investigating and correcting harassing conduct.

It is also unlawful to retaliate against an individual for opposing employment practices that discriminate based on religion or for filing a discrimination charge, testifying, or participating in any way in an investigation, proceeding, or litigation under Title VII.

Sex-Based Discrimination

Title VII protects individuals against employment discrimination on the basis of sex as well as race, color, national origin, and religion. It is unlawful to discriminate against any employee or applicant for employment because of his or her sex in regard to hiring, termination, promotion, compensation, job training or any other term, condition or privilege of employment. Title VII also prohibits employment decisions based on stereotypes and assumptions about abilities, traits or the performance of individuals on the basis of sex. Title VII prohibits both intentional discrimination and neutral job policies that disproportionately exclude individuals on the basis of sex and that are not job related.

Title VII's prohibitions against sex-based discrimination also cover:

- *Sexual Harassment* – This includes practices ranging from direct requests for sexual favors to workplace conditions that create a hostile environment for persons of either gender, including same sex harassment.

- *Pregnancy Based Discrimination* – Title VII was amended by the Pregnancy Discrimination Act (PDA), which prohibits discrimination on the basis of pregnancy, childbirth and related medical conditions. (See below for more on the PDA).

The Equal Pay Act of 1963 requires that men and women be given equal pay for equal work in the same establishment. The jobs need not be identical, but they must be substantially equal. Title VII also prohibits compensation discrimination on the basis of sex. Unlike the Equal Pay Act, however, Title VII does not require that the claimant's job be substantially equal to that of a higher paid person of the opposite sex or require the claimant to work in the same establishment. (See below for more on the Equal Pay Act.)

It is also unlawful to retaliate against an individual for opposing employment practices that discriminate based on sex or for filing a discrimination charge, testifying, or participating in any way in an investigation, proceeding, or litigation under Title VII.

Sexual Harassment

Sexual harassment is a form of sex discrimination that violates Title VII. Unwelcome sexual advances, requests for sexual favors, and other verbal or physical conduct of a sexual nature constitute sexual harassment when this conduct explicitly or implicitly affects an individual's employment, unreasonably interferes with an individual's work performance, or creates an intimidating, hostile, or offensive work environment.

Sexual harassment can occur in a variety of circumstances, including but not limited to the following:

- The victim as well as the harasser may be a woman or a man. The victim does not have to be of the opposite sex.
- The harasser can be the victim's supervisor, an agent of the employer, a supervisor in another area, a co-worker, or a non-employee.
- The victim does not have to be the person harassed but could be anyone affected by the offensive conduct.
- Unlawful sexual harassment may occur without economic injury to or discharge of the victim.
- The harasser's conduct must be unwelcome.

It is helpful for the victim to inform the harasser directly that the conduct is unwelcome and must stop. The victim should use any employer complaint mechanism or grievance system available.

When investigating allegations of sexual harassment, EEOC looks at the whole record: the circumstances, such as the nature of the sexual advances, and the context in which the alleged incidents occurred. A determination on the allegations is made from the facts on a case-by-case basis.

Prevention is the best tool to eliminate sexual harassment in the workplace. Employers are encouraged to take steps necessary to prevent sexual harassment from occurring. They should clearly communicate to employees that sexual harassment will not be tolerated. They can do so by providing sexual harassment training to their employees and by establishing an effective complaint or grievance process and taking immediate and appropriate action when an employee complains.

It is also unlawful to retaliate against an individual for opposing employment practices that discriminate based on sex or for filing a discrimination charge, testifying, or participating in any way in an investigation, proceeding, or litigation under Title VII.

National Origin Discrimination

Whether an employee or job applicant's ancestry is Mexican, Ukrainian, Filipino, Arab, American Indian or any other nationality, he or she is entitled to the same employment opportunities as anyone else.

National origin discrimination means treating someone less favorably because he or she comes from a particular place, because of his or her ethnicity or accent, or because it is believed that he or she has a particular ethnic background. National origin discrimination also means treating someone less favorably at work because of marriage or other association with someone of a particular nationality. Examples of violations covered under Title VII include:

- *Employment Decisions* – Title VII prohibits any employment decision, including recruitment, hiring, and firing or layoffs, based on national origin.
- *Harassment* – Title VII prohibits offensive conduct, such as ethnic slurs, that creates a hostile work environment based on national origin. Employers are required to take appropriate steps to prevent and correct unlawful harassment. Likewise, employees are responsible for reporting harassment at an early stage to prevent its escalation.
- *Language* – An employer may not base a decision on an employee's foreign accent unless the accent materially interferes with job performance. A fluency requirement is only permissible if required for the effective performance of the position for which it is imposed. English-only rules must be adopted for nondiscriminatory reasons. An English-only rule may be used if it is needed to promote the safe or efficient operation of the employer's business.

Title VII and the other anti-discrimination laws prohibit discrimination against individuals employed in the United States, regardless of citizenship. However, relief may be limited if an individual does not have work authorization.

Retaliation

An employer may not fire, demote, harass or otherwise "retaliate" against an individual for filing a charge of discrimination, participating in a discrimination proceeding, or otherwise opposing discrimination. The same laws that prohibit discrimination based on race, color, sex, religion, national origin, age, and disability, as well as wage differences between men and women performing substantially equal work, also prohibit retaliation against individuals who oppose unlawful discrimination or participate in an employment discrimination proceeding.

In addition to the protections against retaliation that are included in all of the laws enforced by EEOC, the Americans With Disabilities Act (ADA) also protects individuals from coercion, intimidation, threat, harassment, or interference in their exercise of their own rights or their encouragement of someone else's exercise of rights granted by the ADA.

There are three main terms that are used to describe retaliation. Retaliation occurs when an employer, employment agency, or labor organization takes an *adverse action* against a *covered individual* because he or she engaged in a *protected activity*. These three terms are described below.

1. *Adverse Action* – An adverse action is an action taken to try to keep someone from opposing a discriminatory practice, or from participating in an employment discrimination proceeding. Examples of adverse actions include:

    - employment actions such as termination, refusal to hire, and denial of promotion;
    - other actions affecting employment such as threats, unjustified negative evaluations, unjustified negative references, or increased surveillance; and
    - any other action such as an assault or unfounded civil or criminal charges that are likely to deter reasonable people from pursuing their rights.

    Adverse actions do not include petty slights and annoyances, such as stray negative comments in an otherwise positive or neutral evaluation, "snubbing" a colleague, or negative comments that are justified by an employee's poor work performance or history.

    Even if the prior protected activity alleged wrongdoing by a different employer, retaliatory adverse actions are unlawful. For example, it is unlawful for a worker's current employer to retaliate against him for pursuing an EEO charge against a former employer.

    Of course, employees are not excused from continuing to perform their jobs or follow their company's legitimate workplace rules just because they have filed a complaint with the EEOC or opposed discrimination.

2. *Covered Individuals* – Covered individuals are people who have opposed unlawful practices, participated in proceedings, or requested accommodations related to employment discrimination based on race, color, sex, religion, national origin, age, or disability. Individuals who have a close association with someone who has engaged in such protected activity also are covered individuals. For example, it is illegal to terminate an employee because his spouse participated in employment discrimination litigation.

    Individuals who have brought attention to violations of law other than employment discrimination are NOT covered individuals for purposes of anti-discrimination retaliation laws. For example, "whistleblowers" who raise ethical, financial, or other concerns unrelated to employment discrimination are not protected by the EEOC-enforced laws.

3. *Protected Activity* – Protected activity includes opposition to a practice believed to be unlawful discrimination. Opposition is informing an employer that you believe that he/she is engaging in prohibited discrimination. Opposition is protected from retaliation as long as it is based on a reasonable, good-faith belief that the complained of practice violates anti-discrimination law; and the manner of the opposition is reasonable.

   Examples of protected opposition include:

   - complaining to anyone about alleged discrimination against oneself or others;
   - threatening to file a charge of discrimination;
   - picketing in opposition to discrimination; or
   - refusing to obey an order reasonably believed to be discriminatory.

   Examples of activities that are not protected opposition include:

   - actions that interfere with job performance so as to render the employee ineffective; or
   - unlawful activities such as acts or threats of violence.

   Participation in an employment discrimination proceeding means taking part in an employment discrimination proceeding. Participation is protected activity even if the proceeding involved claims that ultimately were found to be invalid. Examples of participation include:

   - filing a charge of employment discrimination;
   - dooperating with an internal investigation of alleged discriminatory practices; or
   - serving as a witness in an EEO investigation or litigation.

   A protected activity can also include requesting a reasonable accommodation based on religion or disability.

The Age Discrimination in Employment Act of 1967 (ADEA)

The ADEA protects individuals who are 40 years of age or older from employment discrimination based on age. The ADEA's protections apply to both employees and job applicants. Under the ADEA, it is unlawful to discriminate against a person because of his or her age with respect to any term, condition or privilege of employment, including hiring, firing, promotion, layoff, compensation, benefits, job assignments and training.

It is also unlawful to retaliate against an individual for opposing employment practices that discriminate based on age or for filing an age discrimination charge, testifying, or participating in any way in an investigation, proceeding, or litigation under the ADEA.

The ADEA applies to employers with 20 or more employees, including state and local governments. It also applies to employment agencies and labor organizations, as well as to the federal government. ADEA protections include:

- *Apprenticeship Programs* – It is generally unlawful for apprenticeship programs, including joint labor-management apprenticeship programs, to discriminate on the basis of an individual's age. Age limitations in apprenticeship programs are valid only if they fall within certain specific exceptions under the ADEA or if the EEOC grants a specific exemption.

- *Job Notices and Advertisements* – The ADEA generally makes it unlawful to include age preferences, limitations, or specifications in job notices or advertisements. A job notice or advertisement may specify an age limit only in the rare circumstances where age is shown to be a "bona fide occupational qualification" (BFOQ) reasonably necessary to the normal operation of the business.

- *Pre-employment Inquiries* – The ADEA does not specifically prohibit an employer from asking an applicant's age or date of birth. However, because such inquiries may deter older workers from applying for employment or may otherwise indicate possible intent to discriminate based on age, requests for age information will be closely scrutinized to make sure that the inquiry was made for a lawful purpose, rather than for a purpose prohibited by the ADEA.

- *Benefits* – The Older Workers Benefit Protection Act of 1990 (OWBPA) amended the ADEA to specifically prohibit employers from denying benefits to older employees. Congress recognized that the cost of providing certain benefits to older workers is greater than the cost of providing those same benefits to younger workers, and that those greater costs would create a disincentive to hire older workers. Therefore, in limited circumstances, an employer may be permitted to reduce benefits based on age, as long as the cost of providing the reduced benefits to older workers is the same as the cost of providing benefits to younger workers.

- *Waivers of ADEA Rights* – An employer may ask an employee to waive his/her rights or claims under the ADEA either in the settlement of an ADEA administrative or court claim or in connection with an exit incentive program or other employment termination program. However, the ADEA, as amended by OWBPA, sets out specific minimum standards that must be met in order for a waiver to be considered knowing and voluntary and, therefore, valid. Among other requirements, a valid ADEA waiver must:

1. be in writing and be understandable;
2. specifically refer to ADEA rights or claims;
3. not waive rights or claims that may arise in the future;
4. be in exchange for valuable consideration;
5. advise the individual in writing to consult an attorney before signing the waiver; and
6. provide the individual at least 21 days to consider the agreement and at least seven days to revoke the agreement after signing it.

If an employer requests an ADEA waiver in connection with an exit incentive program or other employment termination program, the minimum requirements for a valid waiver are more extensive.

Americans With Disabilities Act of 1990 (ADA)

Title I of the ADA prohibits private employers, state and local governments, employment agencies and labor unions from discriminating against qualified individuals with disabilities in job application procedures, hiring, firing, advancement, compensation, job training, and other terms, conditions, and privileges of employment. The ADA covers employers with 15 or more employees, including state and local governments. It also applies to employment agencies and to labor organizations. The ADA's nondiscrimination standards also apply to federal sector employees under section 501 of the Rehabilitation Act, as amended, and its implementing rules.

An individual with a disability is a person who:

- has a physical or mental impairment that substantially limits one or more major life activities;
- has a record of such an impairment; or
- is regarded as having such an impairment.

A qualified employee or applicant with a disability is an individual who, with or without reasonable accommodation, can perform the essential functions of the job in question. Reasonable accommodation may include, but is not limited to:

- making existing facilities used by employees readily accessible to and usable by persons with disabilities;
- job restructuring, modifying work schedules, reassignment to a vacant position; or
- acquiring or modifying equipment or devices, adjusting or modifying examinations, training materials, or policies, and providing qualified readers or interpreters.

An employer is required to make a reasonable accommodation to the known disability of a qualified applicant or employee if it would not impose an "undue hardship" on the operation of the employer's business. Undue hardship is defined as an action requiring significant difficulty or expense when considered in light of factors such as an employer's size, financial resources, and the nature and structure of its operation.

An employer is not required to lower quality or production standards to make an accommodation; nor is an employer obligated to provide personal use items such as glasses or hearing aids.

Title I of the ADA also covers:

- *Medical Examinations and Inquiries* – Employers may not ask job applicants about the existence, nature, or severity of a disability. Applicants may be asked about their ability to perform specific job functions. A job offer may be conditioned on the results of a medical examination, but only if the examination is required for all entering employees in similar jobs. Medical examinations of employees must be job related and consistent with the employer's business needs.

- *Drug and Alcohol Abuse* – Employees and applicants currently engaging in the illegal use of drugs are not covered by the ADA when an employer acts on the basis of such use. Tests for illegal drugs are not subject to the ADA's restrictions on medical examinations. Employers may hold illegal drug users and alcoholics to the same performance standards as other employees.

  It is also unlawful to retaliate against an individual for opposing employment practices that discriminate based on disability or for filing a discrimination charge, testifying, or participating in any way in an investigation, proceeding, or litigation under the ADA.

Pregnancy Discrimination Act

The Pregnancy Discrimination Act is an amendment to Title VII of the Civil Rights Act of 1964. Discrimination on the basis of pregnancy, childbirth, or related medical conditions constitutes unlawful sex discrimination under Title VII, which covers employers with 15 or more employees, including state and local governments. Title VII also applies to employment agencies and to labor organizations, as well as to the federal government. Women who are pregnant or affected by related conditions must be treated in the same manner as other applicants or employees with similar abilities or limitations.

Title VII's pregnancy-related protections include:

- *Hiring* – An employer cannot refuse to hire a pregnant woman because of her pregnancy, because of a pregnancy-related condition or because of the prejudices of co-workers, clients, or customers.

- *Pregnancy and Maternity Leave* – An employer may not single out pregnancy-related conditions for special procedures to determine an employee's ability to work. However, if an employer requires its employees to submit a doctor's statement concerning their inability to work before granting leave or paying sick benefits, the employer may require employees affected by pregnancy-related conditions to submit such statements.

  If an employee is temporarily unable to perform her job due to pregnancy, the employer must treat her the same as any other temporarily disabled employee. For example, if the employer allows temporarily disabled employees to modify tasks, perform alternative assignments or take disability leave or leave without pay, the employer also must allow an employee who is temporarily disabled due to pregnancy to do the same.

  Pregnant employees must be permitted to work as long as they are able to perform their jobs. If an employee has been absent from work as a result of a pregnancy-related condition and recovers, her employer may not require her to remain on leave until the baby's birth. An employer also may not have a rule that prohibits an employee from returning to work for a predetermined length of time after childbirth.

  Employers must hold open a job for a pregnancy-related absence the same length of time jobs are held open for employees on sick or disability leave.

- *Health Insurance* – Any health insurance provided by an employer must cover expenses for pregnancy-related conditions on the same basis as costs for other medical conditions. Health insurance for expenses arising from abortion is not required, except where the life of the mother is endangered.

  Pregnancy-related expenses should be reimbursed exactly as those incurred for other medical conditions, whether payment is on a fixed basis or a percentage of reasonable-and-customary-charge basis.

The amounts payable by the insurance provider can be limited only to the same extent as amounts payable for other conditions. No additional, increased, or larger deductible can be imposed.

Employers must provide the same level of health benefits for spouses of male employees as they do for spouses of female employees.

- *Fringe Benefits* – Pregnancy-related benefits cannot be limited to married employees. In an all-female workforce or job classification, benefits must be provided for pregnancy-related conditions if benefits are provided for other medical conditions.

  If an employer provides any benefits to workers on leave, the employer must provide the same benefits for those on leave for pregnancy-related conditions.

  Employees with pregnancy-related disabilities must be treated the same as other temporarily disabled employees for accrual and crediting of seniority, vacation calculation, pay increases, and temporary disability benefits.

It is also unlawful to retaliate against an individual for opposing employment practices that discriminate based on pregnancy or for filing a discrimination charge, testifying, or participating in any way in an investigation, proceeding, or litigation under Title VII.

Equal Pay Act

The right of employees to be free from discrimination in their compensation is protected under several federal laws, including the following enforced by the U.S. Equal Employment Opportunity Commission (EEOC): the Equal Pay Act of 1963, Title VII of the Civil Rights Act of 1964 is the main law enforcing this right but the Age Discrimination in Employment Act of 1967, and Title I of the Americans with Disabilities Act of 1990 also play important roles.

The Equal Pay Act requires that men and women be given equal pay for equal work in the same establishment. The jobs need not be identical, but they must be substantially equal. It is job content, not job titles, that determines whether jobs are substantially equal. Specifically, the EPA provides:

Employers may not pay unequal wages to men and women who perform jobs that require substantially equal skill, effort and responsibility, and that are performed under similar working conditions within the same establishment. Each of these factors is summarized below:

- *Skill* – Measured by factors such as the experience, ability, education, and training required to perform the job. The key issue is what skills are required for the job, not what skills the individual employees may have. For example, two bookkeeping jobs could be considered equal under the EPA even if one of the job holders has a master's degree in physics, since that degree would not be required for the job.

- *Effort* – The amount of physical or mental exertion needed to perform the job. For example, suppose that men and women work side by side on a line assembling machine parts. The person at the end of the line must also lift the assembled product as he or she completes the work and place it on a board. That job requires more effort than the other assembly line jobs if the extra effort of lifting the assembled product off the line is substantial and is a regular part of the job. As a result, it would not be a violation to pay that person more, regardless of whether the job is held by a man or a woman.

- *Responsibility* – The degree of accountability required in performing the job. For example, a salesperson who is delegated the duty of determining whether to accept customers' personal checks has more responsibility than other salespeople. On the other hand, a minor difference in responsibility, such as turning out the lights at the end of the day, would not justify a pay differential.

- *Working Conditions* – This encompasses two factors: (1) physical surroundings like temperature, fumes, and ventilation; and (2) hazards.

- *Establishment* – The prohibition against compensation discrimination under the EPA applies only to jobs within an establishment. An establishment is a distinct physical place of business rather than an entire business or enterprise consisting of several places of business. However, in some circumstances, physically separate places of business should be treated as one establishment. For example, if a central administrative unit hires employees, sets their compensation, and assigns them to work locations, the separate work sites can be considered part of one establishment.

Pay differentials are permitted when they are based on seniority, merit, quantity or quality of production, or a factor other than sex. These are known as "affirmative defenses" and it is the employer's burden to prove that they apply.

In correcting a pay differential, no employee's pay may be reduced. Instead, the pay of the lower paid employee(s) must be increased.

Fair Labor Standards Act (FLSA)

The FLSA requires that a minimum wage be paid to covered, nonexempt employees for all hours that the employees are "suffered or permitted to work." The FLSA also requires employers to pay special premium overtime pay to nonexempt employees who work more than a specified number of hours during the workweek. Overtime pay must be paid at a rate of not less than one-and-one-half times the nonexempt employee's regular rate of pay for each hour worked over the maximum hours standard in a workweek. The maximum hours standard is usually 40 hours in a workweek.

The act generally does not require that an employee be paid overtime compensation for working more than either hours a day, or for work on Saturdays, Sundays, holidays or regular days of rest, as long as the maximum hours standard is not exceeded. If a collective bargaining agreement is in place that limits overtime hours or provides for payment or premium rates, the employer is obligated to follow the terms of the agreement.

The FLSA's basic requirements are:

- payment of the minimum wage;
- overtime pay for time worked over 40 hours in a workweek;
- restrictions on the employment of children; and
- recordkeeping.

The FLSA has been amended on many occasions since 1938. Currently, workers covered by the FLSA are entitled to the minimum wage of $5.15 per hour and overtime pay at a rate of not less than one-and-one-half times their regular rate of pay after 40 hours of work in a workweek. Various minimum wage exceptions apply under specific circumstances to disabled workers, full-time students, youth under age 20 in their first 90 days of employment, tipped employees and student-learners.

Special rules apply to state and local government employment involving fire protection and law enforcement activities, volunteer services, and compensatory time off (instead of cash overtime pay). Employers are required to keep records on wages, hours, and other items which are generally maintained as an ordinary business practice.

The FLSA child labor provisions are designed to protect the educational opportunities of youth and prohibit their employment in jobs and under conditions detrimental to their health or safety. The child labor provisions include some restrictions on hours of work for youth under 16 years of age and lists of hazardous occupations too dangerous for young workers to perform.

Wages required by the FLSA are due on the regular payday for the pay period covered. Deductions made from wages for such items as cash or merchandise shortages, employer-required uniforms, and tools of the trade, are not legal if they reduce the wages of employees below the minimum wage or reduce the amount of overtime pay due under the FLSA.

In order for the FLSA to apply, there must be an employment relationship between an "employer" and an "employee." The FLSA also contains some exemptions from these basic rules. The most significant exemptions are from that part of the law that requires that employees be paid overtime for hours worked above 40 per week. Executives, key administrative personnel, members of "learned professions," and certain creative personnel are "exempt" from the overtime rules. Lengthy new regulations published by the Department of Labor explain the way in which the exemptions can be applied. Some apply to specific types of businesses and others to specific kinds of work.

There are a number of employment practices which the FLSA does not regulate. For example, the FLSA does not require:

1. vacation, holiday, severance, or sick pay;
2. meal or rest periods, holidays off, or vacations;
3. premium pay for weekend or holiday work;
4. pay raises or fringe benefits;
5. a discharge notice, reason for discharge, or immediate payment of final wages to terminated employees; and
6. pay stubs or W-2s.

The FLSA does not provide wage payment or collection procedures for an employee's usual or promised wages or for commissions in excess of those required by the FLSA. The FLSA does not limit the number of hours in a day, or days in a week, an employee may be required or scheduled to work, including overtime hours, if the employee is at least 16 years old. However, many states have laws covering some of these issues, such as meal or rest periods, or discharge notices.

Employee Retirement Income Security Act (ERISA)

ERISA is a federal law that sets minimum standards for most voluntarily established pension and health plans in private industry to provide protection for individuals in these plans. ERISA does not apply to pension and benefit plans established by public-sector employers. Many plans created by religious institutions are also not covered.

On retirement, many workers continue to receive monetary compensation from their employer in the form of a pension. There are mainly two types of pensions. Under a defined benefit plan, the benefit that an employee receives is normally based on the length of a worker's employment and the wages that were received. Each employee does not have a separate account in these programs, as the money to support the pensions is generally administered through a trust established by the employer. In a defined contribution plan, the employer (and often the employee) make regular deposits into an account established for each employee. The employee is not guaranteed to receive a given amount during retirement but only the amount in the account.

Pensions are governed primarily by federal statutory law. ERISA is highly complicated and provides detailed regulations for many aspects of pension and welfare plans. ERISA requires the following:

- That employers provide both the Labor Department and its employees with detailed descriptions of the benefits they are to receive.
- That employees must receive a pension if pensions are offered and that a percentage of the retirement benefits become vested in the employees after they have worked for a given number of years and/or have reached a given age.
- That pension plans provide benefits to an employee's survivors upon his death.
- That employers adequately fund defined benefit plans.

ERISA also establishes fiduciary responsibilities that must be adhered to by administrators and trustees of pension plans. ERISA also establishes the Pension Benefit Guaranty Corporation (PBGC) to insure defined benefits plans. Employers must pay premiums so that their plans are covered by the PBGC. The termination of plans is also extensively regulated.

To encourage employers to provide pension plans that follow congressionally established guidelines such as ERISA, Congress has authorized tax breaks to employers who follow the guidelines. The Internal Revenue Code establishes numerous qualifications and requirements in order for an employer to receive special tax treatment. For example, pension plans must be vested and must meet minimum coverage requirements.

Family and Medical Leave Act (FMLA)

The FMLA requires that private employers with 50 or more employees within a 75-mile radius to provide up to 12 weeks per year of unpaid family and medical leave to eligible employees, and to restore those employees to the same or an equivalent position upon their return. The FMLA allows eligible employees (male or female) to take leave for the birth, adoption or placement in foster care of a child; the care of a seriously ill child, spouse or parent; or the employee's own serious illness. It also requires that group health benefits be maintained during the leave.

The FMLA is designed to help employees balance their work and family responsibilities by taking reasonable unpaid leave for certain family and medical reasons. It also seeks to accommodate the legitimate interests of employers, and promotes equal employment opportunity for men and women.

Not all employees are entitled to leave under the FMLA. The law sets minimum length-of-service and hours-of-work requirements that employees must satisfy. Before an employee becomes eligible for leave under the FMLA, he or she must first be employed by an employer of at least 50 employees within 75 miles of his or her worksite. He or she must also have been employed by the same employer for at least 12 months and must have worked at least 1,250 hours during the 12 months preceding the leave.

If a leave request is based on an employee's own serious health condition or the serious health condition of an employee's family member, the employer can require certification of the need for leave from a health care provider. If the validity of the certification is in doubt, the employer can require the employee to obtain a second opinion (at the employer's expense). If the two opinions conflict, the employer may pay for a third opinion from a provider who must be jointly approved by the employer and employee. The third opinion will be final.

If an employer provides health insurance, it must maintain coverage under its group health plan for any employee who is out on family or medical leave for the duration of the leave at the same level of coverage that would have been provided if no leave had been taken and under the same conditions, *e.g.*, an employee on FMLA leave who paid for all or part of health insurance coverage can be asked to continue to do so during the leave. An employer can also elect to subsidize that cost and recoup it once the employee returns to work.

A number of states have also enacted family and medical leave laws, some of which provide greater amounts of leave and benefits than those provided by FMLA, and/or provide benefits to employees who are not eligible for FMLA leave. In those situations where an employee is covered by both federal and state FMLA laws, the employee is entitled to the greater benefit or more generous rights provided under the different parts of each law. Some employees may also be entitled to protections provided by the Americans With Disabilities Act (ADA).

Consolidated Omnibus Budget Reconciliation Act (COBRA)

COBRA gives workers and their families who lose their health benefits the right to choose to continue group health benefits provided by their group health plan for limited periods of time under certain circumstances such as voluntary or involuntary job loss, reduction in the hours worked, transition between jobs, death, divorce, and other life events. Qualified individuals may be required to pay the entire premium for coverage up to 102 percent of the cost to the plan.

COBRA generally requires that group health plans sponsored by employers with 20 or more employees in the prior year offer employees and their families the opportunity for a temporary extension of health coverage (called continuation coverage) in certain instances where coverage under the plan would otherwise end. COBRA outlines how employees and family members may elect continuation coverage. It also requires employers and plans to provide notice.

Health Insurance Portability and Accountability Act (HIPAA)

HIPAA provides rights and protections for participants and beneficiaries in group health plans. HIPAA includes protections for coverage under group health plans that limit exclusions for pre-existing conditions, prohibit discrimination against employees and dependents based on their health status, and allow a special opportunity to enroll in a new plan to individuals in certain circumstances. HIPAA may also give one a right to purchase individual coverage if there is no group health plan coverage available, and one has exhausted COBRA or other continuation coverage.

HIPAA protects workers and their families by:

- limiting exclusions for pre-existing medical conditions (known as preexisting conditions);
- providing credit against maximum pre-existing condition exclusion periods for prior health coverage and a process for providing certificates showing periods of prior coverage to a new group health plan or health insurance issuer;
- providing new rights that allow individuals to enroll for health coverage when they lose other health coverage, get married or add a new dependent;
- prohibiting discrimination in enrollment and in premiums charged to employees and their dependents based on health status-related factors;
- guaranteeing availability of health insurance coverage for small employers and the ability to renew health insurance coverage for both small and large employers; and
- preserving the states' role in regulating health insurance, including the states' authority to provide greater protections than those available under federal law.

Preexisting Condition Exclusions

The law defines a preexisting condition as one for which medical advice, diagnosis, care, or treatment was recommended or received during the 6-month period prior to an individual's enrollment date (which is the earlier of the first day of health coverage or the first day of any waiting period for coverage).

Group health plans and issuers may not exclude an individual's pre-existing medical condition from coverage for more than 12 months (18 months for late enrollees) after an individual's enrollment date.

Under HIPAA, a new employer's plan must give individuals credit for the length of time they had prior continuous health coverage, without a break in coverage of 63 days or more, thereby reducing or eliminating the 12-month exclusion period (18 months for late enrollees).

Creditable Coverage

Includes prior coverage under another group health plan, an individual health insurance policy, COBRA, Medicaid, Medicare, CHAMPUS, the Indian Health Service, a state health benefits risk pool, FEHBP, the Peace Corps Act, or a public health plan.

Occupational and Safety Health Act (OSHA)

Workplace safety and health laws establish regulations designed to eliminate personal injuries and illnesses from occurring in the workplace. The laws consist primarily of federal and state statutes. Federal laws and regulations preempt state ones where they overlap or contradict one another.

The main statute protecting the health and safety of workers in the workplace is OSHA. Congress enacted this legislation under its constitutional grant of authority to regulate interstate commerce. OSHA requires the secretary of Labor to promulgate regulations and safety and health standards to protect employees and their families. Every private employer who engages in interstate commerce is subject to the regulations promulgated under OSHA.

In order to aid the Secretary of Labor in promulgating regulations and enforcing them, the act establishes the National Advisory Committee on Occupational Safety and Health. The secretary of Labor may authorize inspections of workplaces to ensure that regulations are being followed, examine conditions about which complaints have been filed, and determine what regulations are needed. If an employer is violating a safety or health regulation, a citation is issued.

The act establishes the Occupational Safety and Health Review Commission to review citation orders of the secretary of Labor. The commission's decision is also subject to judicial review. The secretary of Labor may impose fines with the amounts varying according to the type of violation and length of non-compliance with the citation. The secretary of Labor may also seek an injunction to restrain conditions or practices which pose a immediate threat to employees. The act also establishes the National Institute for Occupational Safety and Health which, under the secretary of Health and Welfare, conducts research on workplace health and safety and recommends regulations to the secretary of Labor. Federal agencies must establish their own safety and health regulations. The regulations that have been promulgated under OSHA are extensive, currently filling five volumes of the Code of Federal Regulations.

Under OSHA states are not allowed, without permission of the secretary of Labor, to promulgate any laws that regulate an area directly covered by OSHA regulations. They may, however, regulate in areas not governed by federal OSHA regulations. If they wish to regulate areas covered by OSHA regulations they must submit a plan for federal approval. No state plan may provide for less stringent protections than in the federal law. California is an example of a state that has chosen to adopt many of its own regulations in place of those promulgated under OSHA.

Workers' Compensation – Primarily State Law Controlled

Workers' compensation laws are designed to ensure that employees who are injured or disabled on the job are provided with fixed monetary awards, eliminating the need for litigation. These laws also provide benefits for dependents of those workers who are killed because of work-related accidents or illnesses. Some laws also protect employers and fellow workers by limiting the amount an injured employee can recover from an employer and by eliminating the liability of co-workers in most accidents. State workers' compensation statutes establish this framework for most employment. Federal statutes are limited to federal employees or those workers employed in some significant aspect of interstate commerce.

California's Workers' Compensation Act provides an example of a comprehensive state compensation program. It is applicable to most employers. The statute limits the liability of the employer and fellow employees. California also requires employers to obtain insurance to cover potential workers' compensation claims, and sets up a fund for claims that employers have illegally failed to insure against.

The Federal Employment Compensation Act provides workers compensation for non-military, federal employees. Many of its provisions are typical of most worker compensation laws. Awards are limited to "disability or death" sustained while in the performance of the employee's duties but not caused willfully by the employee or by intoxication. The act covers medical expenses due to the disability and may require the employee to undergo job retraining. A disabled employee receives two thirds of his or her normal monthly salary during the disability and may receive more for permanent physical injuries, or if he or she has dependents. The act provides compensation for survivors of employees who are killed. The act is administered by the Office of Workers' Compensation Programs.

Congress enacted the Longshore and Harbor Workers' Compensation Act (LHWCA) to provide workers' compensation to specified employees of private maritime employers. The Office of Workers' Compensation Programs administers the act.

Unemployment Compensation Laws – State/Federal Partnership

Unemployment insurance provides workers, whose jobs have been terminated through no fault of their own, monetary payments for a given period of time or until they find a new job. Unemployment payments (compensation) are intended to provide an unemployed worker time to find a new job equivalent to the one lost without financial distress.

Current unemployment insurance is based on a dual program of federal and state statutes. The program was established by the federal Social Security Act in 1935. Much of the federal program is implemented through the Federal Unemployment Tax Act. Each state administers a separate unemployment insurance program, which must be approved by the secretary of Labor, based on federal standards. The state programs are explicitly made applicable to areas normally regulated by laws of the U.S. There are special federal rules for nonprofit organizations and governmental entities. Which employees are eligible for compensation, the amount they receive, and the period of time benefits are paid are determined by a mix of federal and state law.

To support the unemployment compensation systems, a combination of federal and state taxes are levied upon employers. State employer contributions are normally based on the amount of wages they have paid, the amount they have contributed to the unemployment fund, and the amount that their discharged employees have been compensated with from the fund. Any state tax imposed on employers (and certain credits on that tax) may be credited against the federal tax.

The proceeds from the unemployment taxes are deposited in an Unemployment Trust Fund (the Fund). Each state has a separate account in the Fund to which deposits are made. Within the fund there are separate accounts for state administrative costs and extended unemployment compensation. During economic recessions the federal government has provided emergency assistance to allow states to extend the time for which individuals can receive benefits. This is accomplished by passing a temporary law authorizing the transfer of money to a state from its Extended Unemployment Account. The ability of a state to tap into this emergency system is usually dependent on the employment rate reaching a designated percentage within the state or the nation.

Some states provide additional unemployment benefits to workers who are disabled. Financing for the California disability compensation program, for example, comes from a tax on employees.

The Railroad Unemployment Insurance Act provides unemployment compensation for workers in the railroad industry who lose their jobs.

Uniformed Services Employment and Reemployment Rights Act (USERRA)

The USERRA was signed into law on Oct. 13, 1994. It is intended to minimize the disadvantages to an individual that occur when that person needs to be absent from his or her civilian employment to serve in this country's uniformed services.

USERRA potentially covers every individual in the country who serves in or has served in the uniformed services and applies to all employers in the public and private sectors, including federal employers. The law seeks to ensure that those who serve their country can retain their civilian employment and benefit, and can seek employment free from discrimination because of their service. USERRA provides enhanced protection for disabled veterans, requiring employers to make reasonable efforts to accommodate the disability.

Under USERRA, an employee is entitled to reemployment rights and maintenance of employment benefits only if the person returning from military service meets five eligibility criteria:

- The person must have held a civilian job with the employer;
- The person must have given advance notice to the employer that he or she was leaving the job for service in the uniformed services;
- The period of service must not have exceeded five years;
- The person must have been released from service under honorable conditions; and
- The person must have reported back to the civilian job in a timely manner or have submitted a timely application for reemployment.

USERRA is administered by the U.S. Department of Labor, through the Veterans' Employment and Training Service (VETS). VETS provides assistance to those persons experiencing service-connected problems with their civilian employment and provides information about the act to employers. The Labor Department has issued a memorandum that clarifies its position on the rights of returning service members to family and medical leave under the Uniformed Services Employment and Reemployment Rights Act (USERRA).

Workers Adjustment and Retraining Notification Act (WARN)

WARN was enacted on Aug. 4, 1988 and became effective on Feb. 4, 1989. It offers protection to workers, their families and communities by requiring employers to provide notice 60 days in advance of covered plant closings and covered mass layoffs. This notice must be provided to either affected workers or their representatives (e.g., a labor union); to the state dislocated worker unit; and to the appropriate unit of local government.

In general, employers are covered by WARN if they have 100 or more employees, not counting employees who have worked less than 6 months in the last 12 months and not counting employees who work an average of less than 20 hours a week. Private, for-profit employers and private, nonprofit employers are covered, as are public and quasi-public entities which operate in a commercial context and are separately organized from the regular government. Regular federal, state, and local government entities which provide public services are not covered.

Employees entitled to notice under WARN include hourly and salaried workers, as well as managerial and supervisory employees. Business partners are not entitled to notice.

Index

A

E

F

G

H

L

M

S

U

V

W